Paradise
Class, Commuters, and Ethnicity in Rural Ontario

What was life like in the 1950s in small communities in Ontario? Lower-class and upper-class residents might have different memories of those days, but on one thing they would agree: it is a much different world in rural Ontario today. The old guard has lost most of its power, displaced partly by 'big brother' in the form of bureaucracy, and by newcomers from the city in search of affordable housing – even if it means commuting daily to work. Unlike their British-origin predecessors, the newcomers who have begun to appear in the countryside represent a wide range of ethnic and economic backgrounds.

Paradise concentrates on the transformed class system of one community in rural Ontario. In a comparison of the decade following the First World War and the 1980s, Stanley R. Barrett analyses the changing face and structure of a town as it has had to adapt to modern social and economic realities. Particular attention is paid to the phenomenon of the commuter in search of affordable housing and the influx of immigrants of varied ethnic backgrounds, and the interaction between these newcomers and long-term residents. What is striking is just how massive the changes in small-town Ontario have been since the Second World War – to the extent of almost obliterating long-assumed distinctions between rural and urban society.

STANLEY R. BARRETT is a professor in the Department of Sociology and Anthropology, University of Guelph. He is the author of *Is God a Racist?* and *The Rebirth of Anthropological Theory*.

Anthropological Horizons
Editor: Michael Lambek, University of Toronto

This series, begun in 1991, focuses on theoretically informed ethnographic works addressing issues of mind and body, knowledge and power, equality and inequality, the individual and the collective. Interdisciplinary in its perspective, the series makes a unique contribution in several other academic disciplines: women's studies, history, philosophy, psychology, political science, and sociology.

Paradise

Class, Commuters, and Ethnicity in Rural Ontario

STANLEY R. BARRETT

UNIVERSITY OF TORONTO PRESS
Toronto Buffalo London

© University of Toronto Press Incorporated 1994
Toronto Buffalo London
Printed in Canada

ISBN 0-8020-0442-3 (cloth)
ISBN 0-8020-7232-1 (paper)

Printed on acid-free paper

Canadian Cataloguing in Publication Data

Barrett, Stanley R., 1938–
    Paradise

    (Anthropological horizons)
    Includes bibliographical references and index.
    ISBN 0-8020-0442-3 (bound)   ISBN 0-8020-7232-1 (pbk.)

    1. Sociology, Rural – Ontario. 2. Social classes –
    Ontario. 3. Urban-rural migration – Ontario.
    4. Ontario – Race relations. 5. Ontario – Ethnic
    relations. 6. Ontario – Rural conditions. I. Title.
    II. Series.

    HN110.06B37 1994   307.72'09713   C94-930247-3

This book has been published with the help of a grant from the Social
Science Federation of Canada, using funds provided by the Social Sciences
and Humanities Research Council of Canada.

Dedicated to the memory of
Dean John Vanderkamp

Academic leader
Scholar
Friend

Contents

Preface

I thought I was never going to find Paradise, at least in this life, but then I discovered it on my doorstep. Paradise is a small town in southern Ontario surrounded by rolling farm land, inhabited by people of British origin who treat each other with dignity, the rich and poor alike, and come to the aid of anyone in need; who never have to worry about the safety of their children because crime in this placid community is virtually unknown.

At least that's the way the town used to be, people claim. Today it is a different story. For the past two decades there has been a steady influx of newcomers into the town from the urban centres to the south such as Toronto, including a not insignificant number of visible minorities, especially African and Asian Canadians. According to the locals, these newcomers, the majority of whom are commuters, have ruined the community. Crime has escalated, community spirit has disappeared, and with it everything that was pleasing and charming about rural life. In short, from the perspective of the people who were born and raised in the town, Paradise has been lost. The newcomers, in contrast, with the city as their measuring rod, enter the town with romantic notions of quaint rural folk, honest and innocent, and settle down to enjoy what life really should be all about: tranquillity, trust, and simplicity in a home of one's own. In their minds – at least initially, for many of them eventually pack up and return to the city, partly because the daily grind of commuting proves to be unbearable, and partly because they simply go bankrupt – Paradise has been rediscovered in all of its glory.

This study, at the most general level, focuses on social change in rural Ontario. Although I have concentrated on one community, I have also attempted to measure the changes that have taken place in other communities in the vicinity, and in the farming community as well. In many respects, then, this is not only a community study, but also a study of a region. No community investigation can be complete, especially if an effort is made to place it in a broader political and economic context, and this one revolves around three major themes: stratification, migration, and race and ethnic relations. In my judgment, these themes go to the root of the most significant changes that have taken place over the past half-century in Paradise and the towns and villages around it. In order to capture these changes, I shall attempt to compare two periods: the era of the 1950s and the decade of the 1980s. During the first period a handful of powerful families ruled the community as if it was their personal fiefdom. By the 1980s all that they had left were their memories; power had swung to the outside bureaucracy, with its increasing rules and regulations, and to a new breed of merchants, most of them well-educated newcomers. During the 1950s young people brought up in small towns like Paradise and on the surrounding farms made the trek to the city in search of adventure and employment. By the 1970s the flow of migration had been reversed; people had begun to move from the city to the rural areas, sometimes in pursuit of a more peaceful environment, but mostly just to be able to afford their own homes. Fifty years ago it was rare to find any resident of Paradise whose origins were not British. By the 1980s not only had Asian and African Canadians begun to settle in and around Paradise, but also people from virtually every part of Europe, including the countries formerly under Soviet domination.

While stratification, migration, and race and ethnicity will be the dominant themes in this study, a fourth one will run somewhat less visibly through the chapters that follow: the exotic and the bizarre. Anthropologists do not need to travel to Borneo or Timbuctoo in search of strange and intriguing customs. The exotic and the bizarre are alive and well in Western society, including southern Ontario.

I have always loved small communities, largely I suppose because I was brought up in one, and the study of Paradise holds a special fascination for me. For a few years as a child I had lived there, and my memories of that period in my life remain warm. Perhaps this accounts for some of the naïveté that characterized my early attempts to understand the town. I had begun this study hoping to discover the nature and meaning of community in today's world. Yet only at the most superficial level, in the geographical and administrative senses, did a community exist. Instead, there were several communities shaped by length of residence, social class, and ethnicity, and to some extent by the different worlds occupied by men and women. As I reflected on the complexity and strain associated with these various divisions, what struck me was just how little separates rural and urban life in the late stages of the twentieth century.

Paradise, the village of my youth, has changed, which may not be a bad thing. Although I began this study out of sheer scholarly curiosity, in the process of carrying it out I have become acutely aware of (and sympathetic towards) the anxieties and frustrations suffered by individuals when their universe seems to lack a firm anchor, or at least a predictable direction. This does not mean, however, that I am unmoved by the various expressions of inequality and oppression that will be described in this book. Whether it is the upper class metaphorically putting the boot to the lower class, or people of European origin erecting barriers against African and Asian Canadians, my reaction is the same: repugnance. Perhaps it is too much to hope for, but I shall be pleased if this book helps the people of Paradise – natives, newcomers, and minorities – to understand where they have come from and where they are today, and to appreciate their common bonds as human beings in a complex world.

Acknowledgments

My basic gratitude goes to the people of Paradise, which obviously is
a fictitious name. I can think of no better way to express my appreciation of these delightful people than to reveal that on so many occasions after finishing an interview, I wished I had the time and opportunity to get to know them as friends, rather than as passing subjects in
a research project. Of course, some of these people had been my
schoolmates and teachers, and it was a rare privilege to re-establish
contact with them after so many years, and to realize why I remembered them with such respect and fondness. As for the newcomers,
representing a wide range of ethnic backgrounds, Paradise today is
intrinsically more interesting and dynamic by virtue of their presence.
Although I cannot possibly name all the wonderful residents of Paradise who helped me with this study – the list literally would run to the
hundreds – I must thank a former resident, E. B., whose keen interest
in local history proved invaluable to my own efforts to understand the
community's past.

While this study is based on a town in rural Ontario, it was written
in another small community on the island of Corsica, where several
friends, champion chefs all of them, helped to keep me sane. I am
particularly indebted to Brigitte and Guy Sintes for introducing my
family to their wide circle of friends, especially Josy, Paul, Conception,
Pascal, Alain, Paulette, Sylvian, Jean-Pierre, Monique, and Rino, who
collectively taught me the real meaning of community. I also must
thank an old friend, Neil Graham, for going out of his way to make
our visit to Corsica a pleasant one.

My students in a course on the sociology of the community suffered
through my initial attempts to analyse this material, and I gratefully

acknowledge their patience and criticisms. Connie Matthews-Cull served as my research assistant one summer for the project. Nan Lustig based her MA thesis on newcomers in Paradise, and Brenda Dusome did her own research for an undergraduate course on an aspect of crime in a neighbouring community; I benefited from their various insights. I am especially indebted to Ken Menzies and Peter Sinclair for commenting wisely on the first draft of this manuscript, and to Ed Hedican and Neil MacKinnon for numerous discussions about life in small communities. This is the third book that I have published with the University of Toronto Press, and my public expression of gratitude and respect towards Virgil Duff, the ideal editor, is long overdue. I also wish to acknowledge the helpful suggestions made by the anonymous reviewers of this study, and the assistance of Joanne Robinson-Duncan in eliciting relevant census information and presenting it in a form that even I could understand. In many respects this book is about the importance of family life, and I have often wondered whether I would ever be able to write without the tolerance, humour, and stability provided by Kaye, Jason, and Mia.

An initial grant from the Research Excellence Fund at the University of Guelph started this project rolling; subsequent grants from the Social Sciences and Humanities Research Council of Canada administered by the Board of Research at the University of Guelph and from Multiculturalism and Citizenship saw it through to completion.

PART ONE

Paradise Lost: Natives

Chapter One

Historical Sketches

Paradise in the 1950s, a Saturday night in summer: life in the fast lane! To the local people, this was no exaggeration, because Saturday night was shopping night, when the farmers and their families came to town, and the stores, at least some of them, stayed open until midnight. Saturday was much more than the day to buy groceries; it was a social occasion, a weekly community event. By early evening, parking spaces along Main Street were at a premium. Some of them, much to the disgust of the shoppers, were occupied by the storekeepers themselves, others by the more gregarious citizens of Paradise who, although their homes might be located only a few minutes' walk from downtown, preferred to park on Main Street, where they could exchange greetings and gossip with the passing cast of friendly actors.

One man, still on his parent's farm today, recalls how much he used to look forward as a boy to the Saturday night excursion; with 25 cents in his pocket, he could splurge on a milkshake, and slowly sip it while sizing up the sophisticated town kids. A woman who had grown up on a nearby farm summed up what Saturday night meant to her when she was young: 'That was about all the social life you had; it was free.'

Paradise, to the surrounding farmers, was not an alien place; it was their own community, where most of them would eventually retire. Nor was the relationship one way. There was virtually no industry in Paradise. Its economic lifeline was the surrounding farming community. Relations between townspeople and farmers were generally amicable, not only because of symbiotic needs, but also because many of the Paradise residents were themselves only one or two generations off the farm.

In the 1950s the division of labour between men and women was still clearly drawn, with most women confined to domestic duties within the home. Their husbands were carpenters and plumbers, merchants, well-drillers and handymen, and clerks and foremen in the grain elevators and creamery. By today's standard, few of them, including the owners of the stores and small businesses, were wealthy, although (unlike the present) even the poorest among them usually lived in a home of their own.

As for leisure activities, fishing was popular, and hunting perhaps even more so – both within and outside the designated season. Children in many families learned at an early age the name of the local game warden, a man to respect and fear. On one occasion, some hunters, among them a local police officer, shot a couple of deer out of season and, to conceal them from the watchful eyes of the game warden, hung them temporarily in the jail. As bizarre as this may seem, it pales next to another hunting story that was related to me: a middle-aged man, so I was told, made a practice of masturbating the hounds so that they would be inclined to chase the fleeing deer in his direction (what he did with the females of the species was left unspecified).

No account of leisure activities in rural Ontario can leave out the place occupied by music. Whether it was at a dance at a local hall or in somebody's kitchen, many cold winter evenings were pleasantly passed listening to the sweet but lively sound of the fiddle and the banjo. These were also the days when ice hockey was the focus of tremendous rivalry among villages. During the playoffs the unheated arenas were jammed with spectators cheering on their heroes, who glided over natural rather than artificial ice. Included among the spectators were people from the farms. One woman recalled that a truck used to drive her and her brothers, along with other farmers, to the hockey games and then take them home, shivering in the back. Such village rivalry is now a thing of the past, reflecting the degree to which community identification has decreased.

One of the most important annual events was the fall fair. It featured farm produce, prize steers and pigs, pies and cakes and jams and jellies by the tableful, horse racing, a merry-go-round and other rides, and contests in which one's throwing arm, or one's ability to swing a sledgehammer hard enough to ring a bell, was tested. At the fall fair in 1951 there was a hog-calling contest. The delicate daughters of the man who won were somewhat less than thrilled by their father's accomplishment; but things could have been worse – their mother could have won the husband-calling contest that was also held that year.

Whereas from the perspective of the farm kids, their counterparts in Paradise lived in the midst of excitement and opportunity, young people in Paradise today would probably regard village life in the 1950s as a barren desert. There was no cinema, except occasionally in a room in the town hall, and no television for most of them, although one could stand outside a store on Main Street and watch a black-and-white screen on a set exhibited by an enterprising merchant. In those days a visit by car to relatives a few miles away counted as an event, and a trip to Toronto was at the end of the universe. The young people of Paradise, of course, did not know they were deprived, and in many respects they weren't. Paradise was in the centre of a snow belt, and in winter there was hockey in the arena and on the frozen ponds. It was not until after 1945 that a serious effort was made to keep the county roads ploughed. Even in 1950 many people still put their cars up on blocks for the winter, and farmers came to town in horse-drawn cutters and sleighs. One of the most delightful experiences that adults today remember about growing up in those days in Paradise is jumping on the back runners of a farmer's sleigh, riding it a couple of miles out of town, and then catching another sleigh for the return trip.

In the summer there were endless baseball games, not organized affairs such as we find today, but simply a handful of kids with a ball and a bat. For girls, the opportunities at that time to participate in sports were much less, except within the school, but both girls and boys gathered together on warm summer evenings to play kick-the-can or cops and robbers.

Drugs in the school yard were unknown in the 1950s. This does not mean that the youth of Paradise were angels. By the time some of them had got to high school they had already become acquainted with alcohol, and had experimented with tobacco at an even earlier age, picking up butts from the street if they had no money. A favourite pastime, mischievous but essentially innocent, was to climb the fire-escapes at the back of the stores on a Saturday night, crawl across to the front, and drop water-filled balloons on the people strolling below. Hallowe'en was also a time to raise hell. Some of my informants recall loading a number of outhouses onto wagons – those were the days when indoor plumbing had only recently been put in place – and piling them in front of the doors of the village's only school. Those also were the days when the teachers were still allowed to use the strap, although few adults today, including those who could still recall its sting, thought that it had been administered injudiciously or cruelly.

Creating Paradise

In order to understand the community of Paradise in the 1950s, and later in the 1980s, we have to step back in history and examine its origins. Most of the early settlers (or invaders, from the perspective of the Aboriginal inhabitants) were Empire Loyalists from New York State. From the 1780s (see Ankli and Duncan 1984), the population of Ontario grew rapidly. Crown land could be had for six pence an acre, plus survey costs and an oath of allegiance. From 1825 to 1851 the province's population jumped from about 150,000 to 925,000. After the War of 1812, migration from the United States slowed to a trickle, while that from Britain rose to a flood. Harris (1975) interprets the massive immigration from Britain as a by-product of the Industrial Revolution. Rather than relocating in the new industrial cities in Britain, some people chose to cross the Atlantic and re-establish farming livelihoods in the new land.

Although Paradise was not granted the status of a municipality until 1878, it began to take shape in 1864. The vast majority of the early settlers were Protestants from Northern Ireland. The county itself was named after Lord Dufferin, the Irish-born governor general of Canada from 1872 to 1878; some of the founding citizens of Paradise wanted to name the community after a town in Northern Ireland from which they had originated.

These early pioneers entered a land containing bears and wolves, with wild raspberries and blueberries to supplement their meagre diet (Kelling 1981), and malaria or swamp fever to test their commitment. On the farms, especially in winter, weeks might pass before a family would come in contact with another human being. The first stores in Paradise were constructed out of wood, with false fronts; by 1885 they had been replaced by brick buildings. The small villages that began to take shape in rural Ontario in those days soon had churches, taverns, general stores, grain elevators, harness shops, blacksmith shops, a sawmill, a grist-mill, a drugstore, a tannery, a bank, a shoemaker and tailor, perhaps a jeweller, plus a medical doctor and a veterinarian.

Stagecoaches were the early form of public transportation; in the swampy areas, they bumped across corduroy roads constructed from earth piled on top of the stripped trunks of trees. Over the decades farmers were obligated to do statute labour on the roads, with one farmer in each area being designated 'road boss.' In 1873 the first train, owned by the Toronto, Grey and Bruce Railway, rolled into Paradise on a narrow-gauge track. In 1884 that company was absorbed by the Canadian Pacific Railway, which continued to operate a passenger service until 1970. As Glazebrook (1968:134) has commented: 'The arrival of a train was not routine but an event, for the train itself was given a personality.' Certainly, train service had a critical impact on the economic life of communities. If they were located on the railway line, they blossomed; if they weren't, they withered. Paradise was counted among the lucky communities.

One of the most onerous jobs in the pioneer days was removing stumps, which convicted criminals could be sentenced to perform. In the last century there also existed a system of indentured apprenticeship (or perhaps more accurately, labour) for children who had been abandoned, or whose parents were unable or unwilling to care for them; these children were bound by court order to an adult until the age of twenty-one, although those who were fourteen or older could refuse to comply (Glazebrook 1968:101). The Paradise area also had its share of Barnardo children, over thirty thousand of whom had been sent to Canada between 1882 and 1939 under a program organized by Dr Thomas John Barnardo to provide a better life for unfortunate youngsters than they could have in Britain (Corbett 1981). One of the most remarkable characters whom I met in Paradise in the late 1980s – at the age of ninety he still operated his own small barber shop and quoted poetry to his customers – had been a Barnardo boy.

The first church services in villages like Paradise were often held in private homes or halls. The Presbyterians, for example, met in a farmer's cabin in the bush near Paradise, the Anglicans in the Orange Hall. The Salvation Army and the United Brethren were present in the village around 1885, as well as the Gospel Workers, whose church was not torn down until 1965. Although church union occurred formally in 1925, it was only in 1939 in Paradise that the Presbyterians and Methodists came together to form the United Church. The church was more than a spiritual centre; it was often used for meetings and plays. Fowl suppers, with goose rather than turkey being the tradition in those days, were annual church events; one man from a poor family recalled how his mother would always tell him not to fill up on bread so he would have room for the meat.

There was no school in Paradise during its first decade of existence, and children walked to a one-room building a couple of miles away (Dodds 1983). A private school that opened in 1875 only lasted five months; later that year, school was held in the Orange Hall. The following year a brick schoolhouse was built. In 1900 it was replaced by a larger structure which, after being renovated in 1925, served as both elementary and secondary school until 1954, when a new secondary school was built (two new primary schools exist today). For the first part of the century, boys and girls from the farms boarded in homes in the village while attending high school. Often there was a wide age range in the classes, because some children only went to school during the winter months. By the 1960s the last of the county's one-room schools had closed. Farm kids, transported by bus, joined town kids in the classroom. A prominent teacher from those days told me that he could tell at a glance if a student came from the town or the country: the latter always were more polite and eager to learn. As the years passed, however, the farm kids, he said, went through several stages. While initially so well-behaved, and so grateful for all the facilities provided to them, in due time they began to take it all for granted. Finally, they started to complain and raise hell like all the other students.

Few among us today would be surprised to learn that the pioneer life in villages like Paradise was one of hardship and challenge. Yet what is striking is the sheer number of organizations and outlets that existed in those early days for the sole purpose of providing people with pleasure. In addition to the church socials and the many taverns, and wood bees for men and quilting bees for women, there were sporting events and a host of clubs covering almost every conceivable interest. Horse-racing, with the main street serving as the track, was popular, and cock-fighting was organized in a nearby village (Huxtable, undated). Several angling clubs existed. A cricket club was established in 1893, and a tennis club – something residents today have been trying in vain to re-establish – made its appearance in 1905, complete with clay courts, only to be abandoned by the 1940s.

Checkers tournaments and spelling bees were popular, as were plays like *Uncle Tom's Cabin*, complete with blackened faces – a practice one could still observe in some small communities in the area even in the 1960s. For the intellectually inclined, there was the Debating Society founded in 1900, and the Victoria Literary Society established a year later. For the musical, a Citizens Band was organized as early as 1876;

one remarkable and talented man was the bandleader for sixty-two years. The Ladies Coronet Band was established in 1888, the Glee Club three years later. Added to these were several voluntary organizations: the Masons in 1879 (they eventually bought the premises of the Methodist Church after church union took place), the Canadian Order of Foresters (with eighty-three charter members) in 1890, the Women's Institute in 1902, and the IODE in 1918. The one type of organization that has never seemed to thrive in Paradise is the businessman's club. A Chamber of Commerce founded in 1919 quickly fell apart, and the same thing happened when another effort was made to establish it in 1955. In 1949 a Business Man's Association existed, but with little clout. It has only been since the late 1980s that a successor to it – the Business Improvement Association (BIA) – has emerged as a viable organization for the town's merchants. No community is complete without its own newspaper. Paradise's first newspaper was founded in 1875, predating the village's status as a municipality. In 1928 it amalgamated with a second newspaper that had been established in 1883. This same newspaper serves the community today. Many citizens of Paradise complain bitterly that it no longer contains much news about the community itself, and put the blame on the publisher, whose father and grandfather had owned the paper before him. What Paradise people fail to appreciate is that the newspaper has merely changed along with the community itself.

No discussion of voluntary organizations in Paradise's pioneer days could possibly avoid the Orange Lodge. By the 1980s, it is true, the Orange Lodge had become an archaic organization, the local Orange Hall only being used by elderly men (and sometimes women) for a place to play cards. Yet only a generation earlier the annual Orange Parade had been one of the most impressive events in the community. The organization, of course, was introduced into Canada by Protestant immigrants from Northern Ireland. According to Saunders (1960), the organization served as the 'valiant champion of British and Protestant supremacy,' upholding the vision inspired by William of Orange. Marshall has written: 'Dufferin Orangemen seldom were as bigoted as some accused them of being.' Many of my informants in Paradise, whose fathers had been members of the lodge, and mothers members of the women's branch (the Loyal Orange Benevolent Association, or LOBA), cannot recall being raised in homes of rabid anti-Catholicism. Nevertheless, everyone certainly knew the identities of the handful of Catholics who lived there, and it is a reflection of the attitudes that prevailed that one merchant was often referred to as 'the man who married the Catholic woman,' even though both of them attended the Anglican Church.

In 1990 I was invited to attend a supper and dance at an Orange Hall a few miles from Paradise. The history of that particular lodge goes back a long way. It emerged in 1922 when two separate lodges, one founded as early as 1830, the other in 1848, were amalgamated. According to a brief document that traces the lodge's high points, one of its earliest responsibilities was law and order among its members. Some of them were fined five shillings for being drunk and disorderly, others 'were expelled for divulging signs and secrets of the lodge to unqualified persons,' or 'for shady deals on fellow Orangemen.' In 1978 a third lodge amalgamated with the original one – a sign of the times, with the membership ever dwindling. In 1922 there had been seventy-four members; in 1990 there were about twenty, only a half-dozen of whom were still active on a regular basis.

On the evening that I was in attendance, about ninety people were present, most of them from lodges in surrounding communities. The average age was about seventy, with less than ten of them being under fifty; the vast majority were farmers or former farmers. Only two of the several speakers mentioned religion. One of them referred to the Orange Lodge as a Protestant organization, and another described it as the defender of Christianity. In many respects, my impression that evening was that I had stepped into a scene from the last century. Yet the overall effect was far from unpleasant. I watched two elderly men, formerly farmers who had lived across from each other, renewing acquaintances with a degree of genuine warmth that was touching. The man who had invited me, himself a farmer nearing retirement age, said it has been the comradeship that he has enjoyed most during a lifetime in the organization. Today the building in which we met, constructed in 1930, is still used as a community hall, a place which baseball teams and other groups can rent at a reasonable rate, and where benefit dances can be held for families in need. But my host was under no illusions about the organization's future. As he explained, there is no longer the same hatred in the area between Protestants and Catholics – a change which he did not lament – and thus history has passed a death sentence on the fraternal association that had been his second home.

Today it is not only the Orange Lodge but also the Women's Institute and the IODE that are dying off. While these organizations once provided the main opportunities for social interaction (albeit possibly of a somewhat narrow-minded variety) and for philanthropic work in the small community, they have been dislodged by their contemporary counterparts. In Paradise, the Rotary Club was established in 1938; its charter members were then among the leading citizens, and even today it is known as 'the rich man's club,' influential and powerful, although somewhat long in the tooth (the Masons even more so). Since then the Lion's Club, the Kinsmen Club, and the Kinette Club have made their appearances, with memberships ranging from twenty to thirty, as well as Horticultural and Agricultural societies. In terms of their impact on life in the small community, however, none of them is in the same league as the Orange Lodge in its heyday.

The surrounding farmers sometimes attended events in town, such as a church supper, but they had their own organizations and sources of entertainment. In most farming districts there was a branch of the Women's Institute, and country churches in those days thrived. There was a collective element in the work sphere, such as during harvest, when neighbouring farmers would join forces. Beef rings, consisting of a cooperative formed by several farmers, each of whom provided a steer, existed into the 1930s. A large part of social life consisted of two or three families getting together for a meal. Often they would listen to the Farm Forum, a popular radio program, and afterwards bring out a deck of cards. The Farm Forum was basically educational in nature, rather than political and economic, which more closely describes the influential organization at the time called the United Farmers of Ontario. The cooperative spirit that existed apparently took an unusual twist on one occasion many years ago: a handful of farmers, with pillows under their arms and the good of the community in their minds, converged on the bedroom of an unfortunate neighbour who had rabies, and snuffed out his life.

Although the trend was for farmers to spend their retirement years in Paradise, this does not mean that they relinquished all their ties to the countryside, or that everyone made the move with the same degree of enthusiasm. Many former farmers whom I met in Paradise continued to attend the churches and organizations located in the countryside where they used to live, rather than joining those in town. One woman, who did just that, described how she felt when she moved into Paradise following her husband's death. For the first couple of years she used to work until after midnight in her new home, building cupboards, cleaning – too unhappy to sleep unless she was totally exhausted. Somewhat introverted and inflexible, but with the strong will and backbone out of which pioneers are made, this elderly woman made it clear that she preferred the solitary life that she had led on the farm. As the years went by in Paradise, she did make friends among her neighbours, and got together with them on a regular basis to play cards. By the time I had met her in the late 1980s, most of these friends had passed away, and she was once again on her own.

Changing Rural Ontario

If the number of people living in a community over time can be taken as a measurement of change or stability, Paradise during the first half of the century was stable indeed. Its population in 1901 was 1188; in 1951 it was 1184. Yet population figures alone do not tell the whole story. Over these same fifty years the telephone, introduced into the village in 1901, eventually reached almost every home; oil lamps gave way to electricity, horses and buggies to tractors and cars, stagecoaches to trains and buses, and young men and women marched off to two world wars, many of them never to return. There is, therefore, nothing new about social change in Paradise, but after Hitler had been burned in effigy at the Fair Grounds in 1945, a new world seemed to emerge. An early concrete sign was simply the establishment of the village's first large supermarket. Its impact on the community was dramatic. Not only did it make the existing small grocery stores obsolete, but it transformed the weekly economic and social rhythm of the village. Up to that time, Saturday night had been the big night, but the new supermarket began to remain open on Friday evenings. Other merchants were up in arms, but Friday-night shopping was the wave of the future, and they had no option but to adjust. Many of them, for a year or two, kept their stores open on both Friday and Saturday nights. Eventually they capitulated, and the social drama of Saturday evening took its place in the dustbin of history.

The close analysis of social change in Paradise will dominate all of the chapters that follow, but before turning to it, I shall briefly describe what has transpired in the surrounding farming community. It was not until after the Second World War that most of the farms in the Paradise area got electricity and tractors. Many of my elderly informants recall how marvellous it was merely to turn a switch and the barnyard and barn itself would light up; as for the women among them, the general opinion was that the greatest invention of all was the electric washing machine.

Throughout the 1950s and the early 1960s the cost of farm land increased steadily, but not sharply; but by the end of the 1960s prices had begun to go wild. Accident plays a large part in life, and whether a farmer sold out in the 1950s and early 1960s, or ten years later, meant the difference between hopefully having enough to live on in retirement or making a fortune. One man, who had scratched out a meagre living on less than one hundred acres, sold his farm around 1950 for the same price he had paid for it about forty years before, and said he was happy he had not lost anything on the deal. Other people were less sanguine. Walking around Paradise today are many men and women who have not been able to forgive their parents for having let the farm go before prices soared into the clouds.

By the 1980s the composition of the population in the countryside had been transformed by land speculators, and by people from the city searching for rural retreats. But the initial stimulus for these changes came from another direction: agribusiness. As one man observed: 'There's been an evolution in the countryside. One hundred acres are no longer enough. Mixed farming is out. They have to have 1000 acres. And they have to specialize.' Many of the retired farmers to whom I talked were fully aware of the dilemma they had faced. One of them said it was no longer possible to find hired hands, and if he did find them, he couldn't afford them. The only options were to borrow money from the bank to buy bigger and better equipment and more land, or get out of the business. He took the latter route.

Some indication of the changes that have occurred in rural society is reflected in statistical material, neatly summarized by Dasgupta (1988). From 1871 to 1971 the population of Canada changed from four-fifths rural to four-fifths urban. In 1931 the urban population exceeded the rural population for the first time in the country's history. These changes were proportional: from 1871 to 1981 the rural population actually increased in absolute numbers from about three to six million (Dasgupta 1988:25). Between 1931 and 1981 the proportion of Canadians living on farms decreased from 31 per cent to 4 per cent; in Ontario, the figures were 23 per cent and 3 per cent. But during this same period the rural *nonfarm* population rose from one-third to four-fifths the total rural population across Canada. Although there has been a decrease since the Second World War in the number of farms, farmers, and acres under agriculture, agricultural productivity, as Dasgputa points out (1988: 81), has steadily increased. The success of agribusiness, however, has been at the expense of the smaller farms, which have been made obsolete. In Dufferin County the proportion of people employed in agriculture shrunk from fifty-three per cent in 1951 to 8 per cent in 1986 (Statistics Canada: 1951 and 1986). Because small communities like Paradise owed their economic existence to agriculture, it is obvious that they must have changed dramatically as well.

The countryside around Paradise today is occupied by several distinct groups: modern farm operators with large tracts of land; wealthy city people on new estates, anywhere from ten to one hundred acres; middle-class newcomers in converted farmhouses or new bungalows on a few acres; and a sprinkle of old-style farmers, most of them at least semi-retired, either holding on to the old life, with a few pigs and cattle, or playing out their hands on a couple of acres severed from the homestead.

How have these old-style farmers reacted to the revolution in the countryside? One man, eighty years old when I met him, remarked: 'The whole place has gone mad. There's a pile of Italians up the line!' His wife left him years ago, and he now lives alone in the family farmhouse on two remaining acres of land (the rest of the farm was sold long ago). There is no electricity or telephone, and only an outside well for water. Like many other destitute people in the countryside, the last part of the twentieth century for this man still means a wood-stove and oil lamps.

A few miles away, a couple in their sixties reminisced about the past: 'This used to be a beautiful part of the country. The fences all standing. There wasn't a patch not planted. Everyone made maple syrup, nearly, that had a bush.' They remembered the buss bees (wood-cutting get-togethers), the beef ring they belonged to, the evenings spent listening to the Farm Forum, as well as to the party telephone line – a gold-mine of gossip. Their farm is the only one still in operation in the area today, and at the time I met them they were trying to figure out what to do with their remaining years. Their marriage had been childless, and thus there were no sons or daughters to inherit the farm, or to persuade them to buy a bungalow next door to them. In the past they would simply have sold the farm and moved into town. But as they pointed out, the town, with all the newcomers, was no longer the familiar place they used to know.

A much younger man, still in his thirties, and unmarried, faced a similar problem: should he sell the farm which his family had owned for three generations and make a bundle, or should he be swayed by his love of the land? In addition to his hundred acres, he rents two hundred and fifty acres nearby, but said it still is not enough from which to make a living (he holds down a part-time job off the farm). Musing about the drastic changes in farming over the past few decades, he remarked: 'If my grandfather had a crop failure, he'd lose a bit of seed, and he'd have to tighten his belt. If he needed more power, he'd take his mare and have her bred, and soon he'd have another horse. But you can't do that with a tractor.' The stakes, he thought, are much higher today, because so much money is tied up in equipment. His 'monster equipment,' as he referred to it, requires that he has access to more land, in order that it pays for itself. He rents additional acreage from city people who have bought old farms but, as he pointed out, there is no guarantee that the land will be available next year, and consequently it is not worth his while to maintain the fences and drains in good repair.

This man had fond memories of what farm life used to be like, but he did not paint it all in rosy colours: 'In my Dad's generation, the competition among the farmers was horrendous. The furrows had to be that straight. Everybody else were the worst farmers. There could be meanness in that competition.' As for the newcomers, his general opinion was that most of them wanted the countryside equipped with city amenities: 'You hear them complain there's no theatre, the cultural events.' Half-laughing, he added: 'You go to an auction sale and you can tell everybody from the city – their jeans are pressed. They all have a jeep, a 4 by 4. Sometimes it's just like a safari around here.'

The fact that this farmer had to hold down a part-time job to make ends meet has become the rule rather than the exception across the country. As Dasgupta (1988: 91) pointed out, in 1981 almost 40 per cent of family farm operators worked part-time off the farm, and another 14 per cent held down full-time outside jobs. In the Paradise area virtually every active farmer whom I met was employed on a part-time basis away from the farm. In some cases the newcomers themselves were a source of supplementary income. One man, for example, who was the only active farmer left around him (and in his words, he only 'semi-farmed'), had been hired to look after the properties nearby that had been bought by city people (these included four medical doctors, an architect, three executives of large corporations, and a lawyer; of the nine people, only one commuted daily to Toronto – the others were 'weekenders'). The farmer in question, still active in the Orange Lodge, did not object to the presence of the newcomers, who after all had provided him with employment and driven up the price of his land. He merely regarded them as a somewhat strange species, whose habits and language precluded meaningful communication.

A polar example of the new breed of farmer, at least among those with only one hundred acres or so, is the character who said to me: 'I'm a wheeler-dealer. I'm self-employed in agriculture. People phone me to cut down trees. I snow plough. I clear bush. I wouldn't call me just a farmer.' As he explained, it is impossible for him to make a living from straight farming. Whereas some of the old-time farmers could not be bothered applying for farm subsidies, this man, in his late thirties, subscribed to agricultural reading material to make sure he wasn't missing any hand-outs. An entrepreneur to his bones, he also had tried, with moderate success, to organize a barter system among his neighbours, trading both labour and equipment. In his words, 'Money's too expensive, so I make deals.' As a comment about economic life, that's not bad, but it's not in the same league as the words from one old rural philosopher who summed up why prices had escalated so much in the area: 'You see,' he said, 'they haven't made any more land for quite a few years.'

Chapter Two

The Framework of the Study

The historical overview that has just been sketched serves as an invitation to enter the world of the people of Paradise. Before we can proceed any further, we must pause to clarify the topics which have been selected as the focus of the study, plus the key concepts and the central arguments.

Focus

STRATIFICATION

As indicated in the preface, at the most general level this is a study of social change in small-town Ontario, revolving around a systematic comparison of two periods: the decade following the Second World War, and the decade of the 1980s. During the first period there was a broad and rigid stratification system in Paradise. Class position and formal power were highly correlated, with members of the elite monopolizing leadership roles on the local council and in the service clubs and churches. The community was physically divided to some extent along social class lines; most of the poor people lived in run-down dwellings on three streets at one end of the town. The normative expectation at that time was for individuals to remain in the class level into which they had been born.

By the early 1980s the stratification system had been transformed. What is most striking is that not a single one of the elite families from the past remains among the elite today. Another dramatic change has been the dissociation of upper-class position and formal power. Members of the town council in the 1980s were recruited from the ranks of the middle and lower-middle classes, and included relative newcomers. People contend that the extreme ends of the class structure have crumbled, replaced by a broad middle class. There has, indeed, been some movement in that direction. Yet what has really transpired is that both extreme poverty and extreme wealth have become less visible. A new generation of poor people has emerged, but is hidden in apartments and rooming-houses. As for the members of today's elite – mostly professionals and successful businessmen who are newcomers to the town – they do not flaunt their wealth or demand deference to the same degree as their counterparts a generation earlier had done. Nor do they seek to verify and exhibit their class superiority by contesting public office.

MIGRATION

Over the last couple of decades it has been apparent that a most significant change, as yet poorly analysed in Canada, has been taking place in the North American countryside. For the first time in history more people have been moving from urban to rural areas than the reverse. Sometimes referred to as the population turnaround, this recent pattern has been the subject of close examination in the United States. Most of the migrants in that country have been described as highly educated, middle- or upper-middle-class people, motivated primarily by the prospect of a better quality of life. The Canadian scene, at least based on my study of Paradise, has been quite different. The newcomers there are not remarkably well educated; most of them are working-class people aspiring to the middle class, motivated less by quality of life than by the sheer desire to own their own homes, or at least to rent an affordable townhouse.

The majority of these newcomers commute to the urban centres to the south, including Toronto itself. Pressed by mortgage payments, drained by the daily drive, they have little time for interaction in the community. The very fact that they are there, however, has modified the quality of social relationships. People born and raised in Paradise complain that they no longer know their neighbours, and many of them have ceased to greet people automatically on the street; some of them, equating strangers with danger, believe crime has exploded in their small town. The newcomers, on their part, are left to grumble about the unfriendly natives and the lack of amenities, unless, as happens to so many of them, the experiment in rural living is abandoned, and they return to rented premises in the city.

RACE AND ETHNICITY

In the decade following the Second World War almost all the residents of Paradise and the surrounding communities were British in origin. By the 1980s this was no longer true. Joining the march from the city to the countryside has been an increasing number of ethnic minorities. These include white ethnics (non-British and non-Western Europe in origin), African Canadians (some of whose roots in Canada go back several generations, many of the others recent immigrants from the West Indies), and Asian Canadians (mostly from India and Pakistan). This part of the research was guided by one basic question: is racism more or less pronounced in rural society than in urban society? Many of the African and Asian Canadians stated that they felt less at home in the countryside than in the city. Before it is concluded that a more virulent form of racism exists in rural society, it must be remembered that Paradise today includes not only the long-term residents of British origin, but also the white newcomers. It seemed to me that prejudice ran deeper among the latter than among the former. The long-term residents, whom I refer to as 'the natives' in this study, tended to be ethnocentric, a condition that sometimes evaporates when exposed to the objects of one's imagination – in this case, the visible minorities themselves. Some of the white newcomers, in contrast, tended to be racists, their attitudes already hardened by their previous experiences in the city. One of the striking revelations of this project, indeed, was the discovery that a motivation (in some cases, the main motivation) for moving away from the city for some people was simply to escape from an environment that included a large number of visible minorities.

The theme of migration from the city, involving newcomers and commuters, will be the focus of Part Two. While race and ethnicity are the centrepieces in Part Three, in a less obvious manner they are on stage throughout the study, in the personage of the British-origin native in Part One and the mixture of European-origin people in Part Two. Similarly, stratification, the dominant topic in chapter 3 and to a lesser extent in chapter 7, constitutes an implicit framework for the entire book. This is because, in the end, two kinds of stratification intersect: that based on class, and that based on ethnicity. At the point where they make contact lie some of the most difficult questions, and potentially the most profound answers, about the nature and dynamics of social life in rural Ontario.

Concepts

NATIVES

How long does it take for a newcomer to become accepted into a community? On one extreme, Strathern (1982) indicates that in the community of Elmdon in England only a handful of families that had lived there before 1914 qualified as 'the real Elmdoners.' On the other extreme, Sinclair and Westhues (1974:89) define natives (oldtimers, in their terminology) as anyone who has lived in the Ontario community they studied for at least seven years. In Paradise, and in virtually every other community that has been investigated by social scientists, that would appear to be an implausibly short time-span. However, seven years was used as the cut-off point by the authors because most of the newcomers had taken up residence in their community within that brief period.

In Paradise one's occupation (for example, successful businessman or commuting factory worker) and one's behaviour (for example, whether a person joined local organizations) influenced how quickly one was accepted, although some people claimed that if you were not born in the community, you were always regarded as an outsider, regardless of other conditions. I arbitrarily defined natives as all people who had lived in Paradise before 1960. Not only was this a reasonably long period – about thirty years at the time of my study – but it also clearly placed the natives in the era prior to the massive invasion of newcomers that began around 1970.

NEWCOMERS

These are defined as all those people who had moved to Paradise after 1960. These newcomers in the rural scene are sometimes referred to in the literature as reverse migrants or inmigrants (as opposed to outmigrants), to distinguish them from the previously dominant pattern in which people moved from rural to urban society.

ETHNIC MINORITIES

The scholarly literature on racial and ethnic prejudice and discrimination is bedevilled by a persistent problem. On the one hand, racial classifications based on observable physical appearance (phenotypes) have long been discarded by the academic world because they lack scientific validity; more recent attempts to employ genes and chromosomes as the basis for classification (producing genotypes) have not fared much better, due to the obstacles against experimental control, and to the measurement problems posed by a complex organism: namely, the human being. On the other hand, lay people often act *as if* a biological classification, especially in the phenotypical sense, is meaningful, and their beliefs, regardless how erroneous, have consequences for social life which the investigator cannot ignore. Even academic specialists who dismiss racial classifications as misleading fictions find it difficult to avoid using common terms like white and black, or Caucasoid and Negroid, and, of course, 'race' itself.[1]

One indication of the meaninglessness of concepts like white people or black people, conceived in biological terms, is that the definition of who is white or black has been a shifting one. Among white supremacists, such as the members of the Ku Klux Klan, the term 'white' has shrunk and expanded over the decades, at one point excluding Greeks and Italians, at another point not only including them but also Slavs, Scandinavians, and the 'Aryan' people of Persia. In Paradise in the past, the terms British and Canadian were synonymous. In recent years, however, as a result of the influx of newcomers, the ethnic conceptual map has been redrawn. The category of 'real' Canadians has been expanded to include a wide range of people of European origin and the term 'British' has given way to a vague image of 'white people,' who are assumed to constitute a separate race, distinct from and superior to the African, East Indian, and Pakistani peoples who have moved into the area.

Finally, there were the attitudes of Paradise residents, both natives and newcomers, towards French Canadians, only a handful of whom lived in the community. Not only did a number of people argue that French Canadians and Quebec in general were parasites within the Canadian fabric, but some of them also defined French Canadians as a separate and peculiar race – the most inferior one of all.

As earlier indicated, when I refer to natives in this study, I shall mean the people of British origin who until recently constituted almost the entire population of Paradise. By newcomers I shall mean those people, including white ethnics, who are now considered part of the expanded version of the white 'race.' By minorities I shall mean primarily the newcomers of Asian and African origin, plus the few French Canadians and Jews who have made Paradise their home, and who are regarded by many of their neighbours as belonging to separate races.

COMMUNITY

What could be easier than defining what we mean by community? Apparently almost anything else! Bell and Newby (1972:21) have pointed out that although sociologists have grappled with the concept for more than two hundred years, there still is no satisfactory definition. In an early review of the literature on community, Hillery (1955) came up with ninety-four definitions; the only element that was commonly agreed on was that community involves people. Wilkinson (1986:1) remarks: 'Community is a most appealing concept ... [but] ... for all of its appeal, the meaning of the concept of community is most elusive.' Stacey (1969:134) arrived at a similar conclusion: 'It is doubtful whether the concept "community" refers to a useful abstraction.'

The conventional definition of community contains two minimal elements: ecology (demarcated geographical area) and solidarity (shared values and a feeling of belongingness). Smuggled into the definition are usually assumptions about social structure, behaviour, beliefs and attitudes. That is, communities are thought to be characterized by particular types of organization (shaped by territory or ecology) and ways of behaving, distinct from other sociological types such as urban society.

The discovery of village-type communities within the confines of the city (Gans 1962 and 1967), along with the recognition that conflict is as prevalent in the small community as solidarity, and that territory is a poor predictor of 'ways of life,' has cast serious doubt on the usefulness of this conventional approach. Quite different definitions have been offered by Cohen, Arensberg, and Weber. As Cohen states (1989:15), 'Community is that entity to which one belongs, greater than kinship but more immediately than the abstraction we call "society." It is the arena in which people acquire their most fundamental and most substantial experience of social life outside the confines of the home.' There is an attractive message in these words, but then

Cohen proceeds to define community in terms of 'meaning' and 'symbolism.' It is not structural type or ecology that represents community, but instead what it means or symbolizes to people. Undoubtedly Cohen is correct in arguing that community is conceived through the lens of symbol and meaning, but if that is all there is to community, the term can be applied to a remarkably wide range of human behaviour; in effect, Cohen's approach does not merely modify the classical focus of study known as the small community: it destroys it.

Some writers such as Arensberg (1954) regard community study as a method, not a field of social behaviour. The small community is said to constitute a naturalistic experiment, life in the raw, which provides the basis for comparative analysis. It is on these grounds that Carstens (1991:xix), in his recent study of a Native community in British Columbia, advocates that we continue the tradition of community studies.

Finally, there is Weber's approach to community which, as Neuwirth (1969) has so clearly demonstrated, constitutes a radical departure from the classical approach. Not only does Weber de-emphasize the ecological factor, but, more importantly, he dissents from the conventional view that communities are characterized by shared values, common interests, and solidarity. In Weber's theory, community emerges from competition for economic, political, and social resources, and internal solidarity is always a function of conflict with competing groups or communities, rather than an expression of shared values generated by common residence. Given the degree of competition and conflict in Paradise between upper-class and lower-class people, between natives and newcomers, and between white people and minorities, Weber's approach appears to be particularly appropriate for this study.

Commenting on why we focus on small communities and villages, Geertz (1973:22) has written: 'Anthropologists don't study villages (tribes, towns, neighbourhoods ...); they study *in* villages.' The implication, with which I am in agreement, is that the small community is not in itself a meaningful basis for sociological theory; that is, we do not get very far in the attempt to build a *theory* of community. But, following Arensberg, the small community, for which we could substitute the terms village or settlement without any loss of meaning – the point being merely to indicate the locus of the investigation – can serve as a useful methodological unit for abstracting relationships among variables from the flow of ongoing social behaviour. The fringe community in particular, where natives and newcomers collide, would seem to be a suitable setting in which to investigate social change in the contemporary world.

Finally, a word about the rural-urban continuum, given early shape by Wirth (1938) and Redfield (1947). The scholarly attack against this continuum has been so extensive as to render further criticisms redundant (see, for example, Hauser 1965, Lewis 1965, Lupri 1967, Miller and Luloff 1981, Pahl 1966 and 1967, and Williams 1973). This is not to say that no differences between rural and urban society exist in relation, for example, to educational attainments, divorce and crime rates. But such variation has over the past several decades been reduced to the point of insignificance, at least in the part of Ontario on which my study has been based. To paraphrase Dewey (1960–1), some differences between rural and urban society may remain, but they are relatively unimportant. In the chapters that follow, then, the rural-urban continuum will be virtually ignored, for the simple reason that it distorts rather than clarifies the data. Ironically, however, as in the case of racial terms, one can hardly avoid the continuing usage of concepts such as rural and urban, plus community itself, even if the meaning they convey is minimal and imprecise.

STRATIFICATION AND CLASS

I have left the most difficult conceptual problem, but one that is absolutely crucial to the study, until the last. How many classes are there in a community? Does the number of classes perceived vary with the actor's position itself? Are classes real, or merely analytic tools? In analysing stratification, should the actor's concepts or the observer's concepts be employed? Of course, one could write a book around these questions, but here I can do little more than indicate my own route through this theoretical maze.

My analysis of stratification in Paradise begins with the ideas of three talented writers: Marx, Weber, and Warner. Warner's approach would appear to be especially relevant because of his extensive investigations of stratification in various communities in America (Yankee City, Old City, and Jonesville). In Warner's scheme (1949), classes are presented as real, empirically existing entities, not merely analytic tools, because they are based on the actor's own subjective rankings; in other words, they reflect the world as perceived by and lived in by people themselves. According to Warner, the number of classes in any specific community is a matter of empirical investigation, for it can vary from one place to another (in his own studies, for example, either five or six classes are identified, depending on the community).

For the anthropologist – and Warner himself was an eminent one – there is much that is attractive about this approach, paramount among which is the priority assigned to the actor's definition of the situation, rather than the imposition of an alien model. Nevertheless, the criticisms levelled at Warner's work (see Bell and Newby 1972 and Mills 1967) have been massive, and in my opinion justified. One criticism is that he privileges the viewpoint of upper-class people, who tend to perceive more classes than do lower-class people. As Kornhauser (1953:249) asks, why should the five or six classes recognized by the former be considered more real than the three or four seen by the latter? Another criticism is that while he contends that his approach and findings can be generalized to all of America, they only are applicable to small, static communities where everyone knows each other. Perhaps the major criticism is that he confuses class and status, a key analytic distinction in Weber's work, and ends up merely probing issues of prestige and esteem, rather than social class per se.

The limitations of Warner's subjective approach to stratification were quite evident in my study of Paradise. Although my starting point was to follow Warner by trying to understand the community as experienced by the residents themselves, their subjective views were not sufficient to construct an overview of the class system. Indeed, their views were inconsistent and sometimes contradictory. For example, the number of classes perceived by Paradise people ranged from two to five, and these did not always vary neatly with the class position of the actor, as Warner would lead us to assume. Moreover, the class position of a specific individual was often ranked differently from one person to another. Finally, people's perceptions of their own class positions often failed to coincide with the positions they were assigned by their neighbours. The implication is clear: the subjective approach to stratification, relying on the actor's view of the world, does not produce a picture of discrete, concrete classes; nor does it, for that matter, provide a profile of an orderly status hierarchy, because status was subject to the same degree of variation and inconsistency. What people's subjective evaluations do give us is some understanding of their symbolic universe, the meaning of which, as Cohen (1989) has so eloquently indicated, can vary from one individual to another.

The approaches of Marx and Weber to social class, which combine both objective and subjective dimensions, are much more sophisticated. For Marx, social class is an objectively locatable entity: people who occupy the same position in relation to the means of production (for example, factory owners versus factory workers) constitute a social class. Central to a Marxian analysis is the principle that class membership is not dependent on the subjective views of the actor. Instead, class is an an analytic tool which enables the investigator to make sense of the phenomenal world of everyday life by identifying the dynamic forces below the surface that produce it. Yet it would be a grave error to conclude that Marx ignored subjectivity. The very fact that people may not be aware of their class interests and positions is from a Marxian perspective subjectively shaped, reflecting false consciousness. As well, Marx separated 'a class in itself' and 'a class for itself.' The first corresponds to the positions people occupy objectively in relation to the means of production. The second is infused with class consciousness, as people become aware of their class interests, and the potential for organized class conflict and revolutionary change increases. The synthesis of objective and subjective dimensions in Marx's conception of class, it should be added, is consistent with his overall theoretical orientation (Marx 1975, Marx and Engels 1970, Schaff 1970, Selsam et al. 1970). Material conditions and the structural arrangements people enter into in order to make their livings certainly are fundamental for Marx, but his actors are active agents whose will-power and emotions help shape the course of history.

Although Marx appears to have presented us with a clear and unambiguous approach to class, that is not quite the case. There is no unified agreement among social scientists, including Marxists, about the number of social classes in capitalist societies, or about who belongs to particular classes. A popular conception of the Marxian scheme is that it divides (and thus simplifies and distorts) society into two opposing classes, the bourgeoisie (capitalists) and the proletariat (workers). Even Marxian scholars who would reject that dichotomous scheme as a gross distortion of Marxism, pointing out that Marx alluded to 'the three big classes of modern society' (Heller 1987:14), and to class divisions or fractions within the major classes, display little agreement about the fundamental character of the class system. For example, whereas Poulantzas (1975) concludes that the working class in the United States is only a small proportion of the population, in Wright's analysis (1987:87) it constitutes about half of the population. To make matters even more complicated, Wright identifies what he calls contradictory class relations which do not fit into his three main classes (the bourgeoisie, the petty bourgeoisie, and the proletariat). The source of confusion concerns the most meaningful way to slot people into classes when distinctions between the propertied and propertyless, the owners and the workers, and mental and manual labour no longer tell us the full story.[2]

We now turn to Weber, whose life work can be portrayed as an endless debate with Marx, and whose writings on social class have probably been more influential than Marx's among social scientists. It is often argued (see Mann and Dickinson 1987) that subjective factors constitute the basis of Weber's general theoretical perspective. It is not difficult to understand why this interpretation has emerged. It was Weber who promoted *verstehen* (subjective understanding) as a cardinal methodological principle. Weber also emphasized motivation, and defined motivated social action as meaningful, in the sense that it is goal-oriented, and based on the individual's conscious interaction with others. But this is only one of the programs in Weber's writings, the other being the historical and comparative analysis of institutions revolving around the material conditions of social life (Weber 1964, Gerth and Mills 1958, Bendix 1962).

What is especially significant is that despite Weber's emphasis on *verstehen* and subjectively intended behaviour, his approach to social class, as Gerth and Mills (1958:57) point out, is essentially an objective one. Unlike Marx, Weber did not define class in terms of the relation of people to the means of production. But economic factors were the basis of his approach: a class consists of people who share similar life chances as determined by the market situation, or by their capacity to accrue goods and income. Class, thus, connotes economic power, and, like Marx, Weber emphasizes the pivotal role played by the possession or lack of possession of property. Weber also took pains to stress that classes are not 'communities.' That is, classes are not characterized by shared feelings of belonging, and are not the basis of collective action. Yet he goes on to state (Weber 1953: 67) that class consciousness, leading to class action, can indeed emerge under certain circumstances.

This last comment suggests that Weber, like Marx, allowed for subjectivity in his conception of class, but it was around his conception of status that subjectivity was most pronounced. Weber separated analytically class, status, and party. These constitute three quasi-independent aspects of power: class power, status power, and political power. It is the first two which concern us most here. Status is defined in terms of

honour, and concerns lifestyle; in contrast to class, status does form
the basis for organized association and action, because people are
conscious of the status group to which they belong. Central to Weber's
framework is the claim that status can vary independently of class, in
the sense, for example, that a penniless woman from a noble lineage
may occupy the same status category as the president of General
Motors.

In my judgment, it is precisely here that Weber's framework
becomes suspect. As Weber wrote (1953: 68): 'Property as such is not
always recognized as a status qualification, but in the long run it is,
and with extraordinary regularity.' If this is the case, and if property
or the lack of property are 'the basic categories of all class situations'
(Weber 1953:65), one can only wonder about the justification for
drawing such a clear distinction between class and status. In Marx's
scheme, status power and political power are consequences of social
class, not independent entities, and this is the manner in which I
prefer to view them. Status, in other words, is an ideological mechanism which helps prop up the class system. This does not mean that
status is insignificant, or that its influence cannot vary in time and
place. It merely implies that class, not status, at least in the long run,
is the bedrock of social stratification.

The Marxian and Weberian approaches to class, despite their ambi-
guities, are considerably more sophisticated than the Warnerian approach. Nevertheless, for the reasons indicated below, I am reluctant
to organize this study solely around the writings of either Marx or
Weber, although I certainly will attempt to draw on their insights
where it is especially relevant to do so. When I undertook my first
anthropological fieldwork – a study of a religious community in West
Africa (Barrett 1977) – I was more interested in engaging in theoretical
debates than in explaining the community that I was investigating.
Now I see my task in exactly the opposite terms, my approach to
ethnography having been influenced by reflections on my earlier
research and by contemporary debates about the ethnographic enterprise. The post-modernists (Clifford and Marcus 1986) are adamant in
their opposition to scholarly investigations that are organized around
macro-theoretical orientations, as are some versions of feminist anthropology (Whittaker in press). Such orientations, from the post-modernist perspective, falsely mimic the image of science, camouflage the
particularism and interpretism inherent in ethnography, and objectify
and estrange the people in one's study. For quite different reasons the

advocates of grounded theory (Glaser and Strauss 1967, Schatzman and Strauss 1973, Strauss 1987, Strauss and Corbin 1990), who have been bent on making qualitative research more rigorous rather than rejecting positivistic social science, are equally disdainful of sociological studies which promote general theory at the expense of discovering theory in one's data. I sympathize with the post-modernists and the grounded theorists, at least with regard to the role of theory, because my main goal is to understand Paradise rather than add to the corpus of theory in the discipline.

What I want is a set of conceptual tools that will enable me to organize the data as close to the ground as possible, reflecting the manner in which Paradise people themselves perceive their community and govern their behaviour. Towards this end, I have turned to the approach spelled out by Krauss (1976). Following the lead of Dahrendorf (1959), Krauss draws a clear distinction between stratification and class. In his words (1976:12): 'Social stratification then is any ordering of society's members, using any convenient criteria such as income, education, style of life, ethnic background. In other words social stratification is merely the *description* of a population in terms of "strata," or categories of people who have similar characteristics.' Krauss explains that strata are not organized, and are not the basis of collective action; moreover (and here the difference between Krauss and Warner is most pronounced), there are as many strata (Krauss 1976:100) as the investigator wishes to introduce. For example, one could divide a community into two strata, the rich and the poor, or into a dozen strata employing income level as the measuring rod.

Social class, in Krauss's approach, is an analytic concept involving conflict groups. Classes consist of organized groups which contest the unequal distribution of valued social goods: power, privileges, and possessions. Krauss's scheme, like those of Marx and Weber, is not devoid of ambiguity. For example, he appears to define social class entirely as 'a class for itself,' based on revolutionary consciousness and organized communal action, while ignoring Marx's concept of 'a class in itself.' It also is unclear whether the distinction between social stratification and class is analytic or concrete. On the one hand, the distinction seems to be analytically heuristic, enhancing the prospect of accurately describing a hierarchical system in terms of strata, while at the same time explaining how the hierarchy is generated by underlying class-based dynamics. On the other hand, the distinction seems to be embedded in the concrete world. Thus, Krauss takes pains to explain how strata transform empirically into classes, giving the impression that both stratification and class are concrete entities, rather than instruments in the investigator's tool-box.

These criticisms aside, the distinction that Krauss makes is very useful for my purposes. Stratification, as he defines it, provides a relatively unobtrusive framework for organizing my study of Paradise, allowing me to present an analysis which should be meaningful to the residents themselves. In this connection, however, there is one little problem. Paradise people did not employ the terms strata or stratum when they talked about their stratification system. Instead, they used the term class, even though its connotation was very similar to what Krauss meant by stratum – that is, an unorganized category of people in a hierarchy with similar characteristics, life chances, and social goods. In order to remain faithful to the manner in which Paradise residents themselves described their community, I shall use the term class rather than stratum throughout this study. It must be emphasized, however, that class will have the connotation of stratum as represented by Krauss. When I do discuss class in the sense that Krauss employs the concept, as organized conflictual action between groups of people structured in relation to the means of production (as I do, for example, in the concluding chapter of the study), or in the more orthodox Marxian and Weberian senses, the change in connotation will be made clear.

In the chapters that follow, a five-level descriptive scheme of Paradise's stratification system will be employed: upper class, lower-upper class, middle class, lower-middle class and lower class. Occasionally I shall add to or subtract from this scheme, depending on the problem at hand. As Krauss indicates (1976:12), the basis of erecting a stratification scheme could be people's subjective evaluations of their own positions, people's reputations as evaluated by others, and objective indicators such as education, residence, occupation, and income. Krauss adds that one's approach to stratification could rest on all of these factors. That essentially describes my procedure in regard to Paradise, but with one important difference: my five-point scheme also reflects my own subjective grasp of the community. The investigator always imposes her or his personal stamp on the data, consciously or unconsciously, because all sociological analysis involves interpretation. One final remark. Knowledge gained through fieldwork is produced by and negotiated between the investigator and the people investigated. Although it is the investigator's voice that unavoidably shapes the

Figure 1. Model of Social Change in Paradise

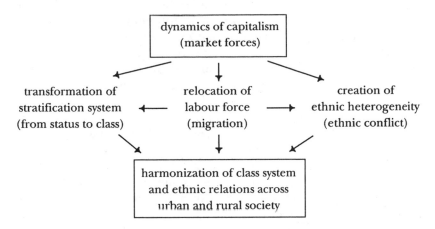

final product of one's work – even Clifford's writings, as Rabinow (1986:244) points out, are monological rather than dialogical – throughout this book I have attempted to give voice to the people of Paradise by presenting their dreams and anxieties in their own words.

Arguments

It may appear that the three topics focused on in this study – stratification, migration and ethnicity – are only loosely connected. To the contrary, my argument is that together they form a tightly integrated system of social change in rural Ontario (see figure 1). At the most general level, the movement of people, including the minorities, from the urban to the rural areas, and the transformation of Paradise's stratification system, have been responses to market forces in capitalism, and the end result has been to bring the class system and ethnic relations of the countryside in line with those in the city.[3]

Let us break the argument down into smaller parts, beginning with stratification. Status, as a principle of stratification, becomes pronounced during periods of social stability, and serves as an ideological mechanism that sustains patterns of power and privilege. In other words, it props up the class system. When rapid social change occurs, as Weber himself suggests (1953:73), the influence of status on the stratification system dissipates, and naked class relations become even more dominant. In Paradise during the decade following the Second World War, status overshadowed class in the minds of the residents (which, of course, does not mean that class was not the bedrock on which status rested even in those days). By the 1980s social class, defined in terms of the market situation, had the field to its own, with one exception. For the remnants of the old elite (the fallen aristocracy), left with little else except memories of past grandeur, status had become even more important, amounting to a sort of private ranking system about which the 'inferior' newcomers were essentially ignorant.

Corresponding to the changes in the stratification system were changes in the structure of authority. Traditional authority, the type that existed in Paradise in the 1950s, is similar to status in that it accumulates under conditions of stability and is ideologically conservative in nature. As class dislodged status in the face of rapid social change, impersonal bureaucratic (or legal-rational) authority – its dynamic centre located in the larger political and economic structures beyond the community – replaced the familiar members of the elite whose leadership had seemed to be divinely ordained.[4]

One consequence of these changes has been to render the subjective interpretations of Paradise people even less incisive than before. Over and over again in the 1980s I listened to people saying that you can't really pinpoint what social classes their neighbours occupy any more. As for authority, the general opinion was that the community was just drifting, with nobody in charge, including the local council. Some of the more thoughtful residents pointed to a hidden helmsman, which took the form of Queen's Park in Toronto, where the provincial politicians charted the waters, and their agencies such as the Ontario Municipal Board manned the oars. The odd person even referred to the power of the market as the invisible hand behind the scenes.[5]

I now turn to the newcomers and minorities. The working-class newcomers, mostly British in origin, and the minorities, mostly Asian and African in origin, are locked in an embrace not of their choosing, and Cupid is none other than the capitalist system itself. Driven by market forces, including the high cost of living in the city and cheaper accommodation in the country, the newcomers and minorities together gravitate to towns like Paradise, with the following consequences. The newcomers provide a jolt to the old stratification system propped up by status, preparing the way for the unfettered market-oriented class relationships characteristic of the wider society. In this sense, their impact, plus that of the wealthy weekenders and middle-class newcomers living on rural acreage, simply consolidates a trend already put in place by the emergence of agribusiness. The combined result is to reshape the rural class system along the lines of its city counterpart.

As for the influx of the visible minorities (plus the white ethnics among the other newcomers), it must be understood foremost as a 'modernizing' movement. The city in advanced industrial societies is pluralistic in terms of ethnicity, and class and ethnicity are two of the central principles of its stratification system. Whether it is simply the weight of a heavier structure on a lighter one, or whether ethnic and racial strains are necessary components of capitalist society, as Niko-linakos contends (1973), the consequences are the same: the migrating minorities provide Paradise and area with a degree of ethnic heterogeneity hitherto absent, and this makes possible the fusion of class and ethnicity in the rural stratification system. Paradise, in other words, with its reconstructed definition of 'white people,' with the visible minorities relegated to the political and social sidelines, and with the potential for ethnic and racial conflict greatly increased, has joined the modern world.

It must be made clear that I did not begin my research with this model of social change as a guide. Instead, it emerged from my efforts to make sense of the data after field work had been completed. The model itself, of course, is only a skeleton. To put flesh on it, to reveal the organs and the flowing blood, it is necessary to introduce real human beings, equipped with emotions, attitudes, and values, manipulating others, contradicting themselves, as they choose their routes around the land-mines of life. The attempt to present the people of Paradise in this matter, and thus to animate the abstract model, will be my goal in the chapters that follow.[6]

Chapter Three

Stratification

Paradise, to paraphrase Dickens, was the best of places or the worst of places, depending on one's perspective. Upper-class people described the community as it existed in the decade following the Second World War as one of harmony and marvellous egalitarianism. When pressed, they admit that there may have been different social levels, but they insist that everyone was treated fairly, even the drunks. There were no obstacles, they claimed, to upward status mobility; those who found themselves in the lowest level were there, and remained there, simply because they lacked ambition. Lower-class people contend that there was an oppressive class system. They remember the poverty, the deference demanded by a wilful elite, and the normative order that kept them in their places regardless of their talents and dreams. To the lower-class people, the community described by those in the upper class resembled a foreign country which they had never had the pleasure of visiting.

Patterns of Perception

Paradise people often remarked, sometimes bitterly, that in the past everyone was ranked. How many classes existed in those days? One man said: 'To me, there was only two; there was the hierarchy, and the rest of us.' Another man asked: 'Was there just two? Was there us and them (poor and rich)?' A woman who was more certain about her opinion declared that there had been three classes: 'the people with money, the in-between, and the ones who didn't have anything.' Many others agreed with her: 'I guess there was always three classes, aye?'

said one man; he described them as upper, middle, and poor. An elderly woman labelled them 'the top, the people who just worked, and poor people on the council' ('on the council' was a local expression for people on relief or on welfare). Another woman described them as 'the élite people, the middle, and the terrible people' ('the terrible people,' she made clear, referred to the lower class – in her mind, mostly drunks living in neglected shacks). Almost as many people thought there had been four classes. One man described them as 'the wealthy businessmen, the middle class, blue collar workers, and the guys that were just existing.' A few individuals insisted the number had been five, roughly corresponding to the class divisions that I had erected for purposes of analysis: upper, lower-upper, middle, lower-middle, and lower.

To add more confusion, the number of classes that people perceived did not simply vary with their own class positions. There was, indeed, a tendency for the poorest people to state that there were only two classes. Yet almost as many people from the upper class thought the same thing. For example, one of the most influential men in the past claimed there were only the high and low classes, with nothing in between. A woman from his circle agreed that there were just two classes, but she labelled them 'wealthy' and 'medium,' and insisted there had been no poor people in the village. Those who perceived three or four classes ranged all the way from the lower to the upper class, although the majority of them hovered around the middle class.

As I listened to the various descriptions of the class system, it became apparent that it was much easier for people to identify the polar positions – the highest and lowest classes – than those in between. Indeed, their standard procedure was to begin by actually naming those who occupied the upper and lower classes, leaving the class (or classes) in between as a vague residual category. Another interesting wrinkle was that almost half the people who initially stated that there were three classes added a fourth after having time to reflect. Thus, an elderly man who had just described the upper, middle, and lower classes commented that his own family was in between the middle and the lower levels, and decided there actually had been four classes. A similar revision was made by a woman who realized her family was not, in her words, 'the upper crust,' but nor was it in the middle of the pack; her solution was to create a fourth category between the middle and upper class.

Not only was it impossible to predict with any consistency how many classes were perceived on the basis of the evaluator's own class position, but there was even variation within particular families.[1] One of the 'terrible people' from the past, to use the previous woman's expression, argued forcibly that there had only been two classes – the rich and the poor. Yet his younger brother was equally certain that four classes had existed – 'the upper crust, middle, below middle, and lowest.' In another family it was the younger brother who said 'you were either rich or poor,' while the older brother added a middle category.

When Paradise people focused on specific families or individuals, their ranking schemes took on even greater variation, although sometimes it was possible to detect the shadow of a pattern based on the evaluator's class position. For example, a well-known family was described as middle class or in between the lower and middle classes by most people. Yet an extremely poor man referred to this same family as 'those rich people,' and an individual from a similar background described the family as high class. In another case, a woman referred to a family that had been consistently placed at the very bottom of the pile as solidly middle class. From this woman's perspective – a single mother living on welfare, and at the time I met her on the verge of losing her dismal rented apartment – even the people normally counted among the lower class seemed comparatively well off.

People's self-evaluations, too, often differed from the manner in which they were ranked by others. The members of a family who thought of themselves as quite poor in the past, although not on the same level as what one woman referred to as 'the stigmatized poor, the really poor,' were consistently placed by their neighbours in the middle class. A more dramatic example concerns a man whom others insisted had come from one of the few upper-class families. Yet from his perspective, his family had definitely belonged to the lower class (he only perceived two classes in the village: high and low). This man's father was well educated, and they lived in a large brick house, but his son remembers eating warmed-up porridge for supper, because his father's business ventures were always on the point of collapse. In this case it appears that the man's neighbours were ranking his family's status, whereas he was ranking its economic well-being.

A reverse example concerns an ambitious individual, who, when I asked how he ranked his own position, boldly placed himself in the upper class. Yet as one of his acquaintances remarked, 'He thinks he's upper class, but he's really middle class.' This acquaintance went on to say that the man in question would denounce his own mother if that would put him in the good graces of the élite, and one of the poorest individuals from the past described the man as 'the most hypocritical person' he had ever met. This brings us to an important theoretical issue: the extent to which a person's behaviour can affect his or her class position. Williams (1969:86), who identified seven classes in Gosforth, England, contended that two of them were based largely on how people behaved.[2] Those in the lower class, he explained, may be better off financially than those in the class above it, but their rough, crude behaviour places them at the bottom of the scale. Similarly, people in what he calls the upper-medial class may be indistinguishable from those in the medial class below them except in one sense: they are notorious social climbers, emulating the behaviour and lifestyle of people in the higher ranks. Within a family itself, Williams suggests, behaviour can make a difference; thus, while a family as a unit may be ranked at one level, one of its members, driven by social ambition, may be ranked at a higher level.

A somewhat similar argument has been pursued by Newby (1977), who draws a distinction between attributional and interactional status.[3] The former refers to the manner in which one's position – for example, engineer or factory worker – is ranked in society in general. The latter refers to how one behaves in the position, which is a matter of local knowledge.[4] For example, Newby states (1977:328) that in terms of attributional status, the agricultural workers whom he studied in England were at the bottom of the hierarchy, but in terms of interactional status, what counted was a person's esteem gained from skill at work in the company of peers. Although Foote (1979:49) does not employ Newby's terminology, he makes a similar distinction in his community study in Nova Scotia. The Protestant ministers there were more highly paid than the Catholic priests, but the latter enjoyed higher status because of their greater involvement and visibility in the community.

Examples of the impact of behaviour on class and status in Paradise were plentiful. In terms of wealth, one prominent businessman clearly qualified for the upper class, but he was never fully accepted by the elite. The reason was clear. He was considered difficult, unpleasant, the type of man who would rub his wealth in the face of others. Another man also qualified for the upper class, but on different grounds: he was one of the few individuals in the community at that time who had a university degree. In his case, the main barrier to elite status was his own temperament. Although quite prominent in business circles, and always willing to contribute his time to community causes, he was not 'one of the boys.' Individualistic by nature, he had no time for small talk, nor did he play bridge, as did most of the members of the elite. This man was far from wealthy, because many of his business interests concerned quasi-philanthropical ventures, such as credit unions for farmers, providing him with more satisfaction than income. Yet given his educational qualifications and his high profile in community affairs, his modest income alone would not have kept him out of the elite had he been determined to join it.

The importance of interactional status is clearly reflected in the following comparison. One unfortunate man went through his entire life either on relief or, when there was work, earning a few dollars as a handyman. But he was honest, sober, and gentle, and enjoyed the respect of his neighbours. The other man was often described as one of the most wealthy persons in the community, and he wielded enormous influence; but he was certainly not loved, partly because of his abrasive personality, and partly because even when he was selflessly serving the community in various political and philanthropical organizations, his own business ventures seemed to emerge in better shape than before. Reflecting on the lives of these two men, one of my informants observed that when the first one died, the funeral home was packed with mourners, but the death of the second man brought a different response: 'I think there were five people at his funeral. Now tell me, who was more successful?'

The moral of this little story is not complicated, but two points must be made. The first man may have enjoyed a much greater degree of respect and esteem than did the second man, but nobody in the community ever forgot that the former's class position was at the bottom of the heap while the latter's was at the top. What I am suggesting is that regardless of one's behaviour, admired or detested, it is one's class position (or attributional status) that counts the most when it comes to ranking people.[5] In more recent years, for example, an individual regularly volunteered his services to almost every community cause that existed, and virtually begged the upper class to accept him into its ranks. Yet he was rebuffed, partly because his social ambitions were too obvious, and he pursued them too aggressively. Even more damaging, he had always had to manage on a very modest salary, and by the time he had retired he still hadn't paid off the mortgage on his house – a fact alone that guaranteed he would never be treated with full respect.

The second point concerns an apparent contradiction within the criteria used to rank people in the community. On the one hand, allowance was made for 'the one bad apple' in the family. On the other hand, it only took a single alcoholic or shifty character to ruin the reputation of an entire family. In practice, this contradiction was resolved on the basis of social class. It was among the lower classes where the actions of a single person were stamped on an entire family. Among the higher classes, a family's reputation could withstand the antics of an irresponsible son or daughter. In other words, the amount of social credit in a family varied from one class level to another. What was curious about the people in the upper class was that they assumed that the individual was the appropriate unit of analysis when it came to understanding the lower class. But when it was a question of understanding themselves, individualism gave way to the larger unit of the family.

Patterns of Social Action

It would be an exaggeration to state that the community was physically divided into rich and poor sectors, because poor people were scattered throughout the village, sometimes in modest houses next to the grand homes of the elite. Nevertheless, three streets at one end of the village were occupied mainly by lower-class people, and one of them, located next to the dump, contained nobody but the poor. An upper-class woman remembers that the air on that street would be blue from all the swearing that went on, and claims that the girls there got into fights just as regularly as the boys. People tended to marry within their own class level. The family histories of the elite could often be traced back to the most prominent founding members of the community. The main families on the street next to the dump were all related by marriage. For example, a generation or so ago, two brothers from one family married two sisters from another. A typical comment made by people in the other classes was that it was inbreeding that produced the (assumed) low intelligence and grovelling poverty among the families on that street. A less typical observation, made by a sharp-minded woman in the middle class, was that perhaps the people there had no other choice than to marry among themselves.

Several families, their names recorded in the village council minutes, were on relief at that time (the village clerk served as the relief officer). In 1951 there were nine families on relief, two of them men, seven of them women (referred to as 'Mrs. Art so and so' or 'Miss'). The average payment was forty dollars per month. In return for relief assistance, the male head of the household, if there was one, was expected to do menial jobs for the village, or road work. One man, now reputedly a millionaire, recalls that when his family had been on relief in those days, his mother was not allowed to buy brown sugar at the general store because it was considered a luxury item. The names of the garbage collectors at that time, also recorded in the council minutes, read like a roll-call of the poorest families in the village. Most of these same people, almost all of them young men, were employed by the community to remove snow in the winter. The council minutes also indicate that older people (some of them retired farmers with little to live on) were paid one or two dollars for cleaning the town hall or burning refuse.

At the other end of the scale was the elite. As one woman explained, 'There was a certain class, rooted in the bridge club. There was a certain toniness.' As a man put it, 'There was a crowd, a group that went around together and held parties and that sort of thing' (he himself belonged to it). Virtually all those in the upper class were successful businessmen, usually the owners of stores, plus some professionals. Yet not all the businessmen were included in the upper class. Their businesses had to be substantial, and there were other qualifications such as family pedigree and proper behaviour. One merchant, for example, did not qualify because his ethnic background was not British. The behaviour of people in the upper class varied from individual to individual; some women were considered to be snooty, walking around with their noses in the air, while others were admired as humble people, despite their high stations in life. Yet a certain degree of arrogance, and expectations of deference from their social inferiors, typified the attitudes of people in the upper class. As was said about one man, 'He'd swing his weight around if he thought you were beneath him.' And about others, 'Back in the old days, there were some people you had to say "yes sir, no sir," just like the army.' An individual who ranked himself in the upper class claimed that neither he nor any of his friends ever spoke disparingly about those beneath him. But he did say that the only time upper-class and lower-class people ever crossed paths was when the former hired the latter to do menial work, such as digging a garden. This same man insisted that there was no discrimination in terms of social class in the school. Yet many of the poor people whom I interviewed felt otherwise; moreover, a repeated claim was that outside school, if one was poor, one never played with the children of the elite, or even entered their backyards. On one occasion a lower-class woman invited several of her daughter's school companions to her birthday party. Parents in the higher classes forbade their children to enter their classmate's home, and the birthday party was held with only two guests in attendance.

The display of wealth in those days varied with social-class level. Nobody was in doubt about the financial status of those in the upper class. They lived in the largest homes, drove the newest cars, and – amazing to the majority of Paradise residents in that era – even could afford to take their holidays in Florida. The middle and lower classes were more difficult to read. One could always find the exceptional lower-class person, who had done well in business, walking around town flashing a billfold full of dollars. Some middle-class people, in contrast, whose businesses had been equally successful, continued to live in woodframe dwellings with the paint peeling off them, purpose-fully concealing their wealth in order not to provoke jealousy among their customers. These people were the exceptions, because most of those in the middle and lower-middle classes were barely keeping their heads above water. One woman said: 'Mom and Dad were so poor that we didn't have a stitch on us that wasn't someone's rags.' Yet she said her family had been middle class, not nearly as badly off as the people who lived down by the dump. Another woman, whose father had been a tradesman, described her family as very poor. But she added: 'I never knew we were poor. We were savers.' Indeed, despite its modest income, this family eventually made it into the lower-upper echelon, and by the time another generation had passed, the daughter, with a university degree for support, was firmly ensconced in the upper class. What is striking about Paradise in the past is just how little money was possessed even by the classes in the middle of the stratification system.

Weber, as we saw in the previous chapter, regarded status as the basis for shared social action or group association. But if that is one of the main differences between status and class, there was very little evidence of it in Paradise. Repeated interaction, whether for instru-mental or expressive ends, only occurred within the upper class, and not all people who occupied that class were included. A small group of upper-class people got together regularly to play bridge in each other's homes, hold dinner parties, and curl. Common membership in voluntary organizations such as the highly esteemed Rotary Club, and in committees set up to run the village, also brought them into regular contact.

At no other class level was there a similar degree of formal or informal association. Middle-class people also participated in voluntary organizations, although to a lesser extent, and not necessarily the same ones as their 'superiors.' For example, a list of nineteen officers in 1948 of the LOBA (the women's branch of the Orange Lodge) reveals that except for two upper-middle-class women, all belonged to the middle class. A list of twenty IODE members in the same year shows that the vast majority of them were upper class (only five were not, and they fell into the middle class; two of these were also on the previous list of LOBA officers). People in the middle and lower-middle classes came together at organized dances and on occasions such as a church supper or an evening of bingo. But they did not meet in each other's homes nearly as much as the group in the upper class.

Lower-class people did not participate in voluntary organizations at all, except for the Orange Lodge and sometimes the Legion. And rarely did they gather in each other's homes. Most of their interaction was kin-based, and indeed it is reasonable to generalize that the lower the class position of people of Paradise, the more probable their social interaction was restricted to their own family and close relatives. Only one other social class was even remotely as fragmented as the lower class. This was the lower-upper class. For a variety of reasons, the people who occupied that class level were relatively isolated in the village. Sometimes it was because they were not welcome in the circles of the elite, perhaps as a result of perceived personality quirks; sometimes it was because they did not *wish* to join the elite, with its accompanying social obligations; and at other times, perhaps, it was because the only option available to them – participating in organizations and groups dominated by the middle-class people below them – held little social benefit.

Politics

Village records indicate that since the last century the local council has been controlled by the most wealthy and prominent businessmen, as well as some professional people such as dentists, doctors and lawyers.

In the 1940s and 1950s the positions of reeve and councillors continued to circulate among members of the elite. Almost all of them were
men, although the village clerk from 1941 to 1947 was a woman. Indeed, only seven men from that era who clearly belonged to the upper
class did not become members of the council. These included two
medical practitioners, a dentist, the publisher of the local newspaper,
the ministers of the United and Anglican churches, and, surprisingly,
one of the most wealthy businessmen whose pedigree went back to the
village's founder. This man, however, was very active in community
associations and in organizations such as the Rotary Club, and there
never was any doubt that he was a bona fide member of the upper
class.

Paradise people who lived in the community after the Second World
War have divided memories about the political elite in those days. One
man remarked: 'I sometimes wonder if they felt the town wouldn't run
without them.' A woman declared: 'Those kind of people wouldn't
want anyone else to be in those places.' She went on to state that in
her judgment, 'the aristocracy,' as she referred to it, got on council in
order to display their class superiority. An elderly man commented:
'The only time the aristocracy would ever speak to anyone was at
election time.' Yet not all people were so negative about 'the aristocracy' (which sometimes meant only the members of the council, and at
other times included all people in the elite). As one person observed,
'I think because they were successful, people thought they could run
the town.' A newcomer to the village in the 1950s expressed great
admiration for the political leaders at the time: 'It's a good job they
had those people. They were the leaders. It's a pity we don't have
them today.'

In the 1940s and 1950s there was only a thin line between formal
and informal leadership. The same small group of men controlled the
community, whether or not they were on the council at the time.
Politically astute residents looking for a favour, such as permission to
put an addition on their houses, never approached the council directly. Instead, they consulted privately with individual members of the
council, and with what one man referred to as 'the power boys' not on
the council. Only after these influential people had been softened up
in the informal realm did it make any sense to place a formal petition
before the council.

One man in particular dominated the community in the period after
the Second World War. He was the village reeve for a total of fifteen

years. Only the individual recognized as the founder of the community in the previous century had served as reeve for a longer time (eighteen years). Nobody who had lived in Paradise around 1950 had much trouble remembering what they thought of the man whose power had touched almost every aspect of village life. An elderly couple recalled how kind he had been to their son when he had been severely injured in a car accident, calling on him daily with a cheery word. This, however, was not the normal reaction to the man. Some people despised him, some respected him, but few liked him very much. A man who had known him well remarked: 'He strutted in with all his glory. A banty rooster.' Others remembered how he used to drive his car around town, surveying his domain, barely slowing down at stop signs, his wary subjects pulling their toddlers from his path.

Even people who respected him – and there were many – did not necessarily love him. One woman who lived next door to him thought he had done a tremendous amount for the village, but she remembered him as a curt and cold individual, who terrified her children (the man's own marriage had been childless). A member of the elite in those days said the former reeve always kept the village finances in the black. But he called him 'a 10¢ and $1.00 man.' What he meant, he said, was that the reeve could be extremely generous or extremely stingy. Apparently during the Second World War a scheme was devised whereby the bank manager would take one dollar a month from the accounts of the most wealthy people, to be used to buy cigarettes for the fighting men abroad. The bank manager thought he had the agreement of the reeve, but when this man discovered that his account was short a dollar, he exploded and refused to cooperate. The embarrassed organizers of the scheme tried to conceal his reaction, so the community at large would not get wind of his selfish act. Months later, the former reeve asked the bank manager how the cigarette fund was progressing, and told him to take fifty dollars from his own account and put it in the fund. Generous the man could be, but he did not like to be pushed around, even gently.

One person who had been a member of the council in those days made no bones about his dislike for the former reeve. Yet he added that he learned to admire the man, because he ran the council like an army sergeant; individuals with cases to present to the council would be in and out before they knew it. He also told me about the occasion when the reeve learned about a reputed child molester. He went to the person's house and ordered him to pack up and leave town. The man complied. As my informant mused, if reeves or mayors did that today, the human rights people would hound them out of office.

The reeve's father has been described by Sawden (undated) as 'one of the most prominent men in business circles' in the area, and his son began his own career with considerable advantage. Yet as one of his admirers pointed out, he did not lose any of his inheritance. In addition to his grain elevator and his numerous properties, he apparently had invested wisely in the stock market. A repeated accusation levelled at him was that he did not want the village to grow in terms of industry, because he was afraid his own control of the market would suffer. As one person remarked, 'There never was any industry in the town because he didn't want it. Unless he owned it.'

There is a well-known musical in which the evil influence of pool on the youth of small towns is explained in no uncertain terms, and in a curious fashion it was the local pool hall that brought the reeve's reign to an end. It all began when a strong-willed member of the community decided to establish a pool hall. He did all the necessary leg work, calling in private on influential people and obtaining their implicit support. But when he went before the council, his project was rejected by the reeve. It just happened that the reeve owned the building in which the existing pool hall was located. Whether he was acting in terms of his own interests, or altruistically protecting the family that rented the building from him and ran the pool hall, the outcome was the same. His competitor decided to call his bluff, not only by going ahead with his plans to open a second pool hall, but also by running against the reeve in the elections which were just around the corner.

The controversy injected a great deal more flavour into the political scene that year than usual, but before the electorate could express its will at the ballot box, the reeve withdrew from the race. His decision to turn down the application for a second pool hall apparently had cast doubts on his integrity as a public servant, which he was not prepared to endure. When the reeve withdrew his name as a candidate for re-election, his opponent was flabbergasted. As he explained to me, he had never seriously believed that he could win the election. He merely wanted to make the reeve dance on a few hot coals. His solution was to recruit a third candidate whose credentials – prominent businessman, British background, Anglican, and Conservative – assured that he would be acceptable to the people. This new candidate went on unopposed to become the next reeve of the village.[6]

That marked the beginning of the end of the former reeve's enormous control over the community. Seven years later, in 1958, he returned once more to the reeve's office. But in 1959 a former farmer became reeve. This was the first time in the history of the village that the reeve was not a member of the elite. His election was a sign of the future. Every reeve who has been elected since then has come from a modest background; indeed, the individual currently holding the community's highest elected office is a woman whose family was usually evaluated as lower-middle class, although since winning the election there has been a tendency among people to elevate her rank to the middle class. Some people today look back on the famous reeve of the 1950s with nostalgia, but also with wry understanding. In the words of a man who did admire him immensely, 'He ran the damn place. You know, there's something to be said for that. But he was sort of like communism. He ruled us.'

Religion

Vidich and Bensman (1960:252), in their classical community study, describe a local minister in these words: 'He was a deeply religious man who was selfless and never did anything to further himself or his own cause.' Universally admired, the minister didn't hesitate to enter the saloons and talk to hard-drinking men and women, or to extend a helping hand to anyone in need, regardless of a person's religious affiliation. If this fine man had a twin, he must have lived in Paradise, because the description bears an uncanny resemblance to the Anglican minister who lived there in the 1950s. The latter's disregard for money was legendary. He repeatedly refused to accept a raise in salary, and on occasions when he travelled to Toronto or other communities, his parishioners had to make sure he had sufficient funds; otherwise he would set off with an empty billfold. After the Second World War the Legion in Paradise developed a reputation for extremely heavy drinking. One evening the Anglican minister walked in and spent the next few hours nursing a beer. Thereafter he became a regular visitor, with the result that the unrestrained drinking ceased. The minister also was in the habit of dropping into the pool hall. One man, a youth at the time, recalls how impressed he had been. The minister would sit there, smoking a cigar, joking with the young people, a sort of grandfather figure, benign and nonjudgmental. Not surprisingly, the Anglican minister's parishioners adored him. But what was most striking of all was the number of non-Anglicans who, when faced with a serious personal problem, would seek out the Anglican minister for advice and guidance.

If one thing stands out in my research in Paradise, it is that no single person is admired (or detested) by everyone. If the fieldworker talks to enough people, sooner or later she or he will encounter someone who has something negative to say about the village hero, or a positive comment about the local villain. This generalization applies to the Anglican minister. One man jokingly put the minister's popularity down to the fact that he delivered notoriously short sermons. One of the poor people from the past suggested that the minister's renowned disregard for money was all a sham; otherwise how could he have managed to send both of his sons to university? Perhaps the most interesting reaction came from a person who had never met the minister. This was a young man who took over the Anglican Church in the 1980s and attempted to rebuild a congregation that had been turned off by the two previous ministers. The new minister was both intrigued and daunted by the reputation of his famous predecessor and, possibly to reduce the man to human proportions, once pointed out to me that the former minister, for all his fame, had done a rather poor job with church records. Perhaps this young minister would have felt less anxious and inadequate if he had known what some of the older people were saying about him: that he was just like the marvellous man who had led them in the 1950s.

Religion in those days was a key institution in the small community, and attendance in the two main churches, the United and Anglican, was high. In the United Church, with the larger congregation, two services used to be held on Sundays, and even then chairs sometimes had to be placed in the aisles to accommodate the overflow. The United Church minister was also highly respected, and he and his colleague in the Anglican Church, in the spirit of ecumenical cooperation, used to exchange pulpits once a year.

Because religion was such an important institution, it is not surprising that to some extent it reflected the broad stratification system of the community. In those days a businessman had to belong to a church, although membership and attendance were two different things. Some upper-class individuals, for example, only put in appearance at Christmas and Easter, yet they were considered valuable members because of their annual contributions (in one of the churches, the names of people and the amounts of their donations, apart from the weekly collection, were published annually for all to see). Other people in that class level, such as the former reeve just described, were powerhouses in the church, exercising enormous influence over it. There was a tendency for people in the upper class to sit towards the front of the church, their places reserved by implicit agreement. When the service was over, the temporary fiction of a community of equals, reduced to a common denominator in the face of a superior force, quickly crumbled. On one occasion, for example, two women from quite different social classes shared an umbrella as they stepped out of the church into a downpour. A car pulled away from the church, and then stopped to offer the upper-class woman a ride. Such was the anger and humiliation felt by her lower-class companion, who was left standing in the rain, that she apparently never returned to the church again.

Middle-class women often did not attend church, but not necessarily because of a lack of faith. They would dress up their children and send them off to Sunday school, while remaining at home to prepare the most elaborate meal of the week, the noon-hour Sunday dinner. As for the lower class, attendance was sporadic. On one occasion a teacher in the elementary school interrupted a lesson in grammar in order to address the students from poor families. He invited them to attend Sunday school, telling them that it didn't matter whether their clothes were ragged. The teacher's intentions may have been sincere, but that is not how everyone interpreted them. A man who had been a student in that class thought the teacher's words amounted to a rather cruel put-down; one of the poorer kids who had listened to the teacher's remarks remembers how humiliated he had felt.

Paradise people often joked that in the past one could never marry into the families of the elite unless one was a Conservative, an Orange-man, and an Anglican. When I began to inquire about life in the 1950s, different people told me that most of the wealthy and powerful people in those days were members of the Anglican Church. As field-work proceeded, it seemed that the generalization needed to be re-fined: the Anglican Church may not only have had a higher propor-tion of the most wealthy citizens, but also of the poorest ones. In order to examine this possibility more rigorously, I turned to the com-munity's assessment records for 1950.

Several qualifications must be made about the assessment rolls. First, not everyone's religious affiliation was recorded there; for purposes of analysis, I only included those people whose religion was clearly indi-cated. Second, the assessments were based on the private property of

TABLE 1
Number of People Assessed by Religious Affiliation, 1950

	Religion Indicated	Assessed	Not Assessed
United	233 (60.3%)	177 (76%)	56 (24%)
Anglican	100 (25.9%)	83 (83%)	17 (17%)
Gospel Workers	37 (9.5%)	27 (73%)	10 (37%)
Catholic	7 (1.8%)	6 (85.7%)	1 (14.2%)
C.e.	9 (2.3%)	8 (88.8%)	1 (11.1%)
Totals	386 (99.8%)	301 (78%)	85 (22%)

Notes:
1 Four ambiguous cases were excluded from the analysis.
2 Although there were a handful of Catholics in the village, there was no Catholic church.
3 C.e. consisted of a small Protestant sect known locally as the black socks, reflecting the way they dressed.
4 Source: Assessment Rolls.

TABLE 2
Assessment Values

	$5,000 or More	$3,000–$4,999	$1,000–$2,999	$500–$999	Below $500	Total
United	2 (1.1%)	8 (4.5%)	95 (53.6%)	61 (34.4%)	11 (6.2%)	177 (99.8%)
Anglican	5 (6%)	2 (2.4%)	38 (45.7%)	25 (30%)	13 (15.6%)	83 (99.7%)
Gospel Workers	–	1 (3.7%)	8 (29.6%)	16 (59.2%)	2 (7.4%)	27 (99.9%)
Catholic	–	1 (16.6%)	2 (33.3%)	–	3 (50%)	6 (99.9%)
C.e.	–	–	1 (12.5%)	6 (75%)	1 (12.5%)	8 (100%)
Total	7 (2.3%)	12 (3.9%)	144 (47.8%)	108 (35.8%)	30 (9.9%)	301 (99.8%)

Notes:
1 The average assessment values from highest to lowest were as follows: Anglican $1,487.00, Catholic $1,367.00, United $1,354.57, Gospel Workers $1,040.00, C.e. $762.00; all religions $1,202.11.
2 Source: Assessment Rolls.

individual household heads (usually males); business property was excluded from the analysis. Third, 22 per cent of those whose religious affiliation was given were not assessed at all; one obvious reason was that some of them did not own property (included here were retired farmers, widows and widowers, living in a rented room or apartment).

Tables 1 and 2 tell the story: the Anglican Church indeed had the wealthiest congregation. The average assessment of the Anglicans was higher than that of any other religious group, and five of the seven wealthiest people in the community (at least with assessment values as the index) were Anglicans. Furthermore, in comparison to the United Church, a greater proportion of the poorest people in the community (16 per cent versus 6 per cent) belonged to the Anglican Church. In conclusion, those people who had told me that the Anglican Church had the wealthiest congregation were correct, although they did not seem to realize that to a greater extent than in the United Church, the Anglican Church attracted people from both extremes of the class system.

Alcoholism

The past, apparently, was full of characters, and the characters were full of booze. The definition of a character, indeed, was a person who hit the bottle hard and likely as not could be found sleeping it off in a ditch. There was a remarkable degree of unanimity among my informants about the identities of these characters. The same five or six men – all from the lower class – were mentioned time after time. Leitch (1975:17), with perhaps a little hyperbole, makes it clear that alcohol had long held its attractions for people in the general area of Paradise: 'At one time, Upper Canada was known far and wide as the drunkenest place in America, and Dufferin [County] gladly helped the reputation along.' In 1864 the Dunken Act was introduced to curb drinking (Kelling 1981), and in 1873 the Canada Temperance Act took effect. It was not until 1965 that alcohol could legally be purchased in Paradise. In the 1940s and 1950s, however, several bootleggers plied their trade. If a man couldn't afford the bootlegger, there was always rubbing alcohol. Its effect on one of the characters was vividly remembered by an elderly person: 'I seen him drinking rubbing alcohol until he strangled. We were pounding him on the back.' If rubbing alcohol wasn't available, vanilla essence apparently was a reasonable substitute. A woman recalled that as soon as she spotted one of the well-known alcoholics outside her store, she quickly hid all the bottles of vanilla. If a man had no money left even to buy vanilla, he could always try to borrow it. Apparently some people discovered how to handle one individual who was continuously pestering them for money. Instead of lending him a dollar or two, they would give him ten dollars. Since he was never in a position to repay the larger sum, he would never bother them again.

The characters were often said to have been 'A-1 men' and 'top-notch tradesmen' when sober, but as soon as they earned a few dollars, off they went on another binge. As one of my informants remarked about a notorious alcoholic, 'There wasn't a smarter man around here. But before he'd take on a job, he's ask for money up front. Well, we knew what that was for. Then he'd be gone for two weeks – drunk.' Another lower-class individual was described as an exceptional entre-preneur, who had established his own business and had begun to lift himself out of the poverty that his family had been stuck in for gener-ations. According to those who knew him well, however, he could never forgive the rest of the world for being born into one of the families that lived on the street by the dump. Apparently handicapped by an enormous inferiority complex, he walked around town flashing hundreds of dollars, and finally drank himself to death. But that was not before he had lost his business and ended up where he had begun – one of the poorest people in the village.

Social-class resentment and feelings of inadequacy seemed to lie at the core of another man's lifelong battle with the bottle. One of sever-al siblings, he grew up in a house equipped with coal oil lamps and potato bags hung over the windows in the winter to keep out the cold. He quipped: 'We were that poor, there was no mice that hung around our house.' By the time he had become a teenager in the 1940s, he already was a heavy drinker. 'In those days,' he mused, 'it was nothing to walk up town and get drunk.' Later in life he joined Alcoholics Anonymous, and for a few years he lived a life of sobriety, only to fall heavily off the wagon as he approached middle age. What he has found most difficult to accept, he said, is the accident of being born poor. He remembers as a youngster not being allowed to play with the children in the higher classes, and being treated as a second-class citizen as he grew into manhood. On one occasion, for example, he and one of his brothers were hired to help move the household pos-sessions of an upper-class family which was leaving the village. At one point, everybody took a break and had a couple of beers; he and his brother were excluded.

Talking about the class system, he remarked: 'I was put on a differ-ent level, and I'm damned if I could accept it.' In this respect, he revealed, he was very different than his parents, who simply swallowed the insults that came their way 'You see, I'm not like my Dad was. I don't take their shit. I remember too much of it as a kid. I grew up with that embedded in my mind. And I thought some day I'm going to tell those bastards what I think of them. And when I got drinking, I did tell them – that's what ruined me.' Alcohol, he explained, provided an escape for his anger and shame: 'I would drink when I didn't like me. When I got drinking, I'd be better than anyone else.' As a result of his alcoholism, he once was referred to a psychiatrist, who told him his problem was that his aspirations in life were too high; he had to accept the cards which he had been dealt.

Over the decades this man, who had quit school in grade six, held a variety of unskilled jobs. About twenty years ago he had begun to work in a little store, intending it only as a stop-gap measure until he could locate something better (he dreamed of moving to a larger community far away). At the age of sixty he was shocked to realize that he was still toiling in the same store, and wondered where all the years had gone. In this respect, his life story touches a common chord. For many people in the Paradise area (and presumably farther afield), especially those struggling to make ends meet, life has a temporary quality. One's dwelling may be a run-down apartment, and one's employment may be at the checkout counter in the supermarket, but one can console oneself with the belief that life hasn't really begun yet. Then, amazingly, a man finds that he is fifty or sixty years old, and what was supposed to be a temporary situation has settled in as the defining feature of his existence.

The man I have been describing lived alone. He had no children, and indeed had never married ('Who would want me?' he asked rhetorically), although for a few years he had had a common-law spouse. His interest in religion had increased as he stood on the edge of old age, and he frequently attended a wide variety of churches, attempting, as he said, to find peace within himself. Blessed with apparent above-average intelligence and sensitivity, plus more than his share of charm (at least when sober), he still bristles when confronted by real or imagined slights from people in the higher classes. If customers treat him with disrespect, he orders them out of the store. Such aggressiveness has not improved his reputation in the town, but it apparently is an unavoidable expression of a lifelong obsession with what he regards as an unfair class system. In his bitter words, 'It hurt. It still does. I don't forget.'

When the subject of alcoholism is raised with Paradise natives, they quickly mention, sometimes with benign amusement, the 'characters'

TABLE 3
Alcoholism by Class Level

Upper class	13
Lower-upper class	4
Middle class	11
Lower-middle class	11
Lower class	20
Total	59

Note:

1 These, of course, were only the ones I learned about; undoubtedly there were others. One further qualification: when I refer to individuals as alcoholics, I do so solely on the basis of their reputations in the community. Obviously I am not qualified to provide a medical assessment of alcoholism.

In statistical terms, fifty-nine reputed alcoholics in a community the size of Paradise, and spread over a period of ten years, is not particularly high. In 1951 alone, there were 859 residents twenty years of age or over in the community (Statistics Canada 1951).

within the lower class. Yet it would be a mistake to conclude that hard drinking was not prevalent at the other class levels. I learned the identities of fifty-nine reputed alcoholics who had lived in the village during the decade following the Second World War. Five of them were women, and eleven of them apparently stopped drinking later in life. The largest number, twenty, fell into the lower class. Yet at thirteen, upper-class representation was not far behind. Indeed, given that fewer people occupied the upper class than the lower class, the number of alcoholics in the former was proportionately greater than in the latter.[7]

What clearly distinguished alcoholism from one class level to another was the degree of visibility. Only the lower-class characters drank openly outside their homes, sometimes in a back alley, at other times along the main streets of the village. And only the hard-drinking habits of lower-class people were publicly acknowledged. At all other class levels, efforts were made both by the individuals themselves and by their families and friends to conceal their dependency on alcohol. Consider the case of a lower-middle-class man who, after his mother died, had been raised by his older sisters until he quit school in grade nine. According to one of his relatives, he was unusually intelligent and talented, but never seemed to possess sufficient confidence to face life head-on, except when under the influence of alcohol. For much of his adult existence, he was either in the process of becoming inebriated or – stiff, stunned, and humiliated – recovering from the previous night's bout. As a result, there was constant strain within the family, and isolation too, because his heavy drinking precluded friendship or even regular contact with the neighbours. Often, of course, the neighbours were perfectly aware of a person's alcoholism. Yet the very fact that one took pains to cover it up was counted in one's favour, because it meant that the person at least had a capacity for shame, supposedly an alien emotion within the lower class.

A middle-class man who had held a prominent position in the village administration revealed that he used to drink all day long on the job: 'Yet there were a lot of people in this town that didn't know I had a drinking problem, because I didn't drink in public.' At the urging of a close friend, he joined Alcoholics Anonymous and pulled his life together. The least visible alcoholics of all were those in the upper class. This was largely because almost nobody talked about them, unless they had lost all control and had begun to turn up inebriated at public functions. Such was the case of a much-beloved medical practitioner. Extremely competent and highly respected for his skills, his addiction to alcohol gradually became public knowledge. At one point some members of the elite attempted to persuade him to join a branch of Alcoholic Anonymous for professional people in the city, assuming that the stigma for him would be reduced. Yet, as one of his friends remarked, he was too proud to seek professional help, and he died prematurely.

Several of these reputed alcoholics were described by informants as having been handicapped by enormous inferiority complexes. It would be ridiculous, of course, to suggest that alcoholism can be reduced to one simple explanation. Yet it would be just as wrong-headed to argue that a lack of confidence only occurs among lower-class individuals. Quite frankly, I do not know what turned the highly admired medical practitioner to the bottle, nor do I know why others in his social class went the same way. In some cases heavy drinking seemed to be triggered by a specific misfortune, such as a marital break-up, or the tragic death of a son or daughter. In other cases, such as a lower-upper-class man who apparently choked to death on his own vomit, there did not appear to be any obvious event that led to his downfall. Then there was the upper-class woman who seemed to possess everything in life she would have desired: a magnificent house, a highly respected businessman for a husband, healthy children, and a social position ranked at the very top of the community. And yet she was said to be a slave to the bottle.

A mark of the success of concealing alcoholism among upper-class people was that many residents of Paradise who had lived there all their lives did not even realize that some of the most highly esteemed men and women were heavy drinkers. Typical of the cover-up was the following interview with an elderly member of the former 'aristocracy.' He informed me that there had only been a half-dozen drunks in the past, and went on to name the characters in the lower class. Understandably, he failed to mention two of his own relatives who reputedly were at the mercy of the bottle. The only individual from the upper class with a drinking problem whom he was prepared to talk about was a woman who had grown up surrounded by luxury, only to watch the family fortune slip away. It was obvious that a lot of people had envied this woman, because they made little effort to hide their satisfaction at her fall from grace. Yet at no time did they refer to her as a character, even when she began to imbibe openly in public places, sometimes in the company of individuals at the opposite end of the social scale; by definition, a character could not possess an upper-class pedigree.

The fact that this apparently unhappy woman, still handsome and alert as she approached old age, occasionally shared a bottle with her social inferiors was not without precedent in Paradise. Alcohol, indeed, was the one instrument that could generate interaction across social class lines. Under the influence of alcohol, people who would normally never associate with each other would temporarily become drinking pals. When they sobered up, however, it was a different matter. Those in the higher classes, scrambling to recover their dignity and to reassert their superiority, would hardly stoop to acknowledge their erstwhile companions if they crossed paths on the street.

Contributing to the invisibility of upper-class alcoholism was the manner in which they were treated by the local police. A lower-class individual found drunk in public might be left to sleep it off in a ditch, be taken home by a compassionate police officer, or be tossed in jail for the night. When upper-class people were found drunk in their cars on a country sideroad, they too were usually returned to their homes, but always quietly. They were never put in jail. Finally, sheer finances had an impact. What was sad about the addiction of lower-class people, remarked many Paradise residents, was that it claimed almost all the money they earned. Yet, as one of my informants observed, people in the upper class probably spent just as much, but it never showed because they could afford it.

In Paradise today long-time residents, as well as newcomers, whose lives revolve around the bottle can still be found. But as an elderly man remarked, one thing has changed: 'You don't have people lying in the ditch any more. I think that's because you can't get away with that sort of thing any more; the law I mean.'

Women

The business and professional sphere in Paradise in the 1950s was a man's world. Except for some of the wives of store owners, a few others who were clerks, and lower-class individuals employed as domestics, women did not usually work outside the home. Their husbands controlled the finances, doling out a weekly sum to their wives for household expenditures. Women who did aspire to one of the few professions open to them, such as teaching, had little prospect of prosperity. As Dasgupta (1988:158) has indicated, that had historically been the case for male teachers as well. In the era of the one-room schoolhouse, before the emergence of teachers' unions, the school board was all-powerful and salaries were low. Those were the days when the teacher was expected to play an active role in the community. One former teacher in Paradise, who was also superintendent of the Sunday school in his church, said he had little choice in the matter if he wanted to keep his job. Teachers at that time who even went away for weekends were labelled 'suitcase teachers.' Today, of course, school boards routinely rotate teachers from one community to another, and teachers themselves generally express little regret that they no longer have to teach in the same communities where they reside.

Female teachers were in an even less enviable situation. Not only were they paid much less than men, which was often why boards preferred to hire them, but in the past, as Dodds (1983:2) has indicated, they were also controlled by particular rules and regulations, 'They could not marry during the term of their contract, and they could not keep company with men. They were not permitted to smoke cigarettes, dress in bright colours or dye their hair.'

Paradise people, of course, did not spend all their waking hours at work, but except for women in the upper and lower-upper classes, leisure had to be avoided. Even the daily routine of those privileged women was shaped by implicit rules. For example, a lower-upper-class woman recalled the occasion shortly after she and her husband, both university graduates, had moved to the community in the 1950s when one of her neighbours, a solid member of the elite, knocked on her door and asked if somebody was ill. The reason for her concern? It was afternoon, and the newcomer to the village had just hung out the washing on the clothesline. As was pointed out to the newcomer in no uncertain terms, people of her class were expected to complete their housework in the morning, and spend the afternoons visiting and drinking tea. They also had to be available to participate in good causes, such as voluntary work with the Red Cross or the IODE. It was because this woman and her husband chose not to conform their behaviour to the rules that guided the upper class that thirty years later they still remained in the class below it.

When the men in the upper classes were not managing their business and professional affairs, they were duty-bound to run the town. Middle-class and lower-middle-class men, when not at work, also had to remain active, whether it was coaching a hockey team or fishing and hunting. If a man was not engaged in some useful activity, his reputation suffered, because shameless indolence was said to be prevalent only among lower-class people. The sole residents of the community who could afford to be seen doing nothing were those who had retired, and even among them there were different expectations for men and women. Elderly men sat in the sunshine in the summer in front of the bank on Main Street, or gathered beside a pot-belly wood-stove in one of the stores in the winter. The leisure time of elderly women consisted of visiting and church work, and was reduced by the same old chores of preparing meals and doing housework that they had always known. The attitude towards work and leisure that prevailed in the 1950s was explained to me succinctly by an individual who had been a young man at that time. 'The important thing,' he said, 'was to be busy. Never mind if you were efficient.' Hard work, his parents believed, kept the devil at bay. Whenever he returned from a night out on the town, his mother would ask: 'Did you have a good time?' His stock answer was 'Yeah,' to which she would retort: 'Well, you'll have to work twice as hard tomorrow.'

Whether at work or play, Paradise men were expected to be in a continuous state of activity. Yet the burden for women, with the exception of those in the upper classes, was equally heavy, and in some cases more so. The home then lacked the conveniences taken for granted today. In the hot summers, cooking was done over a large wood-stove. In the winter the first person to get up in the morning, usually the housewife, would sometimes find the windows frosted over and the frozen cream in the milk bottles jutting over the tops. The first job of the day would be to relight the coal furnace that had died out during the night. In those days women cleaned the floor with mops, and also by getting down on their hands and knees. Then there was the unenviable task of washing clothes. Even in the 1940s the corrugated washing-board, across which one rubbed and scrubbed socks and shirts, was still the standard equipment in many houses. The first electric washing machines, with wringers, reduced the drudgery, but compared to what is available today, they belonged to the dawn of technology. In those days, of course, there were no dryers. In winter the long underwear and the shirts and work pants, arms and legs frozen stiff and straight, would dance on the clothesline like a bizarre company of performing scarecrows. Many elderly women recall what they went through each time they hung out the wet clothes in these conditions; their hands would turn red and blue, and their fingers would be numb and crab-like. Most families at that time had large vegetable gardens, and except sometimes for men in retirement who enjoyed the activity, it usually was the women who tended them.

As they cleaned, cooked and sewed, and looked after the children – all the while scrimping, because one rarely bought anything if it could not be paid for by cash – these women must have had little time to think about the lack of leisure, or about an ideology that lodged their contributions below that of their husbands. Yet it was the lower-class women, especially those in alcoholic families, who suffered the most; not only did they have to run the household while enduring the abuse of their spouses, but they also had to clean the homes of the upper-class residents in order to put food on the table. This does not mean that the wives of alcoholics in the classes above them did not suffer too. But the burden of poverty and the necessity of doing double duty as a domestic outside the home were not added to the load.

In almost every lower-class alcoholic family that remained intact (and many didn't), one found an exceptional woman with a remarkable capacity for hard work and self-sacrifice. Consider, for example, the tragic life of one such woman, as related to me by her daughter. The woman's husband, a builder, actually made a decent living, but as soon as he got paid, he went on a rampage. He would take taxis everywhere, sometimes would get rolled, and always would return with an empty wallet. This man also was the type to become violent when in his cups. At the first signs of another binge, his wife would hide his guns and knives, and then cart the children off to friends or relatives, sometimes for days on end. Often they would walk out past the cemetery to where relatives lived. Even today the cemetery remains a bitter reminder to the daughter of what it was like to grow up with an alcoholic father. On one occasion the guns were not hidden quickly enough, much to the misfortune of the man's faithful hound. The man let off a blast, killing the dog which had taken shelter behind a sofa.

With no money to feed her five children, her mother found work cleaning houses and offices. Her daughter, who also began her working life as a domestic, remembers hating the rich families for whom her mother toiled. Without exception, she claimed, they underpaid her and treated her like dirt. Although she said she didn't realize it when she was young, her family was simply 'white trash.' She grew up feeling immense shame, and remarked that what she can never forgive is the lack of compassion among Paradise people. Not only were the elite women who employed her mother apparently inconsiderate, but so were most of her neighbours. She referred to one unsympathetic neighbour as 'a self-centred bullshitter,' and another as a 'devil' who was in the habit of writing nasty notes to her mother. The daughter only remembers kindness from a half-dozen people in the community – a wonderful family that lived across from them, the bank manager, and the United Church minister. What angers her to this day is that the people who were in a position to help simply turned their backs, either uncaring or unwilling to meddle in a family's private affairs. By the time this woman's mother had reached middle age, she was dead. What killed her, insisted her daughter, was not the hard work and poverty; it was the stress of living with a violent and alcoholic man.

With one exception, this woman's story is typical of those in similar circumstances. For example, another woman, who lived about three miles from the village, used to walk in and out daily to earn a dollar cleaning houses and washing clothes. Later her family moved into Paradise, where for over forty years she continued to work as a domestic. What was different about her case was that she remembered some kindnesses from the people who employed her. When one of the elite families moved to another town, they left her a beautiful dining-room suite, which incongruously adorned her modest home. But her life, too, was hard, and after she died one of her sons remarked to me: 'I hope in the next life mother isn't forced to take up a mop.'

Conclusion

Paradise, with its broad stratification system, is quite different than the villages in England described by Newby (1977:327), where the majority of the wealthy employers, or landlords, lived on farms around the periphery, while a homogeneous class of agricultural workers resided within the villages. Paradise also differs from Crestwood Heights, the upper-middle-class neighbourhood in Metro Toronto made famous by Seeley and his associates (1956). In many respects, Paradise resembles the American community which Vidich and Bensman called Springdale, but there is one major difference. In Springdale, according to Vidich and Bensman (1960:41), there was a public ideology of equality. Springdale people acted *as if* everyone was equal, and only in private, especially through the medium of gossip, were people ranked, and the competitive and negative aspects of the community aired. Similarly, Foote (1979:154) wrote about the town he investigated in Nova Scotia: 'For most residents the perception of social class in the community was "something that didn't exist".'

The familiar ideology expressed in the communities studied by these authors – 'we are all equal here' – has little counterpart in Paradise. As in Everett Hughes's renowned study of a Quebec community (1943: 250), where the lowest class of people, in the judgment of those at the top, were 'less religious' and 'poor, dirty, hard-drinking, lying, stealing people,' the ideology of equality in Paradise only reflected the perspective of the higher classes. Indeed, what was surprising about Paradise was just how thin that ideology actually was. People in the upper classes themselves, when confronted with examples to the contrary, made little effort to argue that the community was classless, although most of them continued to insist that any person with sufficient intellect and ambition could make his or her way to the top. The fictional character of egalitarianism was even more apparent to those in the lower classes; few of them accepted even the watered-down version of unhindered upward class mobility. Yet it would be wrong to presume that today it is only the people in the higher classes who regret the passing of the old ways, or believe that Paradise, transformed by the massive changes of the 1970s and 1980s, has been lost. In one respect the rich and poor people from the past are on the same wavelength: both share a nostalgia for the bygone days when everyone knew each other, and a 'real' community, no matter how imperfect, existed.

Finally, a word or two about 'the aristocracy' in Paradise. By virtue of systematic inequality, whether based on the principle of social class, race, or gender, it is never possible to evaluate the capacities of people who are discriminated against. What can be stated is that many of the people who constituted the elite in the community seemed to be intelligent individuals and gifted leaders. Furthermore, despite the power, authority, and privilege they enjoyed, it would be an error to describe them as moral inferiors to the people below them. Those in the lower classes were not revolutionaries bent on building a just society. Their dream was not to abolish the elite; it was to push aside the existing members and occupy it themselves. If we shift gears here and entertain the Marxian approach to class, we can reasonably conclude that these poor people of Paradise constituted 'a class in itself,' defined in terms of their shared location in the means of production, but they were not 'a class for itself' (which, as I indicated in chapter 2, corresponds to Krauss's conception of class as distinct from stratum). To continue in a Marxian vein, their false consciousness produced envy rather than protest, and in the end led them to support rather than challenge the overall system of institutionalized inequality.

Chapter Four

The Great Escape

Over and over again I heard the same refrain from the poor people of the past: only if they left the community did they have any hope of building a successful life. A woman who grew up in poverty remarked: 'I was dying to leave. I was tired of the stigma.' When she did move to the city, first living in a huge apartment complex, what pleased her was the anonymity; even people with whom she associated did not know her background, and she was finally free from the gossip that had always dogged her. Despite the lack of funds, she persevered, graduated from university, and established a career in the civil service. Although she had left Paradise behind, a part of it followed her to the city: at the least sign of arrogance from upper-class clients or superiors at work, she reacts in anger. As a result, her career has had its ups and downs.

In this chapter I shall take a close look at the pattern of migration from Paradise to the urban areas in the south that prevailed during the decade following the Second World War. Three questions in particular will guide the analysis: who left the community (and conversely who remained), why did they leave (or stay), and what were the consequences for their lives?

Migrants and Non-Migrants

I shall begin by tracing the careers of four men who were teenagers in the early 1950s, born into some of the poorest families in the village. They grew up together, sat in the same classroom in school, played hockey on the frozen ponds, joked and scrapped on the street corner, and then, entering manhood, went their separate ways. Two of them moved away to larger centres, while the other two remained in Paradise, but rarely came in contact with each other.

The first man's parents were raised on farms near Paradise. His father went as far as grade seven, his mother grade six. A year after they married, misfortune struck: the young husband was left disabled by illness, and all thoughts of making a career as a farmer vanished. From that point onwards, they scratched out a living in Paradise as best they could. The man became a shoemaker, repaired harnesses, sharpened skates, and occasionally sold farm implements. The woman worked as a domestic for upper-class people, ran a used-clothing outlet and skate exchange, did baby-sitting, and boarded elderly women.

Their son, thus, was born into a family struggling valiantly to survive. From an early age he displayed the qualities that would eventually take him to the top of his profession. It soon became apparent to his teachers that he was highly intelligent. Equally important was his determination to succeed, his capacity for hard work and self-sacrifice. He delivered newspapers and prescriptions for a pharmacy, and when he became a teenager worked part-time in a grocery store. In those days many kids periodically searched the back alleys and ditches for empty beer bottles, hoping to make 25 cents so they could buy some candy or pay the admission price to the cinema located in a nearby town. The young man in question, however, went about it in a much more sophisticated manner. He organized other kids to collect beer bottles for him, paying them $1^1/_2$ cents a bottle. When a truck load had accumulated, he took them to the nearest beer outlet a few miles away and sold them for $2^1/_2$ cents each. He remembers the occasion when a boy brought him a single bottle. He gave him one cent. A few days later the same boy brought him another bottle, and again received one cent. The boy's mother complained that since her son had delivered two bottles, he should receive three cents. Our young businessman disagreed, insisting that the lower price was justified because two different transactions had been enacted. Entrepreneurial flair, obviously, was not lacking in his make-up.

Just before he was scheduled to write his grade thirteen examinations, his father died. Several elderly people still remember his remarkable courage at that time: he pushed the pain of his father's death to one side, and continued to prepare for the examinations. At one point he drove out to a back road where he could study in peace. The high school principal, worried that his star student might be distraught enough to do something foolish, motored around the country roads until he found him, calmly concentrating on his books. The man himself told me that he can't remember crying when his father died. He reacted stoically, and simply got on with the task at hand. He did, apparently, confuse parts of two subjects when he eventually wrote the examinations, and thought that had been a sign of the stress which he had been under. All this suggests that he possessed a remarkable degree of fortitude and single-minded determination.

His examination marks were sufficiently high to win him a small bursary for university entrance. When he first left the community, he said, he was completely naive. At a university function he showed up wearing a team jacket, adorned with various sports crests. A dignified gentleman mildly suggested that perhaps the next time he could wear a suit like everyone else. He was informed that the man who had commented on his dress was the dean of his college, but at that time he didn't know what was meant by 'dean.' His university years were ones of dire poverty. He no longer could afford to buy meals towards the end of each school year, and would eat at a facility in the city that catered to the down-and-out. At one point, when he was really desperate, out of the blue came a cheque in the mail for one hundred dollars, a gift from a women's organization. Persevering, he was not only awarded a degree in his chosen profession, but also completed a specialized postgraduate program. In possession today of a highly successful practice, he is recognized as a leader in his field and is periodically interviewed by journalists and appears on television.

Despite his family's poverty, his memories of growing up in Paradise were generally positive. As he remarked, 'I never thought I lived on a poor street until I looked back on it.' While he realized that the families located down by the dump were even poorer than his own, he also knew that the homes of his schoolmates in the elite families were off-limits. He did go to one of those homes once to play ping-pong. But he felt out of place and unwelcome, and never went back again. It just so happened that the schoolmate whom he had visited had a particularly nasty habit of reminding his social inferiors of their lowly status.

After completing his university studies, he periodically returned to Paradise when his mother was still alive. Unfortunately, he said, many of his good friends from the past were awkward in his company, awed by his achievements and status. What was ironical, he pointed out, was that the one person who seemed least impressed was the former upper-class schoolmate who took pleasure in reminding others of their humble origins. Although this person's own accomplishments were, to say the least, modest in comparison, his aristocratic background, forged over the generations, apparently gave him the confidence to relate to the highly esteemed ex-resident as an equal.

How can we explain this person's success? A contributing factor was the support he received from other people. His parents, especially his father, encouraged him to strive for the highest goals and provided an example of frugality and determination in the face of formidible obstacles. Some of his teachers, including the principal, recognized his intellectual promise and tried to prepare him for post-secondary education. Others, such as the owner of the grocery store in which he worked, helped him along the way. Yet the key factor was the man's own personal attributes. He insisted that he had not grown up determined to conquer the world. Instead, it was mostly an accident, a product of unfolding circumstances. First, there was the objective measure of his high marks in school. Added to that, he said, was his approach to everything with which he became involved; no matter what the activity – school work, delivering newspapers, or in later years umpiring baseball games – he had to perform at the peak of his ability. He was incapable of doing anything less. His assets, thus, included an above-average intellect, entrepreneurial skills, self-reliance, a perfectionist inclination, and remarkable determination and discipline. This man is the person most often mentioned by high-class elderly Paradise residents when they argue that all that poor people needed to lift themselves out of poverty was ambition.

I turn now to a man who also was raised in a poor family, but who has remained in Paradise all his life. Like the previous individual, he was brought up in the Anglican Church (neither attend any more), and one of his jobs as a boy was to cut the grass and shovel the sidewalks on the church's property. He was bigger than most boys his age, and while he liked to scrap (and still does, according to social workers, even though he has turned fifty), he was never a bully. He quit school in grade nine. Over the years he has worked in construction and as a handyman. He attempted to establish his own small business in town on three occasions, but each time went bankrupt. Some people explained that these failures didn't mean that he was stupid – in fact, they thought that he had a flair for business. But the bottle was always within reach, with the result that he has been on and off welfare for much of his adult life. Although penniless and unemployed, and in poor health, he recently married for the third time (one of his previous wives died of cancer, and the other marriage ended in divorce). He and his new wife moved in with his aging mother (his father had died several years earlier), but with unfortunate consequences. His wife tried to gain control of the household, even forbidding her mother-in-law to use the telephone. After a few weeks the older woman could stand no more. She ordered her daughter-in-law out of the house. As the younger woman departed in anger, she kicked in the glass window of the front door.

This man is widely known today as one of the town bums, and what is significant is that I never met a single person in Paradise who had any sympathy for him, except his own family. Even people who grew up in similar impoverished circumstances declared that he had nobody to blame for his misfortunes except himself. How can you respect anyone, asked one man, who still lives at home at the age of fifty and takes his spending money from his mother's pension? According to another person, the town bum has managed to avoid holding a steady job for years by specializing in relationships with gullible women who have been prepared to support him.

Such criticisms, from the point of view of the man himself and his family, are completely unfair. He fervently believes that he has been a victim of a class-based society. He claimed that 'the Klan,' by which he meant the town council and wealthy merchants, systematically suppressed poor people who attempted to establish a business. The council, according to this man, once tried to force his mother to sell her house at a ridiculously low price, in order that a commercial building could be erected on the site. His mother did not try to deny that her son had a drinking problem, but what angered her was her perception that the poor and the rich were treated differently in the community. Her son, she said, cannot walk out of a restaurant after having a couple of beers without being hassled by the police. But 'the KKK,' as she referred to influential citizens, can get roaring drunk in the Legion and nobody will touch them when they stumble into their vehicles.

There were several children in this family, and all except the one man had moved away from the community. None of them had gone beyond grade eleven, but all of them held down steady jobs, mostly in the trades (one of their children had made it to university), and had gravitated upwards towards the middle class. As the mother of the young woman who went to university explained, she herself had left Paradise at the age of fifteen because her family's reputation meant that nobody would offer her a job locally, or even trust her. Recently one of her brothers and his wife and children returned to live with his mother, only to find that the family's reputation still counted against him. Although he himself did not drink, he could not find work and soon moved to another community where he was not known. As he said, 'If you're poor people, the Klan work together to keep you down.'

If that is so, how can we explain the remarkable success of the previous individual? First of all, although both men came from poor families, the reputations of their families were quite different. The parents of the first man were sober, diligent, and highly respected. The second man's family was always associated with alcoholism, indolence, and rough behaviour. On occasions when I was present, swearing was commonplace, even in front of the mother. One time, for example, the talk turned to a local individual who had been charged with sexual abuse involving teenage girls; as one of the woman's sons quipped, 'He likes to fuck them young.' On that occasion the mother revealed that several years ago the same man had sexually molested one of her daughters, but nothing had ever been done about it because her family lacked power.

A second factor that should not be overlooked concerns the different intellectual capacities of the two men. The one who remained in Paradise was no dummy, but the one who went on to a professional career was clearly gifted. Yet there is the objective fact that all of the siblings of the town bum had built successful lives for themselves in other communities. The implication is that if one left the community, one's chances of success were a great deal better than if one remained. It is precisely here, however, that the argument runs into the first major obstacle. To put it bluntly, it was just as easy to find examples among poor people who had left the community but failed, or who had remained in the community but flourished.

Consider the case of a young man whose parents had been divorced. Raised in poverty by his father, a well-known alcoholic, he quit school in grade nine and left Paradise to seek his fortune. Unfortunately his new environment in a larger centre did not lead him to make a complete break with the past. He too became an alcoholic, and for several years has been in poor health. Today he lives with his wife in a run-down house, the furniture half-broken, looking ten years older than he actually is. Yet he has never been divorced, and like so many other people in the lower class, his family, which includes four grown-up children, is intact. When he first left Paradise, he said, he thought it would just be a matter of time before things started to fall into place. He wasn't sure what went wrong, and wondered if it wouldn't have been better to have simply remained in the community of his birth.

That certainly was the correct decision for our fourth character. He too was brought up in a single-parent household (his father had disappeared), but he was luckier than the previous individual. Although the council records show that his family was on welfare for several years following the Second World War, his mother was one of those strong-willed women who held the family together. His three sisters left the community and have met with success; one of them, by sheer determination, graduated from university and became a teacher. His brother, too, departed for the bright lights, but his life, plagued by alcohol, has not turned out so well. In contrast, the one who remained in Paradise learned a trade, worked hard, and today owns valuable property. Gentle, honest, sober, sensitive, and self-effacing, his success has not inspired the jealousy that sometimes is aimed at upwardly mobile people who were formerly lower class. As I observed on different occasions, he is widely respected, one of the more popular individuals in the community.

There is another major obstacle to the assumption that it was the oppressive class system that drove people out of the community, especially the poor: people from all other social classes became migrants as well; indeed, my impression was that even a higher proportion of upper-class individuals joined the exodus to the south. Moreover, there seemed to be just as much variation in terms of success and failure among these other migrants as in the lower class. In order to examine the migratory situation more systematically, I turned to 135 cases of young people who had entered the workforce for the first time between 1945 and 1960; 77 of them left the community and 58 remained behind.

The General Picture

It must be emphasized from the outset that the figures provided in tables 4 and 5 below are only crude estimates at best. The cases were not selected by simple random sampling procedures, and contain two obvious biases. In table 4 the class composition of the 135 cases of migrants and non-migrants does not correspond to that of the general population at the time. In table 5 there is, unfortunately, a heavy male

TABLE 4
Comparison of Class Composition of 135 Cases to General Population

Class	135 Cases	General Population
Upper	19 (14%)	30 (2.5%)
Lower upper	9 (7%)	79 (6.7%)
Middle	27 (20%)	358 (30.2%)
Lower middle	40 (30%)	516 (43.6%)
Lower	40 (30%)	199 (16.8%)
Totals	135 (101%)	1182 (99.8%)

Note:
The estimated class proportions of the general population around 1950 were derived from interviews with 122 natives. According to the Canadian census, the population of Paradise in 1951 was 1,184, which was the basis for calculating the number of people at each level for the general population. See appendices A and B for more information about these interviews.

TABLE 5
Comparison of Migrants and Non-Migrants

Class	77 Migrants	58 Non-Migrants
Upper	19 (25%)	–
Lower upper	3 (4%)	6 (10%)
Middle	16 (21%)	11 (19%)
Lower middle	24 (31%)	16 (28%)
Lower	15 (19%)	25 (43%)
Totals	77 (100%)	58 (100%)

Note:
The 77 cases of people who left were derived from two sources; most of them had simply accumulated in my field notes over the period of three years of research; an additional 29 were formally interviewed after being traced to their current locations in various parts of Ontario. Among the 58 individuals who remained in the community, 36 were formally interviewed, and the remainder were taken from my field notes.

bias. Among the seventy-seven migrants, fifty-four (70 per cent) were male; among the fifty-eight non-migrants, forty-one (71 per cent) were male.

Despite these biases, the data nevertheless are suggestive. What is most interesting is what we see at the polar class positions. First, a much higher proportion of the people who did not leave Paradise (43 per cent) compared to the proportion of those who did leave (19 per cent) fell into the lower class. Put otherwise, among the forty individuals in the lower class for whom I have information, fifteen (38 per cent) became migrants, while fully twenty-five (62 per cent) stayed at home. That is not the portrait of stampeding lower-class people they themselves painted. Second, every upper-class youth in the period following the Second World War about whom I learned eventually departed from the community.

Lower-class people may certainly have felt oppressed and believed that their only hope was to leave the community, but what was in their heads was not necessarily translated into action. Instead, it was the privileged youth who were most inclined to seek their fortunes beyond Paradise. According to many people in the higher classes, there is a simple explanation: the most intelligent and ambitious people tended to become migrants. While they allowed for the occasional lower-class individual to be included in this select company, such as the young man who started off collecting beer bottles and ended up at the top of his profession, they took it for granted that the vast majority of intelligent and ambitious people came from their own ranks.

What is perhaps surprising is that this self-serving explanation has its counterpart in the scholarly literature. Schnore (1966), for example, refers approvingly to a study done in Sweden on rural to urban migration in which it was argued that migration lowered the average level of intelligence in both rural and urban society. How? This was supposedly because the most intelligent rural people became migrants, leaving those of lower IQ behind; yet these migrants were still less intelligent than people already living in the city. Drawing on the same assumptions, Schnore (1966: 141) went on to speculate that in the USA, blacks (he uses the term 'nonwhites') migrating from the rural South to the urban North lowered the IQ level of nonwhites (he substitutes the slippery expression 'nonwhite education') at both ends of the migratory stream.

Schnore's argument has had a long and contentious history in academic circles. For example, it was found that blacks scored lower than whites on IQ tests given to American soldiers during the First World War. Klineberg (1935) re-analysed those data and discovered that there was a significant difference between blacks from the northern states and blacks from the southern states: the average IQ level of the former was higher. Klineberg concluded that the difference was due to the influence of superior education in the North and a more stimulating environment. Yet others, not all of them racists, retorted that the differences demonstrated that it was the most intelligent blacks who had migrated to the northern states.[1] Further studies showed that northern blacks scored higher on IQ tests than southern whites. This seemed to confirm the importance of environmental influence, but not to those who believed that IQ was the critical factor; their argument was that not only did the most intelligent blacks relocate in the North, but also the most intelligent whites, leaving the South populated by a duller population of whites and blacks.[2]

Quite apart from the dubious assumption that IQ measurements mean much in the context of institutionalized racial and social class discrimination, in my judgment it is simplistic to argue that migrants tend to be drawn from 'the cream of the crop.' The reasons why people decide to try their luck in a new setting are varied and complex. Dasgupta (1988: 31 7) suggests that it has been the lack of opportunities at home, and the availability of jobs elsewhere, together with such extra-economic factors as the glitter and excitement of the city, that have brought about rural depopulation in Canada. This push-pull thesis, essentially an economic model, explains migration as an adjustment of the labour supply to market forces. Other social scientists emphasize status mobility aspirations, risk-taking personalities, and the importance of financial and psychological support provided to migrants by their relatives.

These various explanations penetrate the Paradise scene to some degree, but to get to the heart of the matter a sharper instrument is required. It is too crude, for example, to assign the same motives to lower-class and upper-class migrants. Following De Jong and Fawcett (1981:16), I make a distinction between innovative and conservative migrants. The former consists of people hoping to achieve better lives, and applies to the lower-class individuals who left the community. The latter refers to those people who merely wish to retain the lifestyles which they have always known, and applies to the upper-class migrants. To elaborate, when one examines the family histories of the 'old' families that constituted the elite in the 1950s, one discovers their forebears in various prosaic occupations at the turn of the century, such as shoemakers, blacksmiths, tanners, tavern owners, and especially farmers. It is difficult to know whether these pioneers were more talented and ambitious than their contemporaries. Yet one thing is certain: after people did achieve success, and the community became divided into rich and poor, it was highly probable that the same families would continue as rich or poor in succeeding generations, because privilege had become institutionalized.

In other words, it was vested interests that kept the sons and daughters of the elite in the community during the first half of the century. When the family business began to become obsolete, the offspring of the elite, to conserve their class positions, were forced to pack their bags and arm themselves with college diplomas and university degrees.

The lower-class youth, in contrast, lacking family assets and local business opportunities, had nothing to hold them back; migration for them was an opportunity to move up the stratification ladder. Yet if that was the case, why didn't they all become migrants? Why, indeed, was it the lower class that displayed the greatest reluctance to leave at all? For one reason they lacked the financial support necessary to attend institutes of higher education or to embark on business ventures. To turn this around, it is reasonable to argue that it was precisely such financial support, rather than superior intelligence and ambition, that explained the much higher rate of migration among the offspring of the elite. Other reasons were psychological in nature. Young women and men in the lower class had been socialized to accept modest stations in life; to dream of becoming an engineer or lawyer was a little bit like thinking one was Napoleon. Moreover, it requires a certain degree of self-confidence to embark on a new life in a strange environment, and confidence is the one commodity that is most elusive among poor people. Finally, there is the matter of sheer accident. In many cases, individuals did not make the decision to migrate on the basis of rational calculation. Instead, unforeseen circumstances in their lives took them away from Paradise. Some families were broken apart by alcoholism and scattered in various directions. In others, a financial disaster, such as a business property destroyed by fire, did the trick. One man told me he had no intention of leaving Paradise, but was obligated to do so when the company he worked for moved its operation closer to the city. In a few cases the decision to move was based on nothing more substantial than an inability to get along with the neighbours.

The focus so far has been on why people migrate, but why they do not migrate is equally important. Some hints have already been given. If one had vested interests in the community, such as a robust family business to inherit, one usually remained in place; lower-class people tended to do so too, because they lacked finances, confidence, and great expectations. Personality differences also had an impact. Consider the cases of two brothers who moved from Toronto to Paradise in the 1940s. Their father, a war veteran, was unable to work, and they quickly were assigned a lower-class label. The older brother talked about how much he hated the community from the outset. Nobody, he insisted, put out the welcome mat. On the contrary, he said, he was treated as if he was a city gangster. According to this man, his teachers tried to persuade him not to go to high school. He did complete grade ten. When he quit, he got a job collecting garbage – precisely the line of work, he bitterly observed, that 'the hierarchy' (as he referred to the elite) expected him to do. Eventually he moved back to the city, and made it clear that he had done so because he could not tolerate the shame, oppression and non-existent employment prospects in Paradise.

His younger brother's memory of the class system was a carbon copy. He, too, claimed that his teachers had discouraged him from attending secondary school, and in fact he quit after finishing grade eight. Yet he remained in the community. When I asked him why he had done so, he was not really sure. In my judgment, however, personality made the difference. The brother who left was articulate, aggressive, extroverted, almost flamboyant. The one who remained was shy and withdrawn, the type of person who slips through life unseen from shadow to shadow. For him, there was a wall around the community beyond his capacity to scale.

The same variation in personality was apparent in two sisters, both of whom also expressed rock-hard hatred towards the community in which they had been raised. The one who left was outspoken and aggressive; she rarely returns to the community, even to visit her sister, because of her negative memories. The one who stayed behind can be seen today walking along a street with her head down, too intimidated to look at people, her behaviour and attitudes a throwback to the era of the 1950s when poor people were expected to know their place. Of course, there is also the issue of emotional ties. It would seem reasonable to assume that those people who remained in the community did so partly because of strong ties to friends and relatives, and to the place where they went to school, perhaps met their spouses, and began to raise their own families. These sentiments were expressed by a great many people, especially the elderly. Yet the number of individuals in the middle and lower classes who indicated their intentions of leaving the community on retirement was striking. While their outlooks were partly shaped by the massive changes in the community in recent

TABLE 6

Comparison of Class Positions of 135 Migrants and Non-Migrants with Class Positions of Parents

	Higher	Same	Lower	Unknown
Upper class				
Migrants	–	11 (58%)	8 (42%)	
Non-Migrants	–	–	–	
Lower-upper class				
Migrants	–	–	3 (100%)	
Non-Mmigrants	1 (17%)	2 (33%)	3 (50%)	
Middle class				
Migrants	11 (73%)	4 (27%)	–	1
Non-Migrants	6 (55%)	5 (45%)	–	
Lower-middle class				
Migrants	14 (64%)	6 (27%)	2 (9%)	2
Non-Migrants	9 (56%)	7 (44%)	–	
Lower class				
Migrants	11 (78%)	3 (21%)	–	1
Non-Migrants	11 (44%)	14 (56%)	–	
All classes combined				
Migrants	36 (49%)	24 (33%)	13 (18%)	4
Non-Migrants	27 (46%)	28 (48%)	3 (5%)	
All classes combined				
but adjusted (see note 2)				
Migrants	47 (64%)	10 (14%)	16 (22%)	4
Non-Migrants	27 (46%)	14 (24%)	17 (29%)	

Notes:

1 Four cases among the migrants have been excluded from the analysis in this table because of insufficient information about their class positions, or degree of success; percentages for the migrants have been calculated solely on the basis of known cases (73).

2 By definition, none of the people in the upper class fell into the 'higher' category. I therefore interpreted as successes all those cases that were placed in the 'same' category. Similarly, none of the people in the lower class could be placed in the 'lower' category. I interpreted as failures all those cases that fell into the 'same' category.

In analysing the degree of success of all classes combined, calculations were adjusted to reflect the above interpretations. Thus, among the migrants, 'higher' consisted of 36 cases plus 11 cases that were included in the 'same category (total 47 cases); the 'same' category consisted of 24 cases minus the 11 cases transferred to the 'higher' category, minus three cases among the lower class (total 10 cases); the 'lower' category consisted of 13 cases plus the three lower-class cases that had been placed in the 'same' category (total 16 cases).

Among the non-migrants, 'higher' consisted of 27 cases (no adjustment was required because none of the non-migrants in my sample belonged to the upper class); 'same' consisted of 28 cases minus 14 lower-class cases that were included in the 'same' category (total 14 cases); the 'lower' category consisted of 3 cases plus the above 14 lower-class cases (total 17 cases).

years, the almost total lack of warmth and loyalty towards the town where they had spent their lives suggests that emotional bonds had never been of great importance to them.

I have dealt at some length with the questions of who migrates (or doesn't), and why people migrate (or don't), and I turn now to the third question that guides this chapter: What are the consequences of leaving the community or remaining at home? It is, of course, not an easy thing to decide who has been successful and who has not. Consider the lives of the following two men, both born into lower-middle-class families. Friends from an early age, they grew up playing hockey and baseball together, and went through primary school in the same classes. The one who remained in Paradise showed early signs of being somewhat more clever, at least measured by performance in school. Yet because of a family calamity, his friend moved away from the community, and eventually went to university and became a teacher. Some Paradise people described the man who remained as a narrow-minded individual lacking in ambition. It is true that the person who left has seen the world, and possibly can be considered more sophisticated and worldly; he also enjoys the prestige of a professional occupation. Yet in terms of economic assets there is not much difference between the two individuals. The one who stayed at home has served as a manager of a local enterprise, and today not only has his own small business, but also possesses valuable property. Moreover, he has his roots intact, while the one who left confessed to me that he has no roots. Was it, therefore, ambition and intellect that took these individuals in different directions, or accident, and in any ultimate sense has the one who left been more successful than his friend who stayed? To make the calculus even more complicated, the individual who has spent all of his life in Paradise is one of those who plans to leave the community when he retires.

Because any attempt to measure people's success and failure in terms of happiness, or to estimate the ultimate worth of their occupations and lifestyles, is bound to be imprecise and arbitrary, I have followed a more modest procedure. Success and failure, as indicated in table 6, are defined in terms of a person's class position in comparison to the class position of her or his parents. If people's class positions are higher than those of their parents, I define their lives as successful; conversely, if their class positions are lower, I define their lives as failures.[3]

The overall picture is provided at the bottom of the table (see note 2 in table 6 for an explanation of why and how the figures were adjusted). What is apparent is that there has been a general elevation in class position for both migrants and non-migrants. In each category more people experienced upward class mobility vis-a-vis the class positions of their parents than stayed in the same positions or fell to lower positions. It also is clear that the migrants enjoyed a greater degree of success; in comparison with the non-migrants, a higher percentage of them (64 per cent versus 46 per cent) rose in class position, and a lower percentage of them (22 per cent versus 29 per cent) dropped in class position. A closer look at the fates of the migrants and non-migrants at the various class levels reveals some interesting results, especially at the polar ends. If the 'same' category for the upper-class migrants is defined as a success (by definition, they could not rise higher than the upper class), and if the 'same' category among the lower-class migrants is defined as a failure (by definition, they could not fall below the lower class), then it is evident that a much higher percentage (78 per cent) of the lower-class migrants enjoyed success than of the upper-class migrants (58 per cent). What this implies is that there was more risk involved for upper-class than lower-class people who decided to leave the community. Of course, even a modest drop in the class position of the former still maintained them above the level of the majority of successful lower-class migrants who had climbed towards the middle class. As I explained earlier, I did not learn of any cases of non-migrants among the sons and daughters of the upper class, but there were more non-migrants than migrants among the lower class. While almost half of these non-migrants enjoyed upward status mobility, it is clear that a significantly higher percentage of those who left the community did even better.

To turn this around, while 56 per cent of the lower-class people who stayed put failed to rise above the poverty level of their parents, only 21 per cent of the migrants found themselves in the same boat. It is at the centre of the stratification system, involving the middle class and the lower-middle class, where migration has posed the least risk; only two of the thirty-seven people (or 5 per cent) in these classes who left Paradise actually fell to a lower level.

In summary, it can be concluded that those people who packed their belongings and moved away from Paradise generally made the correct decision, at least if success is defined in terms of upward class mobility. As useful as quantitative data may be for indicating general trends, in order to capture more subtle features, such as the consequences of migrating or not migrating for one's respect and esteem, it is necessary to return to case material.

Who Gets Respect?

Paradise in the 1950s might be characterized as an elaborate code of reputation, and one of the consequences of migrating was to leave behind the collectively acknowledged moral evaluation of one's family. Thus, lower-class people who made new lives for themselves elsewhere, and prospered, often remarked that they now enjoy respect. By the same token, upper-class migrants lost a bit of ground simply because the moral worth of their family background was often an unknown quantity beyond the community. It was quite a different story for those who remained in the town. Upper-class people whose financial statuses had become precarious as they entered old age and were obligated to live frugally, in some cases moving into subsidized apartments, nevertheless continued to be recognized as superior individuals. At the other extreme, lower-class people who had remained in the community – even those who had prospered – found it difficult to counteract their family's reputation. Consider the case of a man who had successfully established a thriving business. By the 1980s he had apparently become moderately wealthy, but one would never had known that by observing his interaction with other people, or listening to their comments about him. People have never forgotten that he was born on the street across from the dump. They are perfectly aware that he has come into money, but some of them put that down to dishonest business practices, and to the fact that people in his class never spend money on what others regard as necessities, such as new furniture, a late-model car, and a vacation in the Caribbean. Of course, facts can always be shaped to fit the stereotype, and in a different context these same lower-class people are said to be lavish spenders, throwing their money away on unneeded luxuries while their children go hungry.

This man's success, albeit admirable, was essentially modest. Could it be that those individuals who remained in the community and achieved spectacular success were duly recognized and respected? To examine this possibility, I turn to the careers of two millionaires.

The soaring land costs and the demand for housing in the early 1970s presented an enormous opportunity to those who were astute enough to recognize it. While a number of local people invested in real estate in a small way, almost all the developers were outsiders; the only major exceptions were the two men described below. The one came from an extremely poor family, the other from a middle-class family. The first man eventually moved away from the community, but not before amassing a fortune. The second man, reputedly a multi-millionaire, still lives near the town. Despite the staggering success achieved by each of these men, it was not often that I met anyone who had anything good to say about them. Riches they may have had in abundance, but respect was quite a different matter.

The first man claimed, with little exaggeration, that there had been no family in Paradise poorer than his own. His childhood story is a replica of several others which have already been described: a father unemployed for much of the time, a mother forced to work as a domestic, alcoholic problems in the family, insults from people in the upper classes, and welfare payments barely enough on which to exist. The records of the council minutes in the early 1950s reveal that his father was paid the grand sums of $1.00 and $2.00 for cleaning the town hall, and one of his brothers received $2.60 for snow removal. He himself, according to these same records, was hired by the town for odd jobs, such as removing the bell from the old school and painting the town hall.

When he quit school in grade seven, he seemed destined to repeat the grovelling life that his parents had known, but his dreams were something else. He remembers as a teenager sitting on porches with three or four friends in similar economic circumstances, talking about how some day they were going to make it. By the time he was in his early twenties, he said, he *knew* he was going to surpass the achievements of all of the elite families. His first big break, he explained, came about by accident. He had purchased an old cupboard for a few dollars. A woman in town saw it in the back of his truck, and asked if he would sell it. She readily agreed to the inflated price he demanded, and requested a couple of other pieces of furniture. Almost overnight he had become fully involved in a thriving antique business. His next major venture was real estate. Lacking sufficient capital of his own, he apparently worked as a silent partner for investors from the city. Unimposing physically, and always associated with the low reputation of his family of birth, this intelligent man, much to the chagrin of those who underestimated him, had little difficulty in playing the role of the rustic innocent. Wheeling and dealing, he eventually achieved precisely what he claimed he would: financial success alongside which most of the elite families of his youth resembled paupers.

His business interests and contacts had gravitated over the years to the larger market to the south, and he eventually left Paradise, but not without considerable satisfaction: 'You see, I defeated them, then I left.' Actually, he insisted that he didn't hold any grudges towards the upper class in the town of his birth. Those people, he said, were understandably just trying to defend the interests of their own families; besides, he added, it was not worth the effort to hate or envy them – it was far better to surpass them. Such admirable objectivity, however, appeared to be mostly on the surface. Underneath, the pain of growing up in poverty remained. It was typical of the community, he pointed out, that the street on which he lived as a boy usually wasn't ploughed in winter until late afternoon, and occasionally not at all, because only poor people lived in that area. Sometimes he got into fights with the sons of the elite who mocked his family. Years later, before he left Paradise, he became part owner of a restaurant. On one occasion the parents of a boy whom he had fought observed that the food was pretty good, especially for someone with his family background. As the man said, he could have exploded in anger, but he controlled his emotions and simply remarked cryptically: 'Things change.'

A talented hockey player in his youth, he commented that sports had been an important factor in his business success, because one couldn't play hockey and drink heavily at the same time. He added that the same aggressiveness needed in sports was an asset in the business world. Even his involvement in hockey, however, brought back memories of his impoverished past. After a game his teammates would relax over refreshments, but he said he could not join them because he did not have any money. One man told me that he once overheard a member of the elite commenting that it would be marvellous if the talented young hockey player could make the game his career, because he certainly didn't have enough brains to go very far in school.

Another reason for his success, he stated, was that he was very good at meeting politicians. He explained that he also had a knack of aggravating people, and once they became angry, he was able to control the business transactions. At one point in the interview I personally experienced his capacity in this regard. Nothing he said made sense for a stretch of several minutes. When I pointed out the inconsistencies and implausible claims, he said he had just been testing me, and congratulated me for being perceptive enough to see through him. Embarrassed he was not, and indeed he went on to say that he didn't give a hoot what anyone thought of him. He was, he claimed, completely self-sufficient, and didn't need anyone's approval, especially the approval of the people of Paradise. If he had any need for their admiration, or wanted to rub his success in their faces, he stated, he would simply dress in a sharp suit and drive through the town in a Cadillac.

Yet here, too, his attitudes were contradictory, for almost in the next breath he commented: 'I don't know if I'll ever get respect there.' Some of his old pals were still fond of him, but they were inclined to regard his financial success as something of a game or lark, rather than as an impressive achievement. Other people were much less generous. For example, when I asked the upper-class man (by then quite elderly), who had apparently said that the developer had not been intelligent enough to go far in school, what he thought of the man's remarkable financial success, he dismissed him as just another crooked developer. One individual refused to believe that the former resident had ever made any money, saying it was all a show. Another person claimed that the man had gone bankrupt simply because he was never smart enough to know when the market was falling. It was true that the developer had had his ups and downs financially, but he remarked that that didn't bother him in the least. If you lose in pennies, he explained, you gain in pennies; if you have the capacity to lose a million, you have the capacity to make another. At the time that I met him, he stated that he was once more in good financial shape.

Earlier I pointed out that the relationships among the members of many of the poor families, even ones plagued by alcohol, were close and supportive. The one great exception was the family of the man whom I have been describing. As he rose to the top of the business world, he apparently cut off all ties with his parents and siblings. When I asked him about the influence of his parents on his career, he said it was non-existent. As for the siblings he had left behind, he had little sympathy for them. In his opinion, they were just as intelligent as he was, but they lacked ambition and had wasted their lives in alcoholic stupors. Like the members of the upper class, he believed that being born poor was no excuse to remain poor; it was up to the individual, he said, to succeed or fail.

Aggressive, clever, and complex, this man may not have gained much respect in Paradise, but his achievements have been outstanding, and only the envy of some people in his past, who prefer their poor to remain poor, has denied him the recognition he has earned. Reflecting on the long road he has travelled from the poverty of his youth, he asked: 'How dangerous would I have been if I had been educated?' Perhaps he would have ended up as an entertaining but (by his standards) underpaid university professor!

Unlike the man I have just described, our second millionaire's life has been profoundly influenced by his father, who probably had more imaginative and innovative ideas for making money than anyone else in the recent history of the community. Many people remember the older person as a wheeler-dealer, his 'hair-brained schemes' often a subject of mirth. Yet if there ever was a man born before his times, it was him. As far back as the 1950s, when Paradise was still a sleepy little village, he had correctly forecast the subdivision boom that would materialize in the 1970s. Yet when he tried to establish the community's first subdivision on his own farm bordering the village, he was frustrated at almost every turn. The reeve in those days, he claimed, had assured him of the complete support of the council, and had agreed that the community would bear the responsibility for installing water and sewage services. Indeed, evidence of that agreement was recorded in the 1959 minutes of the community's Planning Board, an organization that had been established in 1955 to deal with the village's future expansion. In 1956 the Planning Board made tentative plans for two new subdivisions, one to be built by the man I have been describing, the other by an outsider from a nearby town. At the 1959 meeting one of the members of the Planning Board protested that provincial regulations stipulated that the village had to have a subdivision-control by-law, and argued that such regulations required the developer to provide not only roads but also all the services. The local developer, stubborn and inflexible, refused to comply, furious that the terms of the agreement had been rewritten. The developer and the Planning Board squabbled for an entire year, with neither willing to give in, and a cloud settled over the innovator's powerful vision of new streets lined by modern bungalows.

Enter his son. Although only in his early twenties, he realized that they had no option but to capitulate to the demands of the council and the Planning Board. At a meeting of the latter organization in November 1960 he agreed to provide the services in the subdivision; two years later, at another meeting of the Planning Board, permission was formally granted for the sale of lots in the subdivision. In the meantime, however, the other subdivision had already become established, and thus some of the glow surrounding the local man's project was extinguished. To make matters worse, this man died before he could draw satisfaction from the completion of one of his most remarkable enterprises.

His son, having got his feet wet as a developer, plunged into the business up to his neck, buying and selling property, embarking on new development projects, and emerging as the outstanding local person in the business. Along the way he made a lot of enemies, and was possibly even less admired than the previous entrepreneur. One man unkindly remarked: 'He borders on being crooked. If he had a contract with me, I'd want it signed in blood.' Another man said: 'His principles aren't very high; he's slippery and dishonest.' A woman claimed he has absolutely no respect or influence in the town itself. Today, according to a person who has known the developer all of his life, he lives in isolation: 'He has absolutely no friends. He relies on his family.'

The fact is that the man did indeed have some admirers in the community, most of them around his own age and from his same middle-class origins. One person described the developer as the most astute businessman he had ever met. Another individual said he was just like his father – imaginative and innovative; this admirer was perfectly aware of the negative attitudes held by other residents, but dismissed them as envy. Like the first developer, the second one too apparently almost went bankrupt. But as one of his friends remarked, 'He was a goer. He didn't quit, you know. Now he's up there again.'

In the views of some people, the man was simply a rascal. As one person joked: 'I always said I never got up early enough in the morning to deal with him.' Others who admired the man did so while recognizing his aggressive business tactics. One person, himself a successful businessman, commented that the developer is 'like those Toronto businessmen. He was more meant to be down there.' Although the negative evaluations of this man certainly outnumbered the positive ones, a number of factors may help to account for his reputation as a hard-nosed businessman. First, the man has been playing in an arena much larger than the local one, and his opponents have been skilled and experienced. He once told me how, in order to communicate on the same level with the lawyers and investors from the city, he coached himself to drop the local colloquialisms that had been part of his vocabulary. It also is a fact that he has been involved to some extent in the town's affairs, being active in a service club, and playing an important role in the construction of a new recreational facility. Moreover, I observed that when the circumstances were not threatening, his mind turned easily to sentimental escapades of the past, giving the impression that there was much more to him than the ruthless businessman that many people portrayed. Finally, there is the matter of the treatment afforded to his innovative father. It is not implausible to suggest that his father's anguish and frustration shaped his own outlook about how to operate and survive in the world of high finance.

Conclusion

Several observations can be made about lower-class people who overcame their impoverished backgrounds, whether as migrants or nonmigrants. First, some of them have become preoccupied with the task of converting their wealth into status, especially if their routes to the top were via the business world. They have turned to collecting the emblems of success such as books, paintings, and thoroughbred horses. One wealthy man proudly showed me his library, which was not especially impressive, and another man told me in all seriousness that periodically he stops at a bookstore and orders a 'yard' of books – no matter what their titles.

Second, for many of these accomplished people, their hatred of the class system of the past remains not far beneath the surface. At times this has a positive impact, motivating them to overcome new obstacles and strive for even higher goals. At other times it is the source of misjudgment and over-reaction, creating embarrassment for all involved. Again, it seemed to be the people who had clawed their way to the top in business, rather than by college diplomas and university degrees, who were the quickest to fly off the handle at alleged insults, although even those men and women who had entered the professions occasionally exhibited the same reaction. Of course, the tendency to do so also reflected the personalities of the people, independent of their class backgrounds.

Third, upward class mobility sometimes exacted a high price. Ruthlessness, and a disinclination to trust anyone, were among the qualities possessed by some successful people, and when they did reach the top, they often found themselves isolated.

Finally, a source of great irritation in some families was that their children did not possess the same incredible drive and determination that had enabled them to reach the summit. In some cases the parents had been so busy building their careers and fortunes that they had had little time left for their children. In one family the sons bitterly stated that their father had no interest in anything but business and money. In two families some of the children deliberately chose careers of potentially high humanistic value, but of low income potential, driving their parents mad. As one of the mothers in these two families remarked, 'Money, of course, isn't everything, but you've got to have it.' The father of a young man who had dropped out of school at an early age, and refused to hold down a regular job, said he and his wife almost split up because of their constant arguments about how to handle him. In view of his own struggles and sacrifices to provide his family with an elegant home and almost every luxury imaginable, he simply could not fathom his son's complete lack of ambition. Occasionally, however, I encountered a family in which at least one of the children was a chip off the old block. As an extremely wealthy migrant from Paradise observed, as long as his son was alive, everything that he had worked for would be in good hands.

PART TWO

Paradise Found: Newcomers

Chapter Five

Modern Pioneers

By the second half of the twentieth century the spectre of dying towns and villages cast a shadow over rural society in many industrialized nations, and in developing ones too, as people deserted the countryside for the city. But in the 1970s a remarkable transformation in the pattern of migration in countries such as the United States took place; droves of people began to vacate the city in search of the good life in smaller communities. As Schwarzweller (1979:7) has remarked, 'Some years hence we may refer to this as the decade of the Great Population Turnaround in America.' A similar trend has occurred in Britain (Pahl 1970, Newby 1977), and in Europe in general and Japan (Blakely and Bradshaw 1981:30). As for Canada, every census from 1871 to 1971, without exception, has revealed a proportional decline in the rural population. Then came the decade of the 1970s, when for the first time in the country's history the population increase in rural society (14.5 per cent) was higher than in urban society (12.3 per cent); most of the newcomers, as Dasgupta (1988:132) has pointed out, have settled in the towns and villages, or on country estates, swelling the nonfarm rather than the farm population of rural Canada.

The influx of newcomers into Paradise, therefore, is only one instance of a wider pattern. Some indication of the impact of the invasion, if that is not too strong a term, is reflected in the population figures in table 7. From the turn of the century until the beginning of the 1960s there was virtually no increase. Then between 1969 and 1978 the population doubled itself; indeed, most of the growth occurred during the six-year span from 1969 to 1975. By the time the community had become incorporated as a town in 1977, a plateau in the popula-

TABLE 7
Population Growth in Paradise

1881 – 733	1971 – 1,790
1891 – 1,202	1975 – 2,919
1901 – 1,188	1976 – 2,928
1911 – 1,113	1978 – 3,001
1921 – 1,072	1979 – 2,899
1931 – 1,077	1980 – 2,847
1941 – 1,005	1981 – 2,862
1951 – 1,184	1982 – 2,972
1956 – 1,245	1985 – 3,004
1961 – 1,239	1986 – 2,980
1966 – 1,354	1988 – 3,123
1969 – 1,472	

Source: Statistics Canada and local documents.

tion had been reached, although ambitious plans for further growth have been made by the current council.[1]

Who They Are

In order to help us visualize the newcomers more clearly, I have compared them to the natives (see table 8). Almost all of the natives were born in Canada, and indeed nine out of ten of them were born in or around Paradise itself. About one newcomer in five, in contrast, was born outside Canada. Forty-five per cent of them were raised in a city, 25 per cent in a town, 15 per cent in a village and a further 15 per cent on farms; nevertheless, the majority of the newcomers not brought up in a city actually had been living and working in an urban area before they moved to Paradise. By my definition of natives, all of them had resided in Paradise at least as far back as 1960, while 73 per cent of the newcomers had lived there ten years or less, and 52 per cent five years or less.

Most of the natives are Protestants, with only a handful of them Catholics. Among the newcomers, the gap between Protestants and Catholics has significantly narrowed. Another change was that the Protestants in the community were no longer virtually all Anglican or United; 99 of the 102 native Protestants (97 per cent) belonged to these two denominations, while only 32 of the 45 newcomer Protestants (71 per cent) did so.

There was a striking difference between the age structure of the two groups, at least based on the cases in my samples. Not only were the vast majority of natives fifty years of age or older, but also 47 per cent of them were retired. Most of the newcomers were less than fifty years old, and only 11 per cent of them were retired; little wonder that the newcomers and natives seemed to be on different wavelengths.

The newcomers do not resemble the highly educated inmigrants described in the American literature, but they were somewhat better educated (in a formal sense) than the natives. A much higher proportion of the natives had not gone beyond primary school, and a lower portion of them had post-secondary-school training. In terms of occupation, the proportions of newcomers and natives in the professions were almost identical, and the same was true as regards blue-collar jobs. Where they differed was in the much larger number of newcomers in white collar jobs and the much lower number who were farmers. These differences are not unexpected in view of the greater proportion of the newcomers who had formal training in college, technical school, or university, plus the fact that most of them previously worked in the city. It is perhaps surprising that the proportion of newcomers in the professions was not higher than that of the natives. However, a college or technical school diploma no longer qualifies a person automatically for a job at the top nor, for that matter, does a university degree. The vast majority of the newcomers were skilled and unskilled workers, some of them in low-level management positions, but few of them captains of industry. It should be added that there was a significant difference between the two groups in terms of self-employment. Fully 53 per cent of the natives had their own (usually small) businesses. While the percentage of self-employed newcomers was much lower (31 per cent), their businesses tended to be more substantial.

The class composition of the newcomers and natives was roughly the same, with one half of each group occupying the middle rank. They did differ slightly at the extremes; a higher proportion of the newcomers fell into the lower class, and a lower proportion were found in the upper class. No doubt the age difference between the two groups is part of the explanation. The natives, much older on average, had long ago reached the peak of their achievements; besides, they had a tendency to measure their present class positions in terms of the positions that their parents had occupied. Most of the newcomers, in contrast, were still trying to climb up the stratification ladder, and

TABLE 8
Comparison of 122 Natives and 107 Newcomers

	Natives	Newcomers
Country of Birth		
Canada	119 (98%)	84 (78%)
Other	3 (2%)	23 (21%)
Religion		
Protestant	102 (91%)	45 (61%)
Catholic	3 (2.6%)	15 (20%)
Other	7 (6%)	14 (19%)
Unknown	10	33
Age		
50 years or older	103 (84%)	36 (34%)
Under 50 years	19 (16%)	71 (66%)
Education		
Primary	37 (30%)	12 (12%)
Secondary	53 (43%)	50 (49%)
College or technical	18 (15%)	21 (20%)
University	14 (11%)	20 (19%)
Unknown	–	4
Occupation		
Professional	8 (14%)	10 (13%)
White collar	19 (33%)	40 (52%)
Blue collar	22 (38%)	26 (34%)
Farmer	8 (14%)	1 (1%)
Inapplicable	65	30
Social Class		
Upper	8 (6.5%)	4 (3.7%)
Lower upper	20 (16%)	20 (19%)
Middle	62 (51%)	53 (50%)
Lower middle	24 (20%)	18 (17%)
Lower	8 (6.5%)	12 (11%)

Notes:

1 All percentages are calculated in terms of known and applicable cases. Inapplicable cases regarding occupation consist of individuals not in the workforce (unemployed, student, retired, homemaker); homemakers 65 years of age or older were defined as retired.

2 The sample of natives, with 84% of them 50 years of age or older, appears severely biased towards the elderly. However, as Fitzsimons (1991) points out, a remarkably high number of seniors lived in Paradise: 23% of the population compared to the provincial average of 11% (according to Statistics Canada, 22.1% of the residents of Paradise were seniors in 1986). Furthermore, when I calculated the number of people 65 years or over for natives and newcomers combined, the result was 30.1%. The bias,

therefore, is not as great as it appears, and can partly be rationalized by the emphasis in the study on reconstructing the past, which meant interviewing people who had been active in the community around 1950.

3 The sample of natives also is biased regarding gender: 71 (58%) are male and 51 (42%) are female. In this case, the bias is even greater than apparent; according to Statistics Canada, 1986, 47.9% and 52.1% respectively of the overall population (not just natives) of Paradise were male and female. The sample of newcomers, with 52 (48.5%) men and 55 (51.4%) women was almost identical to the Statistics Canada estimates, which means the combined product of native and newcomer gender profiles would not reduce the bias.

4 Although I found that 11.5% of the entire population (average of 2% of natives and 21% of newcomers) were immigrants from beyond Canada, Statistics Canada reports 7.7% of the residents in 1986 were immigrants. While the difference may be due to a bias in my sample, it also may reflect an increase in the number of immigrants in Paradise since 1986, as well as faulty reporting of immigrant status in the census.

5 I found that 15% of the entire population (average of 11% of natives and 19% of newcomers) had attended university, which is similar to the Statistics Canada 1986 estimate of 12%.

6 Not all people completed the level of education indicated in the table. The number of natives who failed to do so are as follows: primary 6, secondary 29, college or technical 7, university 1. The number of newcomers: primary 2, secondary 20, college or technical 7, university 2.

7 Most of the natives in the 'other' category under religion belonged to small Protestant sects which met in private homes. Within the 'other' category among the newcomers we find various faiths such as Jehovah Witness, Islam, and Buddhist. I have not included Jews in this table because they are discussed in Part Three.

8 For further information about these interviews see appendices A and B.

their measuring rod was more likely to be the class system of the city from which they had recently migrated.

Where They Live

Since the mid-1960s six subdivisions have been built to accommodate the newcomers, three of them inhabited by wealthy and middle-income people, the other three by middle- and lower-middle-income people. The most prestigious subdivision consists of magnificent homes on large lots. The residents include three owners of thriving local businesses, a dentist, a fireman, a real estate agent, an assistant manager in a store, and a retired farmer and his wife who had sold their farm for a bundle. Slightly less prestigious is a subdivision built just beyond the boundaries of the town. Again, the dwellings are impressive, and among the residents are a lawyer, a bank manager, the owners of two small businesses, a supervisor in a government office, a policeman, a carpenter, several teachers, and a handful of retired people. The third most prestigious subdivision has only been recently built, and here we find mostly middle-class commuter families, often with both spouses employed in order to afford the mortgage.

Among the three less prestigious (and older) subdivisions, two are inhabited mainly by middle-class people, although some wealthy families who settled in the community fifteen or twenty years ago are scattered among them, as are some lower-middle-class people. The other subdivision, the first to be built in the community, is home to slightly less wealthy people, those who fall mainly into the lower-middle class, including some natives who had bought houses there over the years.

In addition to the subdivisions, seventy-two apartments, many of them in disrepair, exist over the stores in the old shopping district. This is where the majority of the poor people among the newcomers live, most of them young, including single mothers on welfare. Lower-middle-class newcomers, almost all of them commuters, also occupy a block of modest townhouses that were constructed a couple of decades ago. Almost one hundred low-rise apartments and semi-detached homes have been built for a middle-income clientele; and in 1991 forty-five nonprofit housing units, fifteen of them townhouses and thirty apartments, were opened to the public, much against the wishes of some residents. There are also ninety senior citizens' apartments located in two parts of the town. Finally, some of the newcomers can be found scattered throughout the old section of the community. These include middle-class people in renovated homes, and lower-class people in apartments and rooms which have been carved out of some of the stately old dwellings previously occupied by the upper classes. It should be added that another block of low-income units has been in the planning stage for some time, held up by protesting neighbours, as well as a seventh subdivision, held up by the stagnant economy.

Associated with these various residential areas are distinct types of social interaction. Among the six new subdivisions, the least amount of visiting back and forth occurs in the three most prestigious ones. A man who moved from one of the modest subdivisions into the one with the highest prestige remarked that when he used to cut his grass at his previous home it sometimes took half the afternoon, because his neighbours continually stopped to chat. But in his new home, he and his wife live secluded lives, the implicit rule being that people are there because they value their privacy. In the second most prestigious subdivision there are no neighbourhood associations, and what visiting does occur is usually limited to a couple of families getting together for a barbecue. That sort of thing occurs on a somewhat more regular basis in the three less prestigious subdivisions, but it would be wrong to give the impression of tinkling tea cups in the afternoon and dinner parties on the weekend. The fact that the majority of people in these subdivisions commute to jobs miles away, as well as the high turnover rate, mitigate against that scene. Most social contacts there are spontaneous rather than organized, and what passes for 'neighbouring' is basically a wave of the hand and a greeting as one walks by on the street.

When the block of townhouses was first built, the people who bought them with low down payments, or rented them from speculators, quickly got a reputation for hard drinking and uncouth behaviour. As one former member of the town council stated, 'A family could move in there for $500.00. Well, you know what that meant. The scums moved in. And so much fighting – the police had to be up there all the time.' He added that in recent years there has been a complete turnover of the residents in the townhouses, with 'a better class of people' occupying them now. Whether the scandalous reputation of the townhouses at an earlier period was deserved is debatable, since it was not based simply on behaviour: equally important was the fact that the first inhabitants were strangers, and poor ones at that, in a community where newcomers had been rare since the turn of the century. During the late 1980s what marked these same townhouses was the virtual absence of interaction, despite the existence of a townhouse association. Similar to the prestigious subdivisions, the lower-class people in the townhouses, most of them again commuters, went their own ways, except for the occasional friendship between families. As for the lower-class newcomers, they were much more likely to meet socially in one of the greasy spoons, or on the street corner, than in each other's apartments.

Although the older residents of Paradise, people who have lived there all their lives, often complain that neighbouring is a thing of the past, in fact they interact to a greater degree than any other sector of the population, but with a difference: for those newcomers who do enjoy the company of their neighbours, the summer time, with the barbecue sizzling, is the gregarious season; in contrast, most of the social interaction among the older natives occurs during the winter – the season of euchre games, church events, voluntary work in local organizations, and amicable evenings at the curling club.

Why They Come

In the United States it has been the prospect of a less hectic pace of life in harmony with nature, even if it meant a reduced income, that has created the population turnaround. Indeed, as Ploch (1978) has indicated, half of the reverse migrants in his study in Maine earned less than they had in the city. The quality-of-life motive was also evident among the wealthy residents of Toronto who bought farms and built sprawling country homes, complete with swimming pools and tennis courts; however, unlike the reverse migrants south of the border, most of them are weekenders, who continue to live and work in the city. The American pattern is even less applicable to the majority of newcomers in Paradise, among whom there are important differences in motivation depending upon class position. In order to illuminate these differences, I shall employ, with one modification, the same five-level class scheme through which the natives were filtered. The modification concerns a sixth class distinction, which I shall label the aspiring-middle class, inserted between the middle class and the lower-middle class. In terms of financial status, the people in the aspiring-middle class are virtually identical to those in the lower-middle class; in both cases they exist not far above the poverty line. What sets the people in the aspiring-middle class apart are their dreams. Unlike those below them, the struggle is not simply one of survival, keeping a roof over their heads and food on the table. Instead, the move to the countryside is seen as a once-in-a-lifetime opportunity for upward status mobility, and with it the lovely security of middle-class existence.[2]

The vast majority of newcomers fell into the middle, aspiring-middle, and lower-middle classes, and I shall begin with them. With the partial exception of the middle class, the single most important motive for relocating in the small town of Paradise was the possibility of having a home of one's own. In other words, it was not quality of life that made these people become migrants; it was the prospect of increasing their purchasing power by buying into a less expensive market.[3] Those in the lower-middle class usually were content to purchase modest dwellings, or to rent them, while people in the aspiring-middle class often went up to their ears in debt in order to move into a dwelling compatible with their anticipated status. Those in the middle class were somewhat different; for many of them, it was the offer of employment in or near Paradise that took them there, and more so than in the aspiring-middle and lower-middle classes, they spoke enthusiastically about the benefits of living in a small town surrounded by open countryside.

While the desire to own one's home, or to upgrade it, was the fundamental reason why most of these people settled in Paradise, there were several secondary reasons. One of them, a mixture of both economic and quality of life factors, was the wish to have one spouse stay at home to look after the children, which was impossible in the city, since it took two incomes to pay the mortgage (or the rent). Often young couples made the decision to leave the city just before they had their first child, or at least a second child (in every case about which I learned, it was the mother who remained at home).[4] Sometimes such people discovered quality of life *after* they moved to Paradise. They explained that they never had really given much thought to the attractions of the countryside, for it was the dream house that had drawn them. But when they had settled in, they began to realize that they were living on the edge of open fields and rolling landscapes, where one could take a quiet bicycle ride, watch the birds, or even go native and try some fishing.

Two other reasons for turning city people into small-town dwellers were somewhat more unusual, if not bizarre. First, a surprising number of newcomers, mostly men, stated that one of their main motives for moving was in order to be able to have a dog. And it was not just any old dog – in the vast majority of cases, these men got a German shepherd. Second, an equally impressive number of newcomers frankly said that they left the city in order to get away from the visible minorities. Some of them, as I shall show in much greater detail in chapter 10, made it clear that this motive was even more important to them than the prospect of owning their own homes.

One final point. Except for those individuals among the middle class who moved to Paradise because of a job offer, the vast majority of the people in the middle, aspiring-middle, and lower-middle classes ended up in Paradise purely by accident. They did not survey the rural Ontario scene and decide Paradise was for them. Nor did they have relatives or friends already living there. Instead, they had simply driven through the town, perhaps on the way to a camping ground, spotted a house for sale at an attractive price, and bought it; or, more probably, they were lured to the community by a real estate agent's description of bargains to be seized.

The motivations of the upper- and lower-upper-class migrants were quite different. It was not the prospect of owning their own homes that led them to the community, although some of them took the opportunity to upgrade their dwellings. Nor was quality of life the decisive factor, although it was sometimes a secondary one. Almost all those at the upper end of the class system moved to Paradise because they were offered an attractive job, or were able to establish their own businesses. As I indicated earlier, this was the same motive that drew some of those in the middle class, such as school teachers and government employees.

As for the lower-class newcomers, it was neither job opportunity nor quality of life that brought them to Paradise. And certainly it was not the happy prospect of home ownership: virtually all of them lived in run-down rented apartments or dismal rooming-houses. Most of the poor newcomers drifted into Paradise because of some prior family connection. Either they had lived briefly in the town at some point in their lives, or a relative had moved there. The only exception concerned a minority of the new poor who had been sent to Paradise by welfare officials to take advantage of cheap accommodation. Of all the newcomers now living in Paradise, then, only those in the lower class tended to choose the community because to some extent it was familiar territory.[5]

How They Adjust

Just as the motivation for moving to Paradise varied with class position, so did the degree of success. In one category we find people who are in the professions or run their own businesses, who are wealthier than average, who commute only a short distance (if at all), and who are usually forty years of age or older. For these people, which includes all of those in the upper and lower-upper classes and most of those in the middle class, life in Paradise has turned out rosy.

The next category is a mixed bag, half success, half failure. Here we find the aspiring-middle class. These people are younger than those in the classes above them – usually between twenty-five and thirty-five years of age – and in every case they are commuters; that is, at least one of the spouses (and sometimes both) commute long distances to work daily, commanding a city salary. Almost all the wives who don't commute have local full-time or part-time jobs outside the home. The hard-working people in the aspiring-middle class are not only dreamers, they also are gamblers. In almost all cases they are financially pressed. The monthly mortgage payment, albeit low compared to what a similar house would cost in the city, is still daunting. If one piece of the jigsaw puzzle is broken – if the car breaks down, or gasoline prices or mortgage payments sharply climb, or one of the spouses becomes unemployed – it is a disaster. Then, too, there is the sheer physical exhaustion that accompanies the daily grind of commuting, which sometimes brings with it marital problems. For these people the margin between success and failure was treacherously thin from the outset. For the dream to come true, they needed not only unusual determination and fortitude, but also a good dose of luck.

The aspiring-middle class was a pivotal category. Those above it usually were successful, while those below it more often than not tasted defeat. The age span of people in the lower-middle class was wider than in any other category, ranging from the twenties to the fifties. They too wanted a home, and were prepared to pay for it by becoming commuters and by scrimping. But for them a home was often a small townhouse in crowded quarters, or a modest rental property. Like those in the aspiring-middle class, they were exceptionally vulnerable to unforeseen circumstances, such as increased gasoline prices or unemployment. They expressed a psychology different from that of the aspiring-middle class. Not only were their sights set lower, but they also seemed to accept defeat with greater resignation. Perhaps that was because hardship was simply the normal state of affairs for them.

Finally, we come to the lower class. These are people who were penniless before they came to Paradise, remained so after taking up residence in the community, and in fact did not expect anything better. The vast majority of them were in their twenties. While some of them were unmarried, or were single parents (usually but not always women), most of those whom I met were married and had young children. Some held jobs that barely paid the rent; many were unemployed and living on welfare in rented accommodation. If we define successful adjustment to the community in terms of whether newcomers actually remained there, then the majority of people in the lower class had triumphed, because more so than in the cases of the aspiring-middle and the lower-middle classes, they tended to stay in

Paradise regardless of the conditions. But if we qualify the lower-class person's success to mean an elevation in prosperity, then not a single case I became aware of met this criterion. Even among those fortunate enough to have jobs, the prospect of ever rising above the level of poverty, especially if they had children to feed and clothe, was almost non-existent. Indeed, what struck me about people at this class level was the repeated statement that never in their lives, no matter how hard they worked, could they ever expect to have a home of their own.

Case Studies

UPPER CLASS

Merely to state that all the newcomers in the upper and lower-upper classes were successful is redundant and trite. To deepen the meaning, it is necessary to consider the careers of people over time. Except for highly qualified professionals, most of the newcomers who today occupy the upper ranks did not do so from the moment that they stepped into the community. Instead, they rose to the top over a decade or two as their businesses flourished; what is remarkable is that not a single one of them has suffered a permanent reversal of fortunes (although rumours about one entrepreneur's financial woes began to circulate around 1991).

My example from the upper class concerns a man who moved to Paradise fifteen years ago in order to take over a business in a nearby town. He and his wife bought a modest house in Paradise because the prices were lower there than in the community where he worked. After a decade the couple had apparently become wealthy, making it possible for them to move into a mansion in the most prestigious subdivision in Paradise. Although the woman formerly worked as a secretary, she remained at home after her first child was born, because she and her husband believed strongly that was the proper way to raise children, and because they could afford to do so. Although they remarked that even after fifteen years they still regarded themselves as outsiders, they were in fact highly respected in the community and reasonably well integrated. The man's consuming interest, besides his family and his business – he worked six days plus two evenings each week – was the service club in Paradise to which he belonged. Both of these adults, in their late thirties and early forties when I met them, had been raised in or near small villages elsewhere in rural Ontario, and Paradise was precisely the size of community in which they wanted to spend the remainder of their lives. Assisting their adaptation to the community was their combined ethnic backgrounds – Scottish, Irish, English, and German – as well as their Protestant upbringing. Religion, however, was one of their sore spots in the community. Although the man no longer goes to church, and the woman does so basically be-cause she thinks it is important for her children to learn the values associated with religion, they were less than pleased with the local minister, who, on a visit to their striking home, apparently observed: 'Well, some people have their priorities in the wrong place.'

In summary, this couple, hard-working, pleasant, and conservative (they were concerned about the disappearance of the old values and the increase in crime in small towns like Paradise) had several things going for them. He owned his own business and commuted only a short distance, they were brought up in rural Ontario, were active in local organizations, came from the right ethnic and religious back-grounds, and were reasonably well educated (one had gone to grade thirteen, the other to grade twelve). Even had they been somewhat less prosperous, it still is probable that they would have found happiness in Paradise.

LOWER-UPPER CLASS

Like the previous man, the one I turn to now also was raised in rural Ontario, has a British and Protestant background, moved to Paradise about the same time, and worked hard and established his own suc-cessful business. But there were some differences. The lower-upper-class individual, middle-aged when I met him, was raised in a some-what more impoverished environment. He bought his first bicycle after saving money from picking potatoes over a two-year period. In order to establish his business, at first on a modest level, he took out a bank loan and borrowed money from his parents and friends. He chose Paradise because land was cheap, and because his wife had been raised nearby. Over the years his business has gradually increased to the point where he now employs about twenty people in the summer months. A religious man, he attends church regularly, and sings in the choir. Although he thinks that his membership in a service club has been good for business and has brought him respect, he is less enthu-siastic about it than the previous man, resenting the time spent at meetings and functions. A self-made man who quit school in grade ten, he does not live in the previous couple's opulent style. He once remarked that he is even reluctant to spend money on a meal in a restaurant, which perhaps is partly why he is ranked by Paradise people a notch below the upper class.

This man's life is testament to the fact that prosperity doesn't depend solely on luck. In his first few years in Paradise he worked seven days a week. Although the pay-off was the thriving business, there was a certain human cost. As he remarked, even after almost twenty years in the community he and his wife do not have many close friends, because they never had any time to socialize. Paradise for them has not simply been a place in which to make a good living, because they have enjoyed life in the small town and are regarded as people of high morals, worthy of respect. Yet their years in the community have been dominated by work, and as retirement loomed on the horizon, they were seriously considering moving to a more attractive part of the country.

MIDDLE CLASS

While most of the middle-class newcomers in Paradise have enjoyed successful careers, a few failures begin to surface at this level of the stratification system, and examples of both types will be provided. A man who was successful, a university graduate in his early forties, moved to Paradise about a dozen years ago. What led him there was a job in the agricultural field, which involved a considerable amount of travel to surrounding communities. Eventually he established his own small business, cutting the travel down to one day each week. Although raised in a small city in Ontario, he remarked: 'I like the idea of the small town. I'm not one that cares about big malls, and that sort of thing.' His wife, he added, is 'not a shopper.' He particularly enjoys the familiarity that goes with the small town, meeting people whom he knows at the post office, and dropping into stores to shoot the breeze (each one he mentioned was owned by a newcomer). He thinks he and his wife have assimilated so well into the community because he has worked in agriculture for most of his life, and she was born on a farm. Other factors were equally important. He has made a major effort to become involved in the life of the community. He belongs to a service club and has been a member of local political and educational organizations. His wife has been almost as active in recrea-

tional and philanthropical groups. Although conservative in terms of
his values of the small community, he was a strong advocate of even
greater population growth in Paradise, undisturbed by the fact that he
had never met the neighbours who for two years had lived next door.
Neither of these individuals whom I have been discussing attends
church now, but that no longer counts against a person in Paradise,
nor does the fact that he was raised as a Catholic (she was brought up
in the United Church). Well-educated, confident, and respected as a
businessman with a genuine interest in the welfare of the community,
this man had found the appropriate stage – the small town – for his
worldview, talents, and leadership ambitions.

I shall now turn to a middle-class couple, both of them university
graduates in their early thirties, who decided to give up on Paradise
after living there almost three years, and return to Toronto where they
had been born and raised. They said they might have been able to
afford to buy a house in the city if they each worked, but they had
decided to have children, and as the woman stated, 'We were both
quite adamant about mothers staying at home with the children. We're
not believers in day care.' Paradise was selected primarily because
housing was cheap enough to allow them to live on one salary. Their
lives in the community seemed to start off well enough. When they
moved into a house in a lovely old part of the town, an elderly couple
brought them a pot of coffee. The newcomers were surprised and
delighted. Their two children, born in quick succession, became drawing cards for the neighbours, especially during the summer months
when the mother could get out on the street with the baby carriage.
This sensitive woman quickly realized that she had to modify her
behaviour to suit the standards of the small town: 'You can't be
brusque or aggressive. You can't go into the bakery and just say "I want
a loaf of bread." You have to say hello. How are you? That sort of
thing.' Her husband had much less contact with the local people
because he commuted to work about sixty miles away. Yet he was the
type of man to pitch in and help with the household chores when he
returned in the evening and, from his point of view, everything was
unfolding as anticipated. They had their own house, his wife was at
home with the babies, and his income was sufficient for their needs.
What, then, went wrong?

Their decision to put their house up for sale and return to rented
premises in the city was not based on any single disaster; instead,
disillusionment with the small community was the gradual result of

many minor aggravations. When they lived in the city, they could attend films or cultural events on the spur of the moment. Now, the woman said, it is like organizing for a military battle to do so. For example, they recently visited the Royal Ontario Museum in Toronto. They only stayed for one hour, and the round trip took them three hours. In her view, it just wasn't worth the effort involved, especially in winter (which she found extremely depressing in the small town).

Although they both insisted that Paradise people are very friendly, in fact many of their social contacts were superficial. They said that they had got to know people at the grocery store, the bank, and community events, at least well enough to greet them. The woman had attended an organization for women, mostly newcomers like herself, but found it boring and stifling. All they ever discussed, she said, were their husbands and children. Never did they talk about ideas or women's issues. She had been used to being addressed as 'Ms.' and by her maiden name in the city, but in Paradise people insisted on referring to her as 'Mrs.' and using her husband's name; only reluctantly did she conform to the local custom. Both she and her husband complained that there was no suitable place in the community to meet people their own age: 'There's not a lot of places adults can go to. I don't mean a booze place, or a greasy spoon. Just a nice place, where one could sip English beer.' When the woman confessed that she felt isolated, and found it very difficult to make friends in Paradise, her husband responded: 'I wouldn't *want* to develop too many friendships among males here.' He said the local men are 'too red-necked,' and went on to describe an evening when friends visiting them from the city were threatened by some aggressive males intent on starting a fight at a local tavern.

They both insisted that visions of peace and beauty in the countryside had never been much of a factor in their decision to move to Paradise: 'We weren't looking for that peace,' he commented, 'but when we came here we saw the stars and the sky. But you know, you can go camping and get that.' His wife reminisced about the times when they went on bike rides on the back roads. She said it was lovely. She sang at the top of her voice, and her older child actually fed a cow some grass. But she remarked: 'We didn't do that often enough.' In fact, she added, they only went bicycling twice.

At one point the woman blurted out: 'I have nightmares about my children growing up here as teenagers.' At first I thought she was referring to the problems that had emerged with alcohol and drugs.

But she made it clear that what she was worried about was that her kids would be culturally deprived: 'I want cultural things for them. I want them to be worldly. I don't want their experiences to be limited to hot dogs.' In an interesting reversal of the search for fulfilment in rural society by many newcomers, especially in the United States, she asserted: 'I'm looking for a quality of life that's not here.' Her husband, while somewhat less disillusioned with small-town existence, agreed that for quality of life, the city can't be beat.

Like some expatriate sojourners in a Third World country, this couple measured their new life in Paradise against their old life in the city, and defined the differences as inferior. Young and well educated, with yuppie tastes, they found little to attract them on a social or aesthetic level in Paradise, which catered to less sophisticated retired people. Although both had been raised in Christian homes, and he had sung in the choir as a youngster, neither of them attended church any more, and thus lacked even that potential social anchor in Paradise. As I pointed out, the quality of life factor had never been important in their decision to move to Paradise, but it became the central motive in their decision to return to the city. In this respect, both of them pointed out that Paradise was basically a bedroom community, and therefore lacked the charm and cohesion supposedly characteristic of small-town life anyway. Finally, this couple's dissatisfaction with Paradise may partly be independent of small-town existence per se. Since moving to Paradise they have become parents. The woman, admittedly by choice, was stuck in the house with two babies. My impression was that neither parent appreciated the impact of this change on their lives. Perhaps it will require a move back to the city before they discover that it was not merely Paradise's barren cultural landscape that kept them at home more often than they wanted.

ASPIRING-MIDDLE CLASS

This class, as indicated earlier, was pivotal. About half the newcomers in it adapted successfully to rural life, while the others eventually gave up. My example of a success story concerns a couple in their early thirties who had been born in Britain but brought up on the edge of Toronto. Both had gone part-way through high school before entering the work force, he as a skilled tradesman, she as a secretary. According to the man, he had always wanted to get out of the city, but his wife, whom he described as 'a city freak,' was opposed. What brought her around was the prospect of having their own beautiful home. On a drive through Paradise they discovered, almost to their disbelief, how cheap houses were in comparison with the city. One house in particular, modern and impressive, caught their eyes, and they decided they had to have it: 'For my wife, it was the house. She fell in love with it.' With the move to Paradise she had to give up her job, but they had decided the time was ripe to have children, and she wanted to stay at home with them. To help out financially, she established a babysitting service.

Although this couple had only lived in Paradise for two years, they were inclined to regard themselves as old hands in rural society. They were quite aware that not all the local people were enthralled with the newcomers from the city, but blamed the urban refugees for not adjusting. The woman commented that you can tell in an instance who the newcomers are: 'They don't talk. They aren't friendly. Up here, if you walk by someone and don't nod or smile they think you are a snob.' Some of the newcomers, mostly women who couldn't learn to live without shopping malls, she asserted, were less than thrilled with life in small-town Ontario, but she and her husband could hardly conceal their own enthusiasm. When their first child was born, a retired farmer down the street dropped by with a gift. Periodically he also brings them fresh vegetables from his garden. Such kindnesses have almost overwhelmed them, as has the general friendliness of the natives: 'People driving by, they give you a wave. You meet a lot of people. That amazed me from the day we moved up, how different people are.' In Toronto, he remarked, they never walked outside their house: 'Now she (his wife) doesn't feel the day is completed unless she goes for a walk.' Laughing, he stated: 'One of the biggest social events in the town are funerals. I've found it interesting, walking around the graveyard.' He added that he had always wanted a dog, and shortly after moving to Paradise he bought a German shepherd. His wife found it refreshing that people talk more about gardening than the news, and that they treat you like a human being: 'In the city, people don't look you in the eye when you walk down the street. Here they look you right in the eye.' She also was pleased at her reception in local stores: 'I couldn't believe it. You're a person. Where down in the city, you're a number.' But she added: 'There's another side of it; they're nosey.'

The only cloud on the horizon has been the man's commuting,

which he said had concerned him from the moment they decided to leave the city: 'Right away came the question of the drive.' When weather conditions are favourable, the trip takes him about an hour and a quarter each way; when they are bad, it becomes two hours or more. In the winter, he rises at 4:45 a.m. and is on the road by 5:30 a.m. To make matters more difficult, not only does he work every Saturday morning, but also overtime most days, which means he doesn't get home until the evening. As he commented, 'it's a bit of a grind. It always seems longer driving home. I'm tired. That's the number one problem: the drive. The number two problem is having a decent car. You can kill a new car in three years.'

Despite the long hours he has to spend on the road, and the mortgage that stretches their finances to the limit, they think it is worth it. She has her dream house, he his dog. Unlike the previous couple who regarded the small town as a cultural wasteland, this couple believe it offers all anyone could want. In short, they truly have found Paradise.

In sharp contrast to this contented couple is a man who moved to the community four years ago. He was lured to the town by the prospect of making a great leap forward: leaving the employ of a company where he had worked for several years, and taking a gamble by establishing his own small business. Brought up in a poor family, and with little capital of his own, he went in debt up to his ears, only to discover that luck was against him. First of all, the demand for his product was not at the level he had anticipated, and to make matters worse, the town council and established businessmen, he claimed, put every obstacle imaginable in his path: 'If you haven't lived here all your life, you don't have a chance.' He thought it would help if he joined a local service club, but even that backfired: 'That was the worst thing I ever did in my life. They're pathetic.' He insisted that the members in the club were only out for themselves, and claimed that a lot of 'hanky panky' went on. Unlike so many newcomers who eventually threw in the towel because commuting was driving them mad, this individual had the advantage of a local business. Perhaps had the economic climate been more auspicious, he might have made it. As it was, his long-held dream of having his own business and joining the middle class became a nightmare; even his attempt to sell his business and house, in order to salvage something from the gamble, was frustrated by the recession that had enveloped the nation.

LOWER-MIDDLE CLASS

'I'm not really a snotty person. I talk to people. I just don't like them dropping in.' These were the words of a woman in her mid-twenties who found life in Paradise suffocating, and after three years was determined to move back to the city. Her husband loved rural Ontario with the same intensity that she despised it, and was equally adamant that he would spend the rest of his life there. Although in terms of education, occupation, and income there was not a great deal of difference between this family and the two families described as aspiring-middle class, there was a gap in their mental outlooks. The woman who found life in Paradise unbearable was indeed pleased with her new but modest dwelling, yet she was prepared to relocate in a rented apartment in the city in order to realize her version of the good life: shopping malls, cinema, and friends of like mind within telephone reach. As for her husband, he wanted nothing more than a few cows and chickens, and days spent doing the chores and tinkering with machinery.

The woman, who had gone as far as grade eight, had moved to the outskirts of Toronto from another province when she was a teenager. Her husband was brought up in a village near Toronto. After finishing grade eleven, he found a job in a factory on the outskirts of Toronto where he still works. Although each of them attended Protestant churches as youths, neither does so any more. The story of how they landed in Paradise is the familiar one. They didn't have any relatives or friends in the area, and chose the community entirely by accident; while driving in the countryside, they saw an advertisement for a house that they thought was affordable, and made the move from the city. The woman's initial reactions were positive: 'I liked the idea of a small town. I got pregnant, and the thought of bringing a baby up down there (in the city) didn't appeal to me.' One has to worry about kidnapping in the city, she said, adding that neither she nor her husband liked living next door to 'Pakis and blacks.'

It was not long, however, before she became fed up with Paradise. As she remarked about the people there, 'Very friendly, but nosey. And that I don't like. The gossip, that's the part I hate about living in a small town. You can't go into town without someone saying hello and smiling. But I leave it at that. I just can't be bothered having people drop in for a chit chat. As for being in their homes, never.' She went on to state that what she liked about living in the city was that 'you never really got to know people.'

Her husband, who commutes to work, made friends with a local farmer, and most of his spare time was spent at the farm, helping with the chores and the harvest. As his wife remarked, 'We don't see much of each other. If he's not at work, he's over at the farm. I don't remember the last time he had dinner here. He doesn't come home for dinner. He doesn't come home for lunch.' She had begun to work in the evenings in a local business, partly, she said, to cope with the boredom. Sometimes three or four days would pass before she would see her husband. He usually was sleeping by the time she got home, and he departed for his job before she awoke in the morning, remaining in the city with relatives when he had to work on weekends.

This couple, obviously, have begun to go their separate ways, largely because of their polar opposite reactions to life in rural society. As she remarked, 'I couldn't care less if I'm accepted. I don't care what people think. And that bothers my husband.' The man, in contrast, got along well with the local people, especially the old-style farmers, and enjoyed the slow pace of life and the indirect manner in which all topics were approached, from the inconsequential to the significant. What he wanted more than anything else was to buy a few acres and try his luck as a farmer himself. That prospect drove his wife mad, not only because of the financial risk, but also because of her determination to return to the city. Unlike the middle-class couple who did exactly that because they found Paradise to be culturally deprived, this woman merely wanted daily access to shopping malls, and to be able to talk to a friend on the telephone for an hour without having to worry about long-distance charges.

The divided adjustment to life in small-town Ontario experienced by this man and woman was not an isolated case. Such families usually were found in the middle class, or lower, and more often than not it was the woman who longed to return to the urban realm. Several years ago, it is true, a woman who had been brought to Paradise by her upper-class husband fought with his friends and relatives and absolutely refused to remain in the community (the marriage ended in divorce). And I learned about one family in which it was the husband who was agitating to move back to the city. His wife, outgoing and aggressive, had quickly joined local organizations after Paradise became her home, and she soon had a number of friends and acquaintances. The man, in contrast, who commuted to a job in the city, was shy and withdrawn; even under the best of circumstances, he said, it took him a long time to make friends. For the first time in his marriage, almost all his social contacts were with his wife's friends, which did not please him. To make matters worse, he lost his job, and was reduced to sitting at home by himself while his wife went off to her part-time job or to visit friends. Depressed and lacking in confidence, he faced the task of persuading his wife to leave a community which she had decided was the perfect place to put down her roots.

LOWER CLASS

The majority of the newcomers in the lower-middle class struck out in Paradise, although a minority found themselves on a winning team. In contrast, not a single lower-class family (or individual) about whom I learned was successful in the community, if by that is meant an improvement in economic status. Consider the lives of a couple in their late twenties who moved to Paradise three years ago. The woman was born in another province, the man in Toronto. She quit school in grade six, her husband in grade nine. His ethnic background was English, Dutch, and Aboriginal (she wasn't certain of her own, but thought it might be British). For four years as a young boy he had lived in Paradise with his parents, whom he described as destitute, and it was his memories of a quiet and friendly community that brought him back (his parents no longer live there). He works as a labourer about fifty miles away, and said he hates commuting – during the three years, he has gone through four old cars. They have three children. On the weekends the woman works as a chambermaid in a hotel a few miles from Paradise.

Despite the woman's efforts to augment her husband's income, they exist within the shadow of poverty. On more than one occasion generous acquaintances, not much wealthier than themselves, have slipped them a few dollars when they had no food for their children. Their apartment above a store is in disrepair, with the furniture spare and broken. The stairway leading to the apartment is clogged with litter and junk. Yet the one bright spot in their lives is their landlord, who apparently has always been understanding when they were unable to pay the rent on time. Both of them lead isolated lives, partly, the man said, because most of the young people like themselves whom they know are on drugs. Although he had briefly attended school in the community as a youngster, after being back three years he still had not met any of his former classmates.

The woman was raised in the United Church. Deeply religious, today she regularly attends a Pentecostal service. Her outlook on life is essentially fatalistic. Reflecting about what will happen to her family in the future, she remarked, 'I'm not worried. I go God's way. It's up to Him.' This attitude irritates her husband, who was brought up in the Anglican Church but no longer attends. In his opinion, if any improvement were to occur in their lives, it would be at their own hands, not God's. What he wants to do is to take evening courses in order to complete grade twelve and eventually learn a trade. His wife thinks his ambitions unrealistic, and says she will be content if they simply don't fall any lower than their current level in life.

Compared to some of the other families in the lower class, the one I have just described appears prosperous, for at least the man is employed. In another family, in which there were two young children, unemployment insurance was the income source. The husband, who used to work as a security guard and labourer, said he might be able to find a job for $4.50 or $5.00 per hour, but thought it was futile to do so, because it would not pay the rent, let alone provide food and diapers for the children (their monthly rent for a bleak apartment was over $700). The woman's parents, who were not much better off, had moved to Paradise a few years earlier, which is what led the young couple to the town. Feisty, frustrated, but still hopeful of a better future, the woman blamed the rich people in the community for their problems (she defined the rich as 'people who know other people, like a relative, and can get you a job'). Unless one had financial help from a relative, she commented, it was impossible to ever purchase a house. At one point she and her husband tried to arrange for a bank loan in order to buy a trailer, but their application was rejected. This woman had begun to train as a nurse's aide before her marriage, and she thought that her family might have some hope if she completed the course. Her husband, however, was more like the woman in the other lower-class family. He had almost resigned himself to a life of unemployment and poverty, but rather than relying on God for comfort, he was inclined to turn to more worldly diversions.

OTHERS

While the six social-class divisions represent the vast majority of the newcomers in Paradise, three remaining categories of people must be mentioned. The first concerns the newcomer-native combination. Frankenberg (1957:49) indicates that newcomers with local kinship ties in the Welsh village he studied were accepted more readily than those without them, but both he and Gold (1975:69–70) make the point that marriage to a local person does not in itself guarantee a warm welcome. That is essentially what I found in Paradise. In one case, it is true, a young woman who had returned to the town of her birth found that some people who had given her the cold shoulder warmed up when they discovered they knew her parents or grandparents, but they continued to let her husband know that he was an outsider. Similarly, a man who had married a woman who had lived in Paradise most of her life commented that it was very difficult to make friends beyond her family. Both of these cases fell into the lower-middle class, and it seemed that acceptance by the natives was more forthcoming with newcomer-native families in the higher classes. For example, a well-educated couple who live in the most prestigious subdivision in the town apparently have had little difficulty making friends among the natives. In this case it was again the man who was the newcomer, although he now regards himself as more of a native, despite the fact that he has only lived in the community for ten years and spends much of his time commuting to work. Almost all of his social contacts, he said, are with natives whom he has met through his wife. Indeed, when I asked him for some names of newcomers whom I could visit, he could not come up with a single candidate.

The second category consists of retirees (excluding farmers from the surrounding area, whom I treat as natives). For example, about five years ago an elderly couple from Toronto retired to Paradise, where the woman had been born. Her husband had always declared that he would never live in 'a hick town' like Paradise. Yet after a year or so he grew to love the community, partly because his wife's family in Paradise had been respected, and they soon had a circle of friends. Not everyone was so fortunate. A man who had spent his entire life on a farm at the far end of the county moved to a subsidized apartment in Paradise when he was in his early seventies. He knew nobody in the town, and in mid-afternoon one would meet him hanging around the main street, eager to talk to anyone with the time to do so, his breath smelling of alcohol. Another elderly man who had farmed near Paradise for half of his life, only to move away to an urban centre to the south, decided to return to the community for his last years on earth. After a dozen months or so he realized he had made a mistake. He had gone back to Paradise with visions of passing the days in the company of his old pals. What he discovered was that most of his erstwhile friends were dead, and the town had been taken over by people whom he had never seen before.

The people in the third category might will be labelled eccentrics. These consist of newcomers similar to those whom Vidich and Bensman (1960:293–5) described as 'idiosyncratics' in their community, and in Paradise most of them are women. My first example concerns a woman who claimed she had moved forty times, exactly the number of years she had been married. In Paradise alone, their home town for the last eighteen years, they had apparently lived in twelve different houses. Reflecting on her various changes of address, she remarked: 'There was something wrong with every house.' What brought them to Paradise was a squabble with her son, who had decided to marry a woman of Italian heritage. As the peripatetic elderly woman commented, 'I hated Italians. I guess I'm prejudiced.' Paradise, she thought, would be free of Italians, and would serve to put some distance between her and her son. They were reconciled a few years ago, but that gave her little joy. Her son still is married to the woman of Italian descent, and besides, she said, he always is pestering her for money, which she reluctantly gives to him. Although she does not have her own washer and dryer, she apparently has made a bit of money in the course of selling her numerous houses.

This woman, by her own account restless and unhappy, remarked that while she had never been pretty, she used to dress well and look smart, but in the last few years has let herself fall apart. One of her small pleasures is to attend dances: 'It's not that I want to join up with a man. It's just that I want to dance. I want to enjoy life before I die.' By the time that I met her, she was making plans to sell the current house, and move elsewhere – exactly where, she wasn't sure. All that she did know was that she had to move again. As she put it, 'There's gypsy in me.'

Another woman, equally eccentric in her own way, lives on a few acres a mile or so from the community. Although impoverished – her home has no running water or electricity – she takes in stray dogs, estimated anywhere from fifty to a hundred, using the money from her pension to buy food for them. Almost paranoid because of attempts by neighbours to get rid of the dogs, she assumes that anyone who calls on her is a potential enemy. On the occasion when I met her, she ran to meet me at the gate before I had a chance to step inside. Idiosyncratic she certainly was, but she also struck me as a decent human being whose preference for dogs over people was understandable to quite a number of men and women whom I met in the area.

My only bona fide example of a male eccentric doesn't really count, because it concerns a man who has lived in Paradise too many years to be considered a newcomer.[6] His life, nevertheless, has been intriguing. Although not well educated in the formal sense, he was often described as the most intelligent individual who had moved into the community since the Second World War. For most of those years, he had been locked in a running battle with the council. The council, he claimed, had done everything possible to close down his small business; the councillors, in turn, often responding to the demands of the citizenry, periodically attempted to force him to clean up his littered premises, which they regarded as an eyesore. Every election, this gadfly ran for reeve (and later for mayor when Paradise became a town). While he never came close to winning, he drove the opposition mad with his accusations of incompetence and corruption. The game came to an end when the one politician whom he despised above all others failed to get re-elected. Without his perfect enemy to grapple with (on one occasion they even became involved in a fist-fight), the heart seemed to go out of him. The final blow was a fire, rumoured to having been set off by kids with firecrackers, that destroyed the pile of tin sheets, machine parts, and spare boards that he had shaped into a house of sorts. Much to the relief of town officials, he moved to an apartment, and turned his back on the new cadre of politicians that had swept into office.

Conclusion

Nobody, I assume, unless the person is insane, moves to a new community with the hope and expectation that life will turn out miserable and impossible. In this sense, all the newcomers, to varying degrees and at least initially, found their Paradise. The passage of time, however, soon sorted them into winners and losers. Six factors made the difference: class level (the higher, the greater the adjustment); commuting distance (the lower, the better the outcome); self-employment (especially when it eliminated commuting); gender (although men tended to be the commuters in the family, they also seemed to derive more pleasure from the countryside than did their wives, who often lived lonely lives looking after the children); community involvement (joining voluntary organizations); and previous experience in small communities (yet not all people who had been raised in towns and villages found Paradise to their liking; some of them rediscovered the gossip that used to drive them mad). Among these six factors, one had particular importance – social class. Most of the newcomers from the middle class upwards worked in the community, were self-employed, and participated in service clubs and other organizations; they also had the resources that enabled them to live in style, enjoy rustic leisure activities if so inclined (and if they had time), and escape to a fine hotel in the city or a beach in Florida when they felt the community closing in on them. For many of the less fortunate newcomers in the lower classes, debilitating financial strain blinded them to even the simple pleasures of rural living, such as long-lasting friendships, the sun on the new crops in the summer, and contented winter evenings around the wood-stove.

Chapter Six

The Commuting Life

When I asked natives of Paradise how many of the newcomers com-mute to work, the answer usually was 'all of them.' An elderly resident stated that at 5 a.m. the subdivision next to his home is just like a parking lot after a hockey game, with cars criss-crossing in all direc-tions as they charged towards the escape exits. A more precise estimate of the commuting situation can be derived from the place-of-work data in the 1986 census.[1] In that year, 1,208 people who lived in Paradise were active in the labour force; 718 (59 per cent) of them worked in the town, while 490 (40 per cent) of them commuted to jobs else-where. The place-of-work material provides us with a general picture of the commuting phenomenon, but it does not distinguish between natives and newcomers. From my interviews with the 122 natives and 107 newcomers, however, I was able to calculate the percentages of families in which at least one of the spouses was a commuter: 16 per cent of the natives and 63 per cent of the newcomers.[2]

According to the place-of-work data, 300 (61 per cent) of the 490 commuters travelled to jobs beyond the county, while 190 (39 per cent) of them remained within the county; 132 of these 190 people actually commuted to the nearest large town, less than twenty miles from Paradise. My own interviews revealed that it was the newcomers who tended to commute beyond the county, while the natives usually travelled a shorter distance.

Commuting as the Bad Life

It is not difficult to marshall evidence in support of the thesis that commuting is less than a joyful experience. As one man remarked, 'I've never talked to too many people who like it.' His own case is instructive. He was on the road about three hours each working day – longer when the weather was bad. He said he had no energy at the end of the day and no time to play with the kids; his wife added that ever since he began commuting six years earlier, he had been short-tempered. Another man who spent about the same amount of time driving back and forth to work said he too hates the life, but what kept him going was his company's pension plan, even though he was not due to retire for another twelve years. A third individual was somewhat more fortunate. His job in Mississauga allowed him to travel when traffic was not heavy, and to work only four days per week. A commuter for seventeen years, even he had become fed up with the life. Within the past five years, he remarked, there has been a noticeable increase in the volume of traffic, with the result that the round trip took about half an hour longer than previously.

Some people coped with the physical and financial stress of commuting by joining car pools. One man, for example, drove to work with five others and said he enjoyed the fellowship. In another case, several people who worked in the same factory near Toronto travelled together in a van. For individuals who did shift work, however, the car pool was not feasible. Moreover, I learned about cases in which dissension had broken out among the passengers of car pools. Occasionally it was because some of them drank while driving; at other times the source of irritation concerned smoking habits. One car pool fell apart because two of the passengers who had marital problems drove the others mad. Not only did these two men eventually move back to the city, but so did two of the others who decided commuting and small-town life was not their cup of tea. The only one who remained in Paradise concluded that if he hoped to maintain his sanity, he had better drive by himself.

Since the negative side of commuting has already been implied in some of the cases in the previous chapter, I shall only provide one detailed case study here, although it is a particularly poignant one: not only did both parents commute, but their two children were carted along as well. This young couple, part of what I have labelled the aspiring-middle class, moved to Paradise from Toronto for the usual reason: to have a home of their own. The man also saw it as an opportunity to get a dog: 'That's the first thing I said: if we ever get a house, we'll get a German shepherd.' They got their house and their dog, but they had had little money to put towards the mortgage, and to meet the payments both of them held down jobs on the outskirts of the city. They rose at 5:15 a.m. each working day. Everything had to be ready the night before: clothes laid out, the breakfast table set. By 6 a.m. they were on the road with their two children, both under four years of age, who were dropped off at a baby-sitter's house near where the woman worked. The man drove on to his own place of employment, picking his wife up, then the kids, at the end of the day, and arriving back in Paradise about 7 p.m. One of the parents then prepared supper, usually a pizza or a TV dinner, while the other gave the kids a bath. After eating, the children were allowed to stay up for half an hour to play with their toys. When they were in bed, their mother usually watched a soap opera which she had recorded on the VCR. Then it was a few hours of sleep before piling back into the car at the break of dawn.

Less than a year had passed before they decided to put their house up for sale and move back to rented accommodation in the city. What had shattered their dream, the woman stated, was the commuting: 'It's murder. The price of gas is just flooring everybody.' She added that she was always tired, and that her relationship with her husband had become strained.

It is easy to believe that the daily drive, with two young children on board, must have been sheer hell. However, it was not just commuting that had turned them off small-town living. As the woman remarked, 'I think the biggest problem is me. I'm unhappy. I miss my friends. I like to hit the malls every weekend.' She added: 'I like to get on the telephone. The problem is that it's long distance.' Her husband quipped: 'I think she'd stay up here if it's not long distance.' He was much more reluctant to return to the city than his wife. He didn't like the commuting either, but was prepared to put up with it in order to have the house. The prospect of getting rid of his dog was especially distressing for him. At this point, his wife bristled: 'He's a loner. He doesn't need people. But I have to be around people. That's why he's happy here. Me, I like friends, people. I feel that's taken away from me.' .

Given the demanding commuting schedule, they had little opportunity to get to know people in Paradise, nor did they make much effort to do so. From the woman's perspective, the action was in the city. The man did not want action; the peaceful surroundings and his dog were enough. As his melancholic wife explained, they did not really think things out adequately before making the move to Paradise: the driving, the gas prices, the baby-sitting, and the loneliness. Despite her determination to return to the city, she was perfectly aware of the cost: 'I wanted to own a house pretty bad, and this is our only option. If we sell, it'll be the last house we own.'

Commuting as the Good Life

It is perhaps surprising, in view of the evidence presented so far, to find that some people actually enjoyed commuting. There were several reasons: they simply liked to get behind the wheel of a car and watch the miles roll by; when they had lived in the city, they had to drive to work from one part to another, and the trip from Paradise not only often did not take much longer, but it also was more pleasant; they appreciated the time to think and unwind after a hard day at work; they had a need to escape regularly from the small town, and sometimes from spouse and children; some of them were essentially loners, and the commuting provided a convenient excuse for not interacting with the neighbours. This last factor is particularly interesting, because it contradicts the more typical pattern: namely, that those newcomers who did not attempt to become integrated into the community, joining organizations and getting to know their neighbours, were the ones most likely to be forlorn, and eventually to return to the city. In a peculiar manner, commuting was a functional equivalent of the high-rise urban apartment: it provided the anonymity that some people craved.

My first example of a happy commuter concerns a thirty-one-year-old man who had been born in Toronto. His wife, a year younger, had moved to that city from another province when she was a girl. Both of them were raised in poverty-stricken families. The man completed grade twelve, and found a job in a factory on the outskirts of the city. The woman was forced to quit school in grade nine in order to contribute to her family's finances. She too found a job in a factory. Although her husband went through a rough patch as a teenager, running with what he described as an exceptionally wild gang, marriage seemed to settle him down, and he and his wife worked hard, saved their pennies, and eventually were able to put a down payment on a small house in Metro Toronto. When their second child was born, they decided to look for a larger house. They chose Paradise mainly because the price was right. Similar to other cases which I have described, the woman wanted to stay at home with the children, which she could not afford to do in the city. The man, in turn, wanted his dog, and soon after moving to Paradise a German shepherd puppy was bouncing around their new home.

As for commuting, the man commented: 'The first winter was pretty bad. I found out what actual whiteouts are like.' He received a lot of speeding tickets at the beginning, but gradually learned to slow down; he also changed his powerful vehicle for a smaller one in order to get better mileage. He said he had always enjoyed driving, and he soon fell into the routine of commuting: 'It seems that when you do it, you don't even think about it. The drive home actually is relaxing. When you leave sometimes, after a hectic day, the drive relaxes me.' Even the fact that he had to work every other weekend didn't sour him on life in the countryside. As he pointed out, when they had lived in Toronto, it took him thirty-five to forty-five minutes to drive to work at the other side of the city, and the conditions were much more stressful. After two years in Paradise, they had settled contentedly into the community. The woman declared: 'I love this place. I wouldn't want to leave.' It's a good thing she does, she added, because 'once you move out of the city, you can't afford to move back.'

How was it that this couple's move to Paradise has had such a pleasant outcome, while the previous couple whom I described had put their house up for sale and were returning to rented accommodation in the city? A key difference was finances. The first couple had little money for the down payment on their house, and the mortgage payments, even with both of them working, were more than they could handle. The second couple, in contrast, had got lucky. They had sold their house in the city for three times what it had cost them, with the result that they had only a small mortgage on their new home. Another difference, which may partly have been linked to the second couple's greater financial security, is that they made an effort to meet people in the community. In fact, it seemed that their personalities blossomed in the new environment. The woman said: 'I've got to be more of a conversationalist.' She joined an organization through which she met young parents like herself. Her husband began to play darts at the Legion once a week. This amazed his wife, who said he has always been a loner. She was even more astonished when he invited a couple of pals whom he met at the Legion to their home. Never, she said, had he done such a thing in ten years of marriage. Both she and her husband stressed that the quality-of-life factor had never entered their minds when they had considered the move to rural Ontario, but when they got there they bought a snowmobile and actually began to enjoy winter.

Family connections also were on the side of this family. The man's parents and a sister had moved to the Paradise area a couple of years earlier, and indeed that is partly why he and his wife chose that particular community for their new home. His wife's parents continue to live in the city, and on those rare occasions when winter weather makes driving hazardous, he spends the night with them. Finally, there was a significant difference in attitude between the two women in these families. The first woman derived her pleasure from the shopping malls, and from visits and telephone conversations with her old friends. In her opinion, there was nothing to do in small-town Ontario, and nobody to do it with. The other woman commented that if she gets to a shopping mall a couple of times a year, that's more often than she wants; what delighted her was the quiet rural landscape and the circle of friends that had already begun to take shape around them.

My second example involves a couple who had moved to Paradise three years ago, just before their first child was born. Both of them had college diplomas and good jobs near the city. One of the reasons for the move, however, was to allow the woman to remain at home with the infant. This couple did *not* get a dog, but at first they did bite off more than they could chew; they bought a huge house in the elite subdivision, but discovered that with one salary it was not affordable. After two years they moved across the road into a more modest dwelling, and the woman began to work part-time. Reflecting on the life of the commuter, the man remarked: 'It would be great if my place of work was over in the field here [he pointed beyond his house]. I would have more time for my family. There wouldn't be the wear and tear on my body.' But, he added, he had no choice: to afford the mortgage, he had to have a city salary.

Besides, he said, commuting wasn't nearly as onerous as he had anticipated: 'When I first came here, I thought it's such a long way. But after the first month it became all of a sudden not so bad. It was just routine.' Like several other newcomers who commute, he said that even when he had lived in the city, he had had to drive to work, and not only did it take him almost as long, but the traffic was 'insane.' This man was fortunate, because his place of work (he was a supervisor in a retail outlet) was located on the outskirts of the city. Comparing his drive from Paradise to the routine when he lived in the city, he stated: 'It's much more relaxed. Quite often I see wildlife. It's prettier.' In the summer he takes the back roads to and from work, and remarked that he has even begun to enjoy driving, which he had never done before.

Earlier I indicated that a small number of newcomers, who value their privacy, seem to like the commuting life because it insulates them from contact with their neighbours. A case in point is a couple in their forties, each of them immigrants from different parts of Europe, who had met in Toronto and settled in Paradise about fifteen years ago. They chose Paradise after seeing an advertisement about a new subdivision with reasonably priced houses. For the first two years, before they had children, they both commuted to jobs in the city. That experience held few pleasant memories for the woman: 'It wasn't fun. We were just married. We never saw one another.' Her first child was born after the two years, and she remained at home. Her husband, who has been commuting to the same modest job in a large corporation for all of those years, found the routine entirely agreeable: 'It doesn't bother me. It gives you time to think, relax, wind down.' One reason for his positive attitude was that he did not have to travel into the heart of the city. Another reason was that his mechanical flair had enabled him to avoid some of the financial costs of commuting; he buys old cars cheaply, fixes them up, and drives them for a couple of years. A third factor, which for many people might well have turned them off commuting for ever, was that his unusual work schedule enables him to avoid heavy traffic. He rises at 3 a.m., is at work around 5 a.m., returns home about 3 p.m., and goes to bed at 7 p.m.

Such a schedule, his wife pointed out, has made it difficult for them to entertain or get to know people. In addition, she said, she is very shy, and except for a brief period several years ago when she took part in an organization involving her children, she has lived an isolated life in Paradise. At that point her husband broke in: 'Don't get us wrong. We didn't *want* neighbours. We want our privacy.' This does not mean that these individuals, each of whom had completed the equivalent of about grade eleven, were oddballs. To the contrary, they were charming, interesting, and personable. They simply were most fulfilled when they were left alone.

My final example of a happy commuter is a woman who has been able to endure life in the small town because she usually isn't there.

This woman and her husband, solidly middle class, chose Paradise as home because it was halfway between their respective places of employment; they were also attracted by the house prices. The woman had lived in her youth in several towns and cities; the man had been raised in another part of rural Ontario. While he apparently loved living in the country, and in fact wanted to move to a farm, he was not thrilled with the travel required by his job. His wife, in contrast, a computer expert in a Toronto-based corporation, was an enthusiastic commuter. For one thing, she enjoyed driving. And she loved the city, both for its own sake and because it allowed her to escape from the small town: 'I'm not sure if I could enjoy this town half as much if I worked here. I think you'd get locked in a grid.' Her job in the city, she explained, made it easier to avoid social entanglements and boring neighbours; it provided her with a degree of freedom which she otherwise would not have.

Another relevant factor was her relationship with her husband (their eight-year marriage was childless). She described him as 'quiet, introverted, and inoffensive.' She described herself as 'frank and blunt.' She was not the type of woman, she remarked, who liked to be dependent on a man, and indeed, she stated, she dominated her husband. She added: 'I earn as much as my husband, so there's not the breadwinner concept.' She said she had several friends in the city, whom she was able to meet on a regular basis because of her job, adding that her husband didn't seem to mind.

This couple, with their divergent views about rural life and commuting, would appear to be the type who often split up, or at least move back to the city; indeed, the woman revealed that they often joke about getting divorced. In their case, what apparently has made it all work out so far was their solid financial state, plus the woman's commuting, which allowed her breathing room from her husband and the town.

The above case was far from atypical. In another middle-class family, the husband rose at 6 a.m. and returned from the city about 6:30 p.m. He said he liked the drive, since it gave him an opportunity to be alone. His wife described him as an exceptionally quiet man who rarely talks. They don't even talk to each other, she said. When he gets home from work, he immediately begins to watch TV. She, in turn, leaves for her own part-time job a few miles away. According to this woman, she and her husband live separate lives. She quipped that she had her own friends, while he didn't have any friends. Their marriage, nevertheless, she insisted, was healthy, largely because commuting maintained their interaction at a mutually acceptable level.

Former Commuters

For the vast majority of newcomers who disliked commuting, there were only two options: either grin and bear it, or sell out and move back to the city. A few of them, however, found a third way: new jobs in or around the town. Six men who did just that have made successful careers in the community. For five of the six, it meant a new line of work. Three of them went into real estate, two into insurance. All five of these men have become integrated into the community through their jobs and their memberships in service clubs, and are counted among the more prominent citizens today. The sixth man, who was able to continue his trade in a local company, was much less visible, largely because his atypical religious affiliation kept him apart from other citizens. Despite the happy outcome for these former commuters, only one of them intended to remain in the community after retirement. Four of them planned to move to more remote parts of rural Ontario, while the sixth man was considering buying an apartment near the city where most of his relatives still lived. For the majority of these people, then, Paradise itself had apparently never been the main attraction; instead, it had been rural life in general.

Natives Who Commute

While fewer natives than newcomers commuted to work, and the distance was usually no more than twenty miles, a small number of them travelled as far as the newcomers. Four young men in their twenties commuted to family-owned businesses near Toronto, as did a middle-aged man who used to have his own business in Paradise. Another young man was a police officer near the city, and a handful of others whom I learned about worked in factories on the outskirts of the city.

Since the natives usually travelled a shorter distance than the newcomers, it may be thought that commuting had little impact on their lives. In other words, they would return in the evening to the familiar territory of family and friends, and carry on much as they had done before they had become commuters. That was not necessarily the case. To a degree only marginally less than for the newcomers, their social interaction beyond their immediate families was superficial and infrequent, especially if they did not belong to service clubs or similar organizations. Paradise, for the native commuters as well, had become basically a place in which to sleep.

For example, one man whose work was located about fifteen miles away revealed that he almost never stops downtown when he returns in the evening, nor does he chum around with old friends to any degree. Part of the explanation, he said, is simply that he no longer knows many of the people whom he sees on the streets. Also, since he became a commuter he feels like a stranger himself. Another man who commutes about the same distance rarely strays outside his home when he returns from work. He didn't know the names of the neighbours who lived on either side of him (they were newcomers), and even more significantly, a man who had grown up with him in Paradise didn't even realize he still lived in town. My third example is somewhat different. This man too commutes, in his case about thirty-five miles each way, and his interaction with his neighbours and old friends and acquaintances is also severely limited. The reason, however, is his religious affiliation. He has joined a small fundamentalist Christian sect which discourages any association with non-members or unnecessary contact with the profane world.

Reverse Commuting

Most of the commuters head southward to the urban centres around Toronto. By reverse commuters, I mean people who travel from such centres northward to Paradise. Some indication of the degree of reverse commuting can be gleaned from the place-of-work data in the 1986 census, which provides information not only about the destinations of the labour force, but also about its origins. According to these data, 1,847 people were employed in Paradise; 718 of them were residents of the community, which means that 1,129 of them commuted from elsewhere to work in the town. Exactly one thousand of these people lived in Dufferin County itself, and all but 69 of them came from the rural townships surrounding Paradise (these 69 originated from the largest town in Dufferin County). Among the 129 people working in Paradise who lived outside the county, 97 of them resided north of Paradise. For these people, then, employment in Paradise constituted a southern trek just as it did for the majority of commuters who lived in the town. Only 32 of the 129 people who drove to Paradise to work actually originated from urban centres south of Paradise and beyond the county. It is these people who I define as reverse commuters.

Most of the reverse commuters fell into the professional class. They included a handful of teachers who lived in the urban areas near Toronto, some of them preferring to reside there because their spouses were employed nearby. Here, too, we find a man, again a professional, who commuted more than 250 miles daily. For a brief period he had tried apartment life in Paradise, but decided the marathon drive, which permitted him to live in his home town, was preferable, at least until he could locate alternative employment. A woman who commuted to a town near Paradise from the east end of Toronto took the daily trip in stride. Not only did she find the driving relaxing after a stressful day at work (she was a medium-ranked civil servant), but she also was able to travel against the flow of traffic, thus making good speed. Her husband too commuted, but a shorter distance, and according to his wife he hated it. Whoever was home first prepared the evening meal; almost always, the woman said, it was her husband.

The only non-professional reverse commuter about whom I learned was a man who drove from his home near the city to operate a gas station outside Paradise. He rose at 3:30 a.m. every morning, was on the road shortly after 4 a.m., and was open for business by 6 a.m. at the latest in order to catch the commuters motoring towards the city. He finally closed the station at 9 p.m. and drove back to his home. In less than a year he threw in the towel.

A Town for Sale

'Do you know, you can literally put a town up for sale?' These were not the words of just an ordinary citizen; they were spoken by a man who had been a prominent member of the council in the late 1960s. In fact, he said, what decided him to run for council was his disgust at the existing efforts to attract new growth to the community. There are two significant aspects about this man's comment. First, it contradicts a viewpoint held by many natives in Paradise: namely, that the newcomers have forced themselves into the community despite the

opposition of the citizenry; as the former councillor indicated, concert-
ed efforts were made to attract newcomers. Secondly, this same councillor, surveying the community twenty years later, was perplexed and
disappointed with what he saw – exorbitant taxes to pay for new roads
and schools, inadequate basic services such as sewage facilities and
water supply, a once-proud village with a clear identity turned into a
bedroom community.

His reaction was typical. With very few exceptions, those citizens who
had played the leading roles a generation earlier in putting the subdivisions, townhouses, and apartments in place had begun to sing a
different tune by the late 1980s. One of them, a businessman, had
expected to profit from the newcomers, but as he remarked, 'They can
be here anywhere from three to five years before they step foot downtown.' A former reeve, who had wooed the developers and welcomed
the newcomers, seemed surprised that he didn't even know his neighbours any more. Another avid supporter of the town's growth who had
had his finger in real estate concluded sadly that the newcomers, in his
judgment, have not enriched the community; he was particularly
disturbed with his perception that crime had increased and community
spirit had diminished.

A former councillor, again a leading figure in the subdivision boom,
remarked (somewhat naively) that it was a pity that a new industrial
base failed to emerge alongside the housing developments. This
touches directly on one of the most common complaints in the community today – too much housing, too little industry. In answer to a
survey circulated by the town council in the late 1980s, intended to
discover what people liked and disliked about the community, one
citizen voiced this complaint in the clearest of terms: 'Stop promoting
subdivisions. Look after people that already live in town. Encourage
industry (actually give them the land) so both parents can work without the expense of two cars, or people who don't drive. It would make
for a richer environment, then maybe we could afford the tax increase.'

The lack of industry in Paradise is not an entirely new problem,
generated by the demands of a significantly increased population. In
a letter to the editor of the local newspaper in 1945, a writer observed
that their boys overseas would soon be returning from the war, and
would require jobs; he urged the town fathers to offer inducements to
industrialists. This was the period, however, during which the powerful
reeve described in chapter 3 allegedly discouraged new businesses in

order to maintain his economic monopoly. In the early 1960s the village clerk, accompanied by one of the leading businessman, travelled to Toronto as official representatives to lure industries northwards. The venture apparently was fruitless.

The days when powerful figures with vested interests could block the entry of new businesses have passed, but remnants of those days remain. Some of the owners of businesses which have been established during the past decade or so complained about the lack of cooperation from the council, and outright hostility from long-established merchants. Whether true or not, it was rumoured that two industrial plants that were located during the last few years in nearby communities had originally been slated for Paradise, but the owners had been turned off by the obstacles thrown up by the council. A rather interesting exchange of views occurred within the town council during the 1980s. A member of the council introduced a motion to prohibit the establishment of any new businesses in the community if the same types of businesses already existed. Thus, if there was a shoe store or a flower shop, no other shoe stores or flower shops would be welcomed. The motion failed, but the man who told me about it, himself a councillor at the time, expressed amazement that it had been introduced in the first place. There was actually little purpose to the motion. During the 1950s there had been two pharmacies, two hardware stores, in fact two or more outlets for most types of business. But during the 1980s there was only one pharmacy, one hardware, and so on, prompting customers to complain that the merchants ran monopolies.

There has been little change in the downtown business district in physical terms since the Second World War. The number of stores remains about the same. However, in the 1950s most of the buildings were occupied by merchants, whereas in the 1980s the business district consisted of twenty-one merchandising outlets and twenty-seven service outlets (for example, lawyer's office, real estate offices, and travel agent).[3] According to a report prepared by the town council, only half of the twenty-one merchandising outlets were viable businesses. Some indication of the deterioration of the old business sector is reflected in the fact that during the 1980s, seventy-one businesses changed hands. No doubt part of the explanation is that local businessmen have failed to adjust to contemporary marketing practices, such as attractive window displays and periodic sales, but there is more than this to the problem. Despite the complaint that the merchants have virtual monopolies, competition for the customer's dollar is probably more intense today than it was in the past. Local merchants now have to compete with the various shopping malls located in surrounding towns and cities, made accessible by the automobile. Like the old-style farmers on a hundred acres of land, the small-town merchants have been rendered obsolete, and many of them have resigned themselves to relying on the patronage of a few loyal customers, rather than mortgaging their futures for elegant premises in favourable locations.

Finally, it is noteworthy that the only major industry to be established in the community in recent years has been a focus of heated debate and controversy. As a result of an accident at the plant, toxic chemicals contaminated the soil, which caused people to worry about the drinking water. Rumours then became widespread that the plant was a potential fire hazard of major proportions. People began to ask why the plant had been allowed to set up business in the community in the first place, pointing out that it employed few of the locals and thus was not an economic asset. Many also complained that the company not only was given incredible inducements such as tax-free land, but also that there was a lot of shady dealings between the company and the council, including cash pay-offs. When it came to producing proof, however, about all that they could come up with was the fact that shortly after the plant opened, the reeve himself was put on the payroll.

A company representative angrily denied these allegations. He claimed that the council had not gone out of its way to attract the plant. He also insisted that his organization was extremely environmentally conscious, and had spent millions of dollars to assure the plant would be safe, as well as several thousand dollars to clean up the chemical spill. In the old days, he pointed out, the spill would simply have been covered over without fanfare and nobody would have been the wiser. As for the charge that his company did not give jobs to the local people, he remarked bitterly: ' We hired all the rowdies here, all the drunks. We must have gone through 150 of them in the first two years.' He stated that they now have a stable labour force, consisting of about thirty full-time employees, twenty of them locals. Reflecting on all the controversy (and expense) that had reared up since the plant was built, he commented, 'If I was looking at this place today, and what it's like, I probably wouldn't have come.' But, he added, they have invested too much to pull out now.

The Fiction of Choice

One of the politicians who had begun to regret his earlier efforts to attract newcomers asked: 'What choice did we have?' As he went on to say, house-hungry people from the city, like it or not, were invading the countryside, and to have attempted to build a wall around the community would have been to brand it as backward. Besides, he argued, growth *ought* to equal progress. In his judgment, the real problem was not the population increase per se, but the fact that most of it had occurred during a brief five-year spurt.

I only met one local politician who had been adamantly opposed to subdivision developments from the outset, and he was not a resident of Paradise but lived in a township that bordered the community. This man was in favour of single-dwelling units on two or three acres of land, complete with their own wells and septic systems. But subdivisions, in his judgment, simply increased a community's taxes and decreased its cohesion. Often, he said, developers from the city with grandiose plans telephoned him and treated him like a 'local yokel,' which did not please him. Not surprisingly, he was hardly the darling of the county council. He was dismissed as a man behind the times, lacking in vision. Despite his efforts to limit and control the influx of newcomers, they eventually did penetrate the small villages and hamlets in his township, some of them moving into old frame houses, others into new subdivisions that had sprouted up in defiance of his better judgment.

If the residents of the small towns and villages on the commuter fringe had little choice but to put out the welcome mat, was the situation any different for the migrants themselves? In his sensitive analysis of newcomers who have moved from London, England, to the towns and villages surrounding that city, Pahl (1970:115) states: 'A very dangerous fallacy has arisen in recent years. This assumes that the expansion of residential areas in the outer London region is a result of consumer preference ... The man who leaves home at 6:30 a.m. and returns at 9:10 p.m. each day is said to be doing it because he wants to ... I think such arguments are pernicious. Young married couples in London with perhaps one or two children, earning up to 30 pounds a week and wanting somewhere to live, have remarkably little choice.'

Pahl makes it clear that the motivations of the middle-class newcomers and the non-manual newcomers (the lower-middle and aspiring-middle classes in my study) are quite different. The non-manual workers are attracted less by the pleasures of the countryside than by the possibility of having their own house. The wealthier people in the middle class, on the other hand, aren't looking for village or community life; what they want is half an acre of land, stately trees, and privacy (Pahl 1970:60–7). In contrast to the lower-middle-class newcomers, who are described as 'the reluctant commuters,' the middle-class newcomers had some choice in whether or not to move to the countryside.

In almost every respect, Pahl's words resonate well with what has been said about Paradise, especially regarding the lower-middle class and the aspiring-middle class. Like the natives who received them, either with pleasure or with protest, these newcomers were to a large extent puppets on strings manipulated by the unseen hands of the political economy. In this context, power is the capacity to exercise choice, and only the newcomers in the middle class or higher possessed it.

Conclusions

According to many of the natives of Paradise, the turnover rate among the newcomers was staggering, and what caused it was the daily grind of commuting. In one man's words, 'There generally is a five-year burnout. They sell, and new commuters take their place.' This picture of commuting as the bad life is certainly representative, but a number of qualifications are in order. First, not all the commuters were newcomers. Secondly, not all the newcomers who did commute eventually packed their bags and left the town; those among them who fell into the middle class or higher, and whose financial states were solid, tended to stick it out. In addition, some of those in the aspiring-middle and lower-middle classes had adjusted by changing their large homes for more modest ones in Paradise, rather than leaving the town. Thirdly, not all people moving away from Paradise were newcomers; within the past decade, there has been an increasing tendency for natives to do so as well when they reached retirement age. Fourthly, commuting itself – the sheer physical act of the drive – was usually not the problem; as I pointed out, many of the newcomers had had to commute previously from one part of the city to another. The problem was a number of factors directly and indirectly associated with commuting. There was, for example, the financial factor. The costs of keeping in touch with former friends in the city by telephone were high, as were gasoline prices and vehicle maintenance. One real estate agent stated that many newcomers discover that life in the small community, dream house and all, is only deceptively a bargain.[4] Commenting on those who return to the city, he said: 'There's a lot more would like to go back, but they find they can't afford it.' In fact, he added, for some newcomers the rise in interest rates in combination with their low down payments meant that their houses had actually become worth less than their mortgages.

Commuting also took a toll on one's body; people were often fatigued after the long day, and had little time for family life; the strain on their marriages was sometimes evident, especially in families where both spouses had to commute to jobs in order to afford the mortgage. Many of the newcomers had not anticipated what it would be like to drive in a snowstorm. Less direct factors concerned the problem of adjusting to the pace of small-town life, and the feeling of isolation that some people, especially women left at home, experienced. Many of them simply could not adapt to a life without shopping malls, and others pined for the cultural activities available in the city.

It must be stressed that the factors related to commuting, either directly or indirectly, were not the only ones that motivated newcomers eventually to leave the community. As another real estate agent observed, some people are simply rootless; within three or four years in a town, they trot off to a different community, and before long they will leave it as well. Some newcomers, he continued, 'don't neighbour.' In his judgment, this type always fails to stick it out in communities like Paradise, but we have seen that that is not necessarily true. For a small number of newcomers, what has pleased them about Paradise has been the opportunity to live in splendid isolation from their neighbours. This brings us to the final qualification about the hard life of the commuter. Some people – very definitely a minority – did not find the life bad at all. For a variety of reasons, it was commuting, in fact, that had created their Paradise.

Chapter Seven

Growing Pains

Paradise, it appears, has always been shaped by some sort of dualism. A century ago, in the days of the pioneers, it took the form of raw nature against technological change, as the forests gave way to cultivated fields and fenced-in pastures replaced the hunt. Over the passing decades, farmers and townspeople have gazed curiously at each other across a slender psychological divide, while rich people and poor, and men and women have acted out their destinies. Eventually a new dichotomy made its appearance: natives versus newcomers. The purpose of this chapter is to examine the combined impact of natives and newcomers on the community today. What is evident is that to some extent Paradise constitutes two communities: the one in the minds of the natives, the other in the minds of the newcomers.

Divided Visions

Many of the newcomers marvel at the friendliness of the community. In one man's words: 'I was surprised at first. You'd walk down the street and people say good morning. You know, just like you see on the Little House on the Prairie.' The natives, in contrast, claim that the newcomers don't 'neighbour.' All they do is wave and say 'Hi' as they pass by on the street. It must be added that the natives themselves no longer interact in the way they formerly did. One retired couple complained that their neighbours, whom they had known all their lives, departed for the winter in Florida without saying goodbye. A woman could hardly believe that when her mother died her old friends next door did not even drop in to express sympathy. As one long-time resident stated, 'I don't know anybody that's talking to their neighbours really well.'

According to the natives, the newcomers have no loyalty to the town; it is just a bedroom community for them – they don't even shop there. As some of the older businessmen explained, it used to be almost a sin to shop outside the village. Yet two points must be made. First, some newcomers remark that they would prefer to do their shopping in the town, but they can't because the stores are usually closed by the time they get home in the evening from their jobs in the city. Second, the natives themselves no longer automatically buy their groceries in Paradise. As one man observed, he meets more of his old friends at the shopping mall in a nearby town than he does in the community itself.

Some of the natives described the newcomers as an immoral bunch, living outside wedlock and rarely stepping into church. In actuality, there was not much difference between them in marital status; 71 per cent of the natives and 77 per cent of the newcomers whom I inter-viewed were still in their first marriages, and 6 per cent and 7 per cent of them respectively were single. A somewhat higher percentage of the newcomers were divorced (10 per cent versus 6 per cent), and a signif-icantly greater proportion of the natives were widowed (16 per cent versus 3 per cent). Although some of the newcomers thought that the churches were packed with natives ('Oh, it's such a religious communi-ty,' one woman enthused), the two groups were similar in this respect as well. Among the natives, 27 per cent attended church regularly, 9 per cent occasionally, and 64 per cent never; the figures for the new-comers were 28 per cent, 11 per cent, and 60 per cent.

The natives often complained that the newcomers did not partici-pate in community life, and here there was a difference between the two groups, at least in terms of membership in voluntary organizations. Among the 122 natives who were interviewed, 38 per cent belonged to two or more organizations, while only 22 per cent of the 107 new-comers did so. Fully 57 per cent of the newcomers were not members of any organizations at all; the comparable figure for the natives was 30 per cent. It is well known that participation in voluntary associations varies according to class position. Among both the natives and the newcomers in Paradise, almost none of those in the lower class be-longed to a voluntary organization (indeed, not a single one of the newcomer poor did so, whereas in the past some of the native poor had been members of the Orange Order and the Legion). There has been some change at the upper-class level. A generation ago it could be taken for granted that virtually every prominent man and woman was active in at least one organization. That is no longer the case. Among the twenty newcomers who had university degrees, six belonged to two or more organizations, three to one organization, and ten to none at all.[1] Although the participation rate of newcomers in voluntary associations did not match that of the natives, it had not dropped to zero. In fact, about one-third of the members of the major service clubs in the town around 1990 were newcomers.

Voluntary organizations do not always serve to bridge the gap between natives and newcomers. In a community in England (Pahl 1970:35) there were separate Women's Institutes for working-class natives and middle-class newcomers. For a brief period in Paradise there were two IODE organizations, one catering to elderly natives (which eventually disbanded), the other to younger newcomers.

NIMBY Issues

The newcomers have a reputation of being more aggressive and less respectful of authority than the natives.[2] As one woman remarked, 'There's a definite pegging of us as being complainers.' Although she thought it was unfair to pin that label on them, she talked about how much she resented buying withered fruits and vegetables in the local stores, and revealed that on some occasions, much to the embarrassment of other shoppers, she had made a scene. Another woman recounted her experiences with the town employees. Apparently when repairs had to be done to the water system, their customary practice was to shut off the water in an area without notifying any of the residents. When that happened on the street of the woman in question, she confronted the workmen: 'Look, I want some warning.' The man in charge replied, 'That's not common practice. Maybe where you're from. But not here.' Nevertheless, her complaint paid dividends. The next time the water was to be shut off, the man dropped by to forewarn her. But, as she later discovered, he didn't bother to tell anyone else on the street.

Another example of newcomer aggressiveness concerned taxes. In 1989 two of the wealthiest newcomers in the town, both residents of the most elegant subdivision, led a revolt against high property taxes (one of them said he paid $4,800 on his house). Supporters marched to the town hall. Although taxes were not reduced, the organizers of the revolt nevertheless thought they were victorious, because taxes were not raised the following year.

In most cases, the term 'NIMBY' was associated with controversies surrounding non-profit housing. For example, plans were made to convert the town's old school into subsidized apartments. The outcry was immediate, with newcomers making the most noise. A woman who had lived in the community for two years helped to organize a petition: 'We wanted to have the school saved as a heritage property.' Concerned about the impact of subsidized apartments on real estate values, she remarked: 'Everyone was for non-profit housing, but "not in my backyard".' The school was eventually purchased by a private individual and the premises converted into a community centre. Ruminating about her active involvement, despite her brief residence in the town, the woman remarked: 'I saw myself as not having any right to do what I did.' Ironically, she added that there were certain rules for successfully adapting to small-town life: 'You don't try to rock the boat from day one.'

Not all newcomers were prepared to speak up when something failed to meet their approval. The woman who led the petition against subsidized apartments in the school was solidly middle class; indeed, in every case in which there was a confrontation between the town and the newcomers, whether it concerned taxes, non-profit housing or some other issue, the person complaining was middle class or higher. For example, a man who was a college graduate spearheaded a petition against low-cost apartments in a new subdivision. He expressed support for the concept of affordable housing, but thought it was a mistake for everyone involved to locate such housing in the midst of expensive homes. What worried him was that 'a poor class of people' would move into the apartments, driving property values down and creating social problems. When he attempted to organize a petition, he clashed with the council, which had flip-flopped back and forth for a year about whether to allow the apartments to be built. He also discovered that the natives were much more reluctant to support him than were fellow newcomers. The natives, he stated, have a defeatist attitude. One of them told him: 'You're going to learn that you can't change council.' Another commented: 'We'll sign it (the petition), but you'll never get anywhere.'

Although he believed his efforts to halt the construction of the apartments was justified, he was concerned about his reputation in town: 'People will think, there's another guy we're going to have to hear from every time it rains.' Yet after an article appeared about his petition in the local newspaper, he was invited to join two service clubs. Some people also suggested that he run for mayor but, as he remarked, 'I don't think I'd get elected, because I haven't lived here long enough.' In fact, he had only been in Paradise two months before organizing the petition.

Crime and Social Problems

Some people who have lived in Paradise all their lives still think the streets are safe, but the more prevalent view among the natives is that there has been an alarming increase in crime in recent years. As one man stated, 'The hoodlums and gangs on the street corners are something else.' Another man claimed that, relative to population size, there is more vandalism in the community now than there is in Toronto. A retired teacher confessed that she was afraid to walk downtown at night by herself. While at first she said it was the rampant crime that worried her, it soon became obvious that what made her uneasy was the presence of so many strangers: 'It's not that we've heard anything, but it's just that, well, who's out there? We don't know.'

This last case is a classical example of xenophobia, and indeed the natives tended to equate the newcomers with the increase in crime and lack of safety: 'You got a lot of people coming up here from the lower social scale. I know our crime rate went up 200 per cent.' A particular type of person, argued one middle-aged native, moves from the city to small towns like Paradise: 'They have an inability to cope. They thought moving here would solve their problems, but it didn't. They were running away from their problems.'

Most of the vandalism, according to the natives, was perpetrated by the offspring of the newcomers. You can see it in the school, fumed one teacher. The entire student body, she contended, had become disobedient and foul-mouthed since the kids from the city had appeared in the classrooms. She and others believed that a large part of the problem was that the newcomers in the subdivisions neglected their children and allowed them to run around the town unsupervised. It is true that in those families in which both spouses worked away from home their children were sometimes left on their own for a brief period after school, but that situation increasingly included native families as well. Moreover, there was no hard evidence, such as police statistics, to link the newcomer youth to vandalism. As Lustig (1990) has pointed out, not once during the period of her fieldwork on newcomers in Paradise did she observe children being neglected by their parents. There was a time when young people in the community did run wild, but that was a generation ago, back in the 1950s and earlier, and the kids on the loose then were the unruly offspring of the natives.

Although many of the newcomers moved to Paradise partly in order to bring their children up in a better environment, they often came with a city mentality. This meant, among other things, that they rarely accepted that their neighbours could be fully trusted. One couple revealed that they enjoyed greeting people on the street, even if they didn't know them, but at the same time they cautioned their young children not to talk to strangers. They appreciated the contradiction, but were at a loss as to how to handle it. Another newcomer expressed the same dilemma: 'How do you say don't talk to strangers? You've got these older people who say "Hi, how are you"?' Her solution was to tell her seven year old daughter to say 'Hi' back when people greet her, but to keep on walking.[3]

Some newcomers assume initially that Paradise is remarkably crime-free but later change their minds. For example, when I asked one woman if she thought the community was safer than Toronto, she stated: 'I did when I first moved up here. But things I've heard and things I've seen. You know, I've just got a bit afraid about walking.' On one occasion a ruckus broke out in a variety store just as she was entering. Several teenagers – all drunk, she claimed – poured onto the street. Although she was only subjected to verbal abuse when she stepped outside and walked past the teenagers, the encounter prompted her to revise her opinion about the differences between the city and the town.

Another woman said: 'I used to be little Miss Brave in the city.' What has surprised her is that she is actually more apprehensive in Paradise. She stated: 'You know what makes me scared up here? A lot of people who are a bit odd, outcasts, live out here.' She had heard that a young man with mental problems had attempted to abduct a child from the local school. She was also told that a man whom she had seen working around town was a former convicted rapist. She stated: 'I thought it would have been a better place for the kids to grow up.' Then this woman made an acute observation. Perhaps the difference between the city and the small town is that what crime does occur in the latter becomes public knowledge so fast, giving an exaggerated impression of the level of crime: 'Because it's a small town, you hear about it the next day.'

Both natives and newcomers believe that alcohol and drug abuse have become rampant in the community, especially among those living on welfare. A young newcomer discouraged his wife from using one of the public laundromats during the evening because it was a hangout for people on drugs. Commenting on why drinking was so rampant among teenagers, one of them stated: 'It seems to be the only thing there is to do.' Of course, hard drinking is not a new phenomenon in Paradise, but drugs are. A report in 1972 in the local newspaper suggested that drug abuse was becoming more widespread in town. In the late 1980s there was a drug bust nearby involving local people who were dealers. One young man confided: 'I had a lot of money, because I was dealing in drugs.' He added that he had turned over a new leaf, and now sticks to alcohol, but claimed that many of his acquaintances in Paradise use drugs regularly.

Hard drinking apparently still occurs at all levels of the stratification system, as do efforts to cover up for those in the higher classes, but some things have changed. The bootleggers have disappeared, and it is rare now to find people lying inebriated in the ditch or lurching out of control along the streets. This does not mean that the 'characters,' as lower-class alcoholics used to be called, have entirely disappeared. It merely means that they no longer are tolerated in the public sphere. Consider the case of a couple in their sixties, described by a prominent native as relics from the past. Both were raised United, although neither attends church any more. The man, who referred to himself as a jack of all trades, quit school in grade eight and worked as a farmer and carpenter until his back gave out and he began to receive a disability pension. His wife, who quit school in grade ten, formerly was employed as a domestic.

The man made no attempt to conceal his drinking habits: 'I love my alcohol. My problem's I've got to have the whole bottle.' On two occasions he had been taken to institutions to dry out. His wife also was reputedly an alcoholic. Periodically, when they go on a binge, they beat each other up. When the police investigate, neither will press charges against the other. When I was in their home, they continuously yelled and cursed back and forth at each other. After one heated exchange, the man confided: 'I wouldn't think of leaving that old goat. I'd shoot myself first. She is a blessing to me.' Taking down a picture of his wife from the wall, he said: 'There's the old heifer when she went to school.' At that point, the telephone rang. After listening for a few minutes, the man whispered that it was one of his grand-daughters, adding: 'It's her first motherhood.' To illustrate that he meant her first menstruation, he clutched his crotch. Later the man took me downstairs to a little room in the basement containing a cot. He said this is where he hides out 'when people get mad at me.'

Like other members of the lower class, this couple maintained close contact with their children, all of whom had left home and had families of their own. Pictures of their children and grandchildren were everywhere in the house, and the man, sober when I first met him, declared that he loves his grandchildren, and lives for them. Their house, located in the old part of the town and surrounded by the renovated homes of the newcomers, was dilapidated, but they owned it, and in the summer it was ringed by attractive flower gardens, one of their simple pleasures in life (they did not have a car and rarely left their property).

'Everyone tells me I'm no good,' confessed the man. Most of his neighbours were in agreement. One of them, a resident in Paradise for two years, thought the town council should force the man and woman to either fix up their property or sell it and leave town. In order to maintain the alcoholic couple at arm's length, another neighbour insisted on addressing them as 'Mr. and Mrs.' Reacting to such treatment, the two 'relics from the past' remarked that people aren't nearly as nice as they used to be. Forty years ago this couple would have been at the bottom of the heap, acutely aware of their low station in life, nevertheless they would have *belonged* to the community. Today they still are at the bottom of the heap, but with one difference: there no longer is a place for people like them in Paradise.

The View from the Police Department

An obvious source of information about crime and social problems was the local police. In the 1950s the Police Department in Paradise consisted of the chief (who also served as the town foreman) and one night-watchman. By 1988 the force had expanded to a chief of police, a sergeant, three constables, three auxiliary police, and a part-time secretary. The current chief, who had served in that capacity for more than twenty years, remarked that his job had changed dramatically over that period. There had been a sharp reduction in respect towards the police, and the job had become much more bureaucratic. People nowadays, he said, had so many rights, or at least were so much more aware of their rights, that his workload had doubled. Formerly, if someone was drunk the person would just be tossed in a cell for the night. Now, however, it was necessary to go by the book, which meant hours of paperwork. Another major change, he thought, was that individuals had abdicated responsibility. In the past, citizens tended to solve their own minor disputes. Now they even telephoned the police when their neighbour's dog got loose.

The chief of police stated that the number of cases which his department had to deal with had increased sharply in recent years, but they did not include much violent crime; instead they consisted of impaired driving, possessing liquor in public places, public mischief, and domestic disputes. Although he did not keep separate statistics for natives and newcomers, it was his impression that juvenile delinquency and vandalism were especially widespread among the newcomer youth in the subdivisions. Other police officers, including members of the OPP, painted a different picture, with scenes of robbery, rape, and even murder, especially in the countryside surrounding the community. As one officer commented, there was nothing innocent about this area any more, although he added that much of the violent crime was committed by transients rather than by local residents.

In order to try to measure changes in the crime rate in recent years, and to verify the alleged increase in violent crime, I turned to two sources of information. The first was the 1965 annual report to the town by the chief of police, recorded in the council minutes. The report noted thirteen convictions under the Criminal Code (six break and enter, two taking motor vehicles without consent, one assault, one wilful damage, one driving under suspension, two causing a disturbance); thirty-seven convictions under the Liquor Control Act; thirty-seven convictions under the Highway Traffic Act; thirty-four motor vehicle accidents; fifty-four doors of business places 'found insecure during night checks'; forty-one dog tags sold; and thirty other charges still pending before the courts, including twenty for break and enter and one case of counterfeit money.

Since 1965 represents life in Paradise just before the rapid influx of the newcomers, it serves as a reasonable comparison with the other source of data, which consisted of the statistics kept by the police in Paradise for the years covering 1981 to 1988. The average number of charges per year were as follows: seven break and enter in businesses, four in residences; eight shoplifting under $200; nine thefts of bicycles; twelve frauds by cheque; sixty cases of wilful damage to property; seventeen cases of intoxication in public; 128 cases of having liquor in a public place; thirty cases of minors with liquor; fifty-one cases of impaired driving; sixteen cases of domestic disputes. During this period, there were no charges of murder, manslaughter, or rape, no bawdy house or betting house charges, and only ten cases of cannabis possession and three cases of cannabis trafficking for the entire eight years. In addition, there were no sexual assaults under the 'Aggravated' or 'with Weapon' categories, but under 'Sexual Assault – Other' there were two cases in 1986, eight in 1987, and seven in 1988 (in this last year, the perpetrator on six of the occasions was the same man).

In summary, although the records do not indicate a turn towards violent crime in Paradise, there has been a sharp increase in vandalism, alcohol-related charges, and domestic disputes. Whether the first can be laid at the feet of the offspring of the newcomers is unclear in the absence of statistics differentiating them from the natives. A similar degree of ambiguity concerns the apparent increase in alcohol-related offences and domestic disputes, because the police in recent years may simply have been more prepared to level charges than previously.

The streets of Paradise, it would seem, are still relatively safe, despite some claims and fears to the contrary, but the same thing apparently cannot be said about a larger town nearby, which has also been inundated with newcomers. The deputy chief in this other town expressed concern about the dramatic rise in crime, which he placed squarely on the shoulders of the newcomers: 'We're just about double the average rate. There's a lot of violent crime.' He produced a document, prepared by his department, which indicated that crimes of violence in the town rose by 22.4 per cent annually from 1985 to 1989. Indeed, the document revealed that the town has the third highest crime rate for its population (about eighteen thousand) in all of Canada. On the bright side, the police department's clearance rate of crimes of violence, despite being understaffed, was higher than the national average. It was evident, however, stated the authors of the document, that there was an urgent need to hire additional officers.

Yet there was a peculiar thing about the crime rate in this town. When it was compared to twenty-one other Ontario communities of similar size, rather than to the communities that had been arbitrarily selected by the Police Department, it was just about average, both for crimes against property and crimes of violence. One possible explanation is that an innocent mistake had been made by individuals unversed in statistical analysis and census material. Another possibility, I suppose, is that the misleading statistics were intentional, part of a ploy to justify increased resources and manpower. If it was indeed a ploy, it was an effective one, because citizens of the town were predisposed, with strangers all around them, to believe that danger stalked the streets.[4]

Gender Relations

Paradise in the 1950s was a man's world. Is that still the case today? According to Dasgupta (1988:141), relationships between husband and wife on Canadian farms have become more democratic in recent years. The man is no longer the sole figure of authority, and the woman, liberated by modern household technology, has thrown herself into new roles, including running the farm while her spouse holds down an outside job. Evidence of changed attitudes towards gender relations in Paradise were less clear cut, especially among the elderly, including women. One person thought that it was wrong for a wife to earn more money than her husband. She also could not understand why some women wanted to keep their maiden names after marriage. In her own life, she stated, her husband came first, her children second. Pointing to the high divorce rate, which she linked to the trend for both spouses to work outside the home, she remarked: 'They're both so thundering independent. Each have their own salaries. If she don't like her situation, she can just walk out.' Another elderly woman, referring to media reports of increased violence towards women, contended that women themselves were responsible, because they were taking jobs away from men, and were insisting on becoming engineers rather than nurses.

Gender equality, at the level of both attitudes and behaviour, it might be assumed, would be much more prevalent among the newcomers. Certainly some of the evidence pointed in that direction. For example, when I interviewed both spouses together in native families, especially if they were elderly, it was usually the man who did the talking, sometimes even answering for the woman when a question was directed at her. But when both husband and wife among the new-comers were present during an interview, more often than not the dominant partner was the woman. Nevertheless, it must be remembered that in the majority of newcomer families, one of the motives for moving to the countryside was to allow the mother to remain at home with the children. In this respect, the newcomers constituted a conservative force in rural society.

This last statement must be qualified. Some of these women who opted for the role of mother rather than breadwinner were assertive and liberated, especially the well-educated among them. In their cases, the decision to remain at home seemed to be based on philosophical considerations regarding child-rearing, rather than on role stereotypes. One such woman had been brought up in Toronto in a traditional household. Her father, she angrily revealed, had treated her mother like a hunk of dung. He would flop himself into a chair on return from work and yell to his wife for a beer, which she would bring on the run. Every now and then he would give her a black eye. What drove the daughter mad was her mother's attitude: she deserved the beating, she would say.

The daughter came to Paradise with a keen sensitivity towards gender relations, picked up in her home and later at university. What she encountered shocked her. Young women, she claimed, still accepted traditional roles. They dressed in 'frilly things,' and had no ambition other than to become secretaries and housewives. This woman's experiences with local men reinforced her judgment that gender relations in the area were 'prehistoric.' What she found particularly annoying was the refusal of some men to deal with her in business matters. She and her husband had established a small enterprise near the community. On one occasion when her husband was away, a sixty-year-old employee abruptly quit, largely, the woman thought, because he was simply unable to cope with a female boss, even temporarily. Her experiences when renovating her house were similar. Her husband, she said, was absolutely hopeless when it came to carpentry or the building trades, whereas she enjoyed that type of activity. Yet the local tradesmen who had been hired to undertake renovations insisted on dealing with her husband, no matter how insignificant the issue.

This woman's experiences and opinions notwithstanding, there have indeed been some significant changes involving gender in Paradise. On the positive side, women have begun to occupy high-profile public positions previously reserved for men. On the negative side, a new role has become institutionalized: that of the single mother. To elaborate, from 1941 to 1947 the village clerk had been a woman, and from 1966 to 1969 one of the members of the council was a woman. These were exceptions. All other clerks and councillors up to that point in the community's history had been men. By the late 1980s, however, not only was the clerk-treasurer a woman (and not simply because of wartime scarcity of qualified men), but in addition the office of the mayor was occupied by a woman. How did the citizens of Paradise react to a female leader? One man, who confessed great concern about 'political women,' remarked: 'I can see a drift to women trying to take over.' When I asked another man what he thought about a female mayor, he replied: 'That end don't bother me none.' This was the more typical reaction among men, and in fact it was other women who tended to make the least flattering remarks about the mayor. The clerk-treasurer, with the lower profile, was not subjected to as much criticism, although numerous people described her as 'a nice little girl.' Once again such back-handed compliments were made more often by women than men. As for the mayor's own views about her high-profile position, she remarked: 'I had to ask, were they ready for a woman as mayor? I had to tread lightly, because this has been a man's world.' Significantly, she added: 'I felt I had to go in as one of the boys.'

At the other end of the social scale are the single mothers on welfare: one example concerns a woman in her early thirties who looked ten years older. Raised near Paradise, she had never married, and lived with her two young children in a broken-down apartment in one of the old houses in the town. Having left school in grade ten, she worked for a while in a factory, but quit when her second child was born. She said she was unable to take a job now because she can't afford a baby-sitter. The hallway to her apartment was filled with junk, and one had to pass through the bathroom and a makeshift entrance in order to reach the living-room. She had taken in a boarder to supplement welfare payments, but he lost his job and was unable to pay the rent. The women lived an essentially isolated life. None of her relatives remained in the area. The neighbours on one side refused to speak to her; those on the other side were commuters and she had never met them. She had been raised in the United Church, but no longer attended.

This woman's prospects certainly seemed dismal, but what was impressive about her was her self-reliance: 'I can eat leeks out of the

bush, and fiddleheads. I do a lot of preserving myself. And baking.'
She said that she lived for her children, and thought they were happy.
'For eleven years,' she remarked, 'I've been dying to get off mother's
allowance.' She talked about the possibility of finishing high school
and getting a decent job, but didn't know how she could manage it.

Some people in similar circumstances, however, have shown that it
was not impossible to climb out of the ghetto, such as a woman who
had been kicked out of her parent's home when she was twelve years
old. She made her way to Toronto, lived off the streets, and became
pregnant at the age of fifteen. For an entire summer, when her daughter was two years old, she slept in the back seat of a car. Gradually she
pulled her life together. She returned to high school, fought against
the attempts of some teachers to keep her in the general program of
studies, and excelled. To help out financially, she took in boarders in
her rented apartment. Her sights were set on university, and she was
confident that she would make it.

Even back in the 1950s there had been single mothers with a house-
ful of children, but those situations were regarded as temporary break-
downs within the normal social order. What must be appreciated is
that the role of the single mother living on the edge of poverty with
two or three children is no longer an exception. To the contrary, it
has become as much a part of the small town as the roles of teacher,
merchant, and minister, and it is a product of the same dynamics that
have put a woman in the office of the mayor. In a pattern remarkably
similar to the history of racism in North America (see Piven and
Cloward 1979:184), as new opportunities for women have emerged,
they have been accompanied by new forms of suppression.

Incest

A repeated complaint among the newcomers was that they could never
say anything negative about one native to another because they were
all related. The natives themselves usually operated with the same
assumption, engaging in subtle inquiries to make sure that the person
to whom they were speaking was not a relative of the person whose
character they were about to attack. Sometimes the complaints of the
newcomers went a step further: the charge that incest was widespread
in Paradise. As one woman stated, 'The mentality of the people. I was
shocked. There's a lot of people here that are backward, stupid. I

understand there's a lot of inter-marriage.' Ironically, this middle-class woman said she doesn't read a newspaper; instead, she gets the news from her husband, who reads a city daily and tells her what's going on in the world. A man who had moved to Paradise about ten years ago claimed that the suicide rate in the area was exceptionally high, and thought it was caused by inbreeding. Referring to the many poor people in the area, another newcomer, a former teacher, remarked: 'A lot of people put it down to inbreeding.' She agreed.

I learned about five cases of incest among natives in Paradise. Two of them involved father and daughter, two others close relatives, and the fifth mother and son. I only learned about one case of incest among newcomers. The victim, now a woman in her sixties, stated: 'My brother raped me when I was fourteen. I never told my mother about my brother. He always offered me money. I'd say no, no, no.' This woman had also been attacked by a stranger when she was sixteen years old. She fought back and managed to escape. Until this day, she revealed, she can still remember the shiny buttons on the man's coat.

Whether incest was as widespread as newcomers believed is difficult to know, but I do have two other sources of information. A Protestant minister who had served the area for several years stated that among distraught elderly women who came to him for comfort and guidance, the root problem for a high proportion of them was the same: either they had been victims of physical abuse as children, or they had been victims of incest. What was most remarkable, the minister commented, was that the memories of such physical abuse and incest remained alive in the minds of these women sixty and seventy years later, to the extent of reducing their capacity to cope.

The other source of information is a facility for the victims of family violence in the county. According to the director of the facility, a study of all the women who had been admitted to the shelter in 1989 – about one hundred of them – revealed that almost half had reportedly been sexually assaulted at some point in their lives by family members. As the director pointed out, this estimate of the range of incest in the county is flawed by virtue of the fact that women from the rural areas do not seek shelter and assistance in the facility, nor do women from the higher classes who live in the towns and villages.

In summary, it seems reasonable to assume that incestuous relations have existed and continue to do so in the area. However, comments suggesting that incest is at the root of poverty and low levels of intelligence are nonsensical. The newcomers who make these charges, like most people unversed in modern genetics, assign more explanatory weight to incest than it can carry.

Hillbilly Ontario

Just as some newcomers regarded Paradise as a backward little community, characterized by obsolete male-female relationships and widespread incest, so some Paradise natives held similar attitudes towards an impoverished rural area nearby. One man stated: 'It's what I call hillbilly Ontario.' He described the residents as 'hard-drinking, greasy, dirty people,' and claimed that whenever you see a person dressed in filthy clothes in Paradise, you can be certain the person is from 'the hillbilly triangle.' It is common knowledge, remarked a businessman, that the people who live there couldn't be trusted. Never, he added, would he accept a cheque from one of them. 'The number of morons,' commented another person, 'is staggering.' Almost everyone in that area, he claimed, is inter-bred.

A professional man with some training in social work, whose business took him regularly into 'hillbilly country,' agreed that incest there was widespread: 'You can see it in the slow mental capacity of some people.' He also thought there was a great deal of alcohol abuse: 'You buy booze before you buy groceries.' This man's views on gender relations in the area were particularly interesting. 'There's those families,' he stated, 'where it's basically matriarchal. The women rule the roost. But in what we'd call the troubled situations, the men are the bullies.' Elaborating, he explained that wherever the women are strong and in control of the household, the families are in better shape. That happens, he added, only in the middle-class families, or higher. At this class level there is a large gap between the public and private domains in terms of who is in control in families. In public the men are boss, but behind closed doors it is the women who rule the roost. In the lower-class families, the women make little overt effort to control the household, either in public or in private. If they did, the man said, they would quickly get slapped around. Yet he added: 'Even in the broken homes, it's still the women who keep things going. The men are drunk. It's the women who get the kids to school.' As he concluded, 'There's almost like a male rage. Men out of control. Women just to be taken. To me, there's a strong spiritual obsession, or possession, coming from Satan.'

Occasionally newcomers held similar attitudes about the people in the hillbilly triangle. For example, a divorced woman, without children, who moved into that region a couple of years ago recounted how her attitudes underwent a 180-degree turn. When she first moved up from Toronto, people warned her not to walk down a particular street because a dangerous individual lived there. She just laughed. She was also cautioned to be careful when she jogged at night. Her reaction was to dismiss such warnings as ridiculous. After all, she had coped nicely with the city environment, where one did have to be alert, and could not believe that the little village where she now resided posed any threat. As the months went by she began to revise her opinion. Referring to some of her experiences with men, she commented: 'In this area, people don't get the message – hands off.' What really frightened her, she stated, was that the local men didn't adhere to the conventional rules of conduct. In fact, she said, there didn't seem to be any rules. Although she continued to jog, she no longer thought that rural Ontario was innocent and safe: 'I've never faced a fear or never truly worried for my safety as I have up here.'

What are we to make of all this? I have no doubt that hillbilly Ontario does contain its share of hard-drinking men, battered women, and incest. However, a couple of qualifications are in order. First, the foregoing description of the area would be unrecognizable to the vast majority of people living there, who hold down jobs and raise families just as people do in Paradise. Secondly, the village down the road is almost never as pleasant or safe as the one we live in, nor is the town or the city. The human propensity for parochialism, ethnocentrism, and xenophobia dictates that judgment. Thirdly, the rules by which people live in the hillbilly triangle may not be identical to those in Paradise in some minor way, reflecting its more agrarian and economically deprived setting, but they still constitute rules. To argue otherwise is implausible: all social interaction by definition is rule-directed. Finally, xenophobia is not a one-way street. Put otherwise, it is not only the natives of small communities like Paradise who tremble in the presence of strangers. The same reaction can overcome city people to whom rural Ontario may resemble a foreign country.

In conclusion, since a heavy charge has been laid at the feet of men in Paradise and the surrounding region, perhaps it should be pointed out that the perpetrators of violence are not always male. One young woman, a newcomer, remarked: 'By the time I was twelve, my mother had broken every bone in my body. I'd come home from school every day and I'd get a beating.' One of her younger sisters used to covertly clean her room, hoping that her mother wouldn't find another excuse to beat her older sister. The latter claimed that on one occasion her mother tried to kill her by inserting an overdose of sleeping pills into her food. She recovered in a hospital to find that her mother had accused her of attempting to commit suicide. Another woman, also a newcomer, stated: 'I've had a very hard life. My mother, she was a very cruel mother. She threw me out of the house. I was only twelve. She wanted me to die. She used to beat me and beat me. She was a very cruel mother to me. I hated her.' This unfortunate woman said that her father would warn his wife that if she wasn't careful she was going to kill her daughter. The woman's answer: her daughter deserved to die.

Religion

In the 1950s religion was a central institution in the community, closely linked to the stratification system, with almost everyone being at least nominal members of the Anglican Church or the United Church. By the 1980s the religious landscape was hardly recognizable. A wide variety of other religious organizations had been established, but overall attendance had dropped to about one-quarter of the population, including both natives and newcomers. At the same time the diffuse influence of religion, filtering into other institutions such as politics, education, and economic life, had dried up. In fact, to the extent that religion continued to have an impact on the community, it had become as much a source of controversy as cohesion.

The Anglican and United churches, of course, remain in the community. Their greatly reduced congregations prompted one elderly woman to remark: 'I wouldn't get along out there today. Maybe I'm too straight-laced. Religion is gone. I think you've got to have a belief – some belief that you can tell your troubles to.' The Gospel Workers, who were present in the community in the 1950s, have become the Nazarene Church, while the small sect that existed then called C.e. has disappeared. Taking its place are a number of new organizations, most of them fundamentalist in orientation, including evangelicals and Pentecostals: Bethel Chapel, founded in 1918 in a nearby village and established in Paradise in 1960, with about eighty members; the Alliance Church, with about fifty members, which separated from the

Nazarenes; Jehovah Witnesses, with approximately sixty-five adult members; Christadelphians, with about fifty-five baptized members and thirty-five unbaptized children, who used to meet in the Orange Hall in town, but recently built their own church in the countryside. Also in the countryside are a group of Buddhists with an old farmhouse as their meeting place, and two congregations of black people, although the church in which one of the congregations worshipped recently burnt down.

In addition, there were many newcomers in Paradise who had to travel elsewhere to worship: Catholics, Presbyterians, Christian Reformeds, Muslims, Hindus, and Sikhs. There also were a couple of 'no-name' churches in the community. One of these did not have a church building. Members met in each other's houses, and occasionally in rented premises. An elderly couple who belonged to this faith explained that it had no name on theological grounds. They simply worshipped the true God, and no further description was necessary. This woman and man had been raised on farms near Paradise, where their parents had embraced the same faith, apparently established in farm country around the turn of the century. Because of their faith, this elderly couple had lived isolated lives on the farm: 'We didn't visit. We didn't dance.' They didn't play cards either, which brought many farm families together. There is nothing wrong with cards per se, they remarked, but card-playing leads to smoking, drinking and gambling. They sold their farm about a dozen years ago and moved into Paradise, but not with much enthusiasm. As the woman stated, 'I know when I first came in, I just hated to wash the windows or cut the grass, because everybody could see you.' Her husband added: 'We're quite content in town now. Not when we first came here, I can tell you. I missed those little calves.' The move to town had not changed their policy on interacting with the neighbours. They said they didn't know any more people in town now than when they moved in a dozen years ago.

The second 'no-name' church was founded by an immigrant from Europe who was strongly opposed to organized religion. In her judgment, people who attend the historic churches are not true Christians. The power of God, she glowed, is everywhere: God had cured her of cancer, and God had sent AIDS to punish those who sin. This woman ran a drop-in centre for people with alcohol and drug problems; indeed, she declared, the messier a person's life, the more the person is welcome: God exists for such people. Religious services were held, not always regularly, in the same spacious room that served as a drop-in centre. There was a wide variety of opinion about this woman. One elderly couple stated they were indebted to her for leading them to God. A young couple respected the woman, but said that when she gets on the subject of religion she drives them mad. The gossip was that she slept with the men who frequented the drop-in centre. One prominent citizen who believed this gossip revealed that when he visited her on a business matter one day, he thought she was going to rape him (perhaps a case of wishful thinking). Nobody with whom I discussed this matter had any evidence to support the gossip, and it may merely have been based on the fact that sexual matters were often the subject of conversation with the woman. She talked repeatedly about whores and whoredom, and how God's wrath would descend upon them. Intoxicated with her own peculiar brand of Christianity, this woman, to use an expression, was a godsend for the disciples of a lesser deity: Freud.

The diminished impact of religion in Paradise had a number of causes. One concerns a secularizing trend in Canadian society in general. As Bibby (1987:81) has indicated, Canadians no longer attend the mainline churches on a regular basis, and there has been a shift from religious commitment to the selective consumption of religion, such as for weddings and funerals. The new evangelical and fundamentalist congregations also have significantly altered the impact of religion on other institutions. Unlike the Anglican and United churches, they attempt to insulate themselves from the political and social life of the community; in other words, they have been instrumental in blocking the pipeline between religion and stratification that flowed smoothly during the 1950s.

Another factor has been the changing role of the religious leader. Some people remarked that the quality of ministers today seems to be lower compared with the past, reflected in the fact that they no longer seem actively to guide the town's morality in everyday affairs. In view of the several religious organizations now in Paradise, that is hardly surprising: no single religious leader can presume to represent the entire community, or even a significant part of it. Others complained that the ministers no longer visit people in their homes; just as in the case of the medical practitioner, house calls are becoming a thing of the past. But that is partly because many people do not wish the minister's influence to extend beyond the doors of the church, at least in the mainstream denominations. What has happened, in fact, as a result of the general process of secularization, is that the role of the minister has become more focused and specific, not only in the sense of ceasing to spill over into other institutions, but also in the sense of interaction with the congregation. At the same time, ministers today are allowed an incipient private personality, following the footsteps taken by the contemporary school teacher a generation ago.

A concrete example of the minister's transformed relationship with the community concerns housing. A major problem in the past, explained one minister, was that people in his profession were provided with parish houses, which meant that they reached old age without any financial assets. He referred to several ministers who had worked into their eighties, not because they wanted to, but because they had no choice: they were broke. In his own case, he could see the handwriting on the wall a few years ago. He bought a house, which has since increased in value, and now possesses financial security for his old age. Another minister who faced the same problem had worked out the following solution: he continued to live in the rectory, but was paid an extra thousand dollars a year, to be placed in an RRSP, which would serve as a down payment on his own house in the future.

One minister found that having his own house did not endear himself to everyone. A member of his congregation donated land on which he built a beautiful new home. Rumour had it that the house too was a gift, but he denied it: 'I'm mortgaged to the hilt, far more than any pastor should be mortgaged. But it's my retirement investment.' Shortly after the building was completed, he held open house, but half-regretted doing so: the gossip then centred on the opulent furniture. As the minister observed, people think there's something wrong about a person in his position living in luxury: 'I think the bottom line is the house is too big. Too nice and too big.'

An issue specific to the United Church was the controversy over homosexuality. According to Motz (1990), fifty-five congregations left the United Church in 1989 alone to protest against the ordination of gay pastors. The issue smoldered under the surface in Paradise, but was contained by the minister. In two communities nearby, however, the controversy had burst into the open, dividing the one congregation, and almost terminating the other. In the latter situation, the minister, a gentle and compassionate man, decided his beliefs did not allow him to support gay ministers. He denied that he was a homophile, pointing out that he had regularly visited a young gay man who had AIDS. He added that he knew first-hand about homosexuality among his own relatives. On the verge of being fired from his ministry, he resigned, and founded his own evangelical church. About 80 per cent of his former flock followed him, as did the accusation that he had destroyed the town's United Church.

The Anglican Church in Paradise has not had to grapple with the issue of homosexuality, but it has been racked by internal dissent even more than the United Church. The main problem has been the unpopularity of the ministers. While the man in charge in 1990 was highly respected, and indeed sometimes was compared favourably to the outstanding Anglican minister in the 1950s, his three predecessors had been considerably less popular. As a member of the United Church remarked, 'They got three ministers who were more priestly than the Catholics. That just didn't go over.' One of these men, who had entered the profession late in life, apparently was curt and authoritarian, and alienated his flock by changing the hymn book. An elderly couple who stopped attending church complained that 'everything seems to be High Anglican now.'

Things reached a boiling point, and influential members of the Anglican Church decided the minister had to go. As one man, a minister himself, commented, 'If you're not wanted there's some pretty ugly things done to get you out.' In this case, he said, the man in question was told bluntly: 'We're going to starve you out.' Shortly thereafter he was gone. The minister before him, equally unpopular, was also escorted to the edge of town and sent on his way. In his case, ugly rumours had circulated about the behaviour of his wife. The man who took over the Anglican Church in the late 1980s, perfectly aware of the fates of his predecessors, cautioned his wife not to linger over a coffee with men after finishing work, in case gossip drove them out as well. He also attempted to lure back people who had stopped attending church, and to give them a renewed sense of power and control which his predecessor had destroyed. Despite the minister's personal popularity, the church remained half-empty, and severe strains divided those who did attend regularly. One of the most influential families in the congregation was regarded as 'uppity' and enjoyed little respect in the community. Some people snubbed each other even when gathered informally in the basement for coffee.

The Anglicans, it must be stressed, didn't have a monopoly on unpopular ministers, although they had more than their share. The minister in one of the evangelical churches was recently eased out of the pulpit, and not everyone in the United Church was enthusiastic about its leader. One elderly woman commented: 'I think he's a good man. I think, but I'm not sure.' More cutting was another person's evaluation: 'He's a lame duck, a nonentity. He's just coasting until he retires.' Perhaps the most controversial religious figure of all was a retired United Church minister, born on a nearby farm, who continued to live in the town. As one woman commented, 'He's a please everyone man. He likes to socialize and party.' Some people described him as cocky and money-hungry, and another minister remarked sadly: 'He doesn't know Jesus.'

The man himself certainly gave the impression of being somewhat out of the ordinary, if not Elmer Gantry reincarnated. At one point he remarked: 'I've got nothing against people praying.' He just didn't like to see them flaunting their faith in public. What became clear was that the opposition to this man was based primarily on his unconventionality. All his life, he said, he had fought against the stereotype of the minister. He did not attempt to deny that he enjoyed a good time, but added that not everyone realized that he had often been more effective sitting in a tavern than preaching in the pulpit. Although many Paradise residents were critical of the former minister, his admirers were just as numerous. He had a tremendous capacity to relate to people, partly, one man thought, because his weaknesses made him more human. He was also generous of his time when it came to community causes, compassionate towards those in need, and when he had been an active minister he had drawn a full congregation. Admired by some, detested by others, he aptly summed up his own life: 'I cut my own furrow. I'm unique.'

Stratification

Who would have anticipated a generation ago that the elite would become an endangered species? The facts, nevertheless, are clear: by the 1980s not a single family that was counted among the elite in the past enjoys that reputation today. In two cases, the old upper-class families were childless; the family names just died away. In two other cases, merchants failed to innovate as social change swept across the community; they stuck with the old ways, and as a result outsiders saw the opening and slipped in to establish the wave of the future: the big supermarkets. Another highly successful family business fell apart because the offspring were indolent and alcoholic; within a few years of their father's death, the family fortune was depleted. In yet other cases, elite families relocated in different communities; sometimes this was as a result of a calamity, such as disastrous investments or a fire that destroyed business premises; in one case, the family business had simply outgrown Paradise, although a branch of it continued to operate there. I do not mean to imply that no semblance of the old elite remains in the community. About six to eight families continue to be recognized by Paradise natives as special, and regard themselves in that light. Most of the members of these families are elderly (in almost every case, their children have moved to other towns and cities). They possess only modest wealth by today's standards, and their influence on the political and social life of the community is minimal. These people constitute the fallen aristocracy, but with one important qualification. The elite status of most of them in the past was borderline. With the disappearance of the powerful families that had been ranked above them, a vacuum was created which they quickly filled.

In the past, residents of Paradise had little difficulty identifying the extremes of the stratification system – the rich and the poor – but found the middle more amorphous. Today it is exactly the opposite. They readily recognize the middle class, but are vague about the extremes. Their explanation is that the stratification system has become much more homogeneous, with the vast majority of people now occupying the middle ground. The following comment was typical: 'I don't think there are as many classes now as there were thirty years ago.' As another man put it, 'You don't see your extreme poor and your extreme wealthy like we had. I think maybe the government had a lot to do with that. Welfare and that.'

In an attempt to verify these comments, I compared the class positions of the 122 natives today with their class positions (or those of their parents) in the 1950s. As table 9 indicates, from the middle class upwards there has been a general increase in the proportion of people, while below the middle class there has been a general decrease. The most remarkable changes concern the lower-middle and middle classes. Whereas the majority of people in the past fell into the lower-middle class, today these same people are apparently primarily middle class. When added to this is the fact that 50 per cent of the newcomers (see table 8 in chapter 5) also are middle class,[5] the remarks made by Paradise people to the effect that the stratification system has become more homogeneous and that most residents now occupy the broad middle class appear credible.

TABLE 9
Comparison of Class Positions of 122 Natives in Past and Present

	Past	Present
Upper	3 (2.5%)	8 (6.5%)
Lower upper	8 (6.7%)	20 (16.3%)
Middle	36 (30.2%)	62 (50.8%)
Lower middle	52 (43.6%)	24 (19.6%)
Lower	20 (16.8%)	8 (6.5%)
Unknown	3 –	– –
Total	122 (99.8%)	122 (99.7%)

Notes:
1 Percentages are calculated in terms of known cases.
2 These estimates were derived from the subjective rankings provided by the 122 individuals themselves, supplemented by what information I possessed about their past and present family reputations, plus objective indices such as their past and present occupations.

A few sceptical observations, however, are in order. First, part of the ideology of Canadian society (like American society) is that it is classless; usually this translates into a tendency for people to rank themselves in the middle class, regardless of objective facts such as education and income, or regardless of the contradiction with the notion of a society without classes. Second, it was not only the middle class that had grown in size, but also the lower-upper and upper classes. As for the lower class, 6.5 per cent of the natives still fell into this category, and the figure for the newcomers was 11 per cent. It should also be recalled that each of the new subdivisions had its own dominant class character, ranging from the upper class to the lower-middle class. Relevant as well is the fact that during Christmas of 1989, thirty-three hampers of food were distributed to destitute families.

The implication is that the class system in Paradise remains somewhat less than homogeneous. What has contributed to the false impression to the contrary has been the tendency for both poverty and wealth to become less visible. The shacks where the lower-class residents used to live are gone. Today's poor are tucked away in apartments and rooming houses. Most of them, as I have indicated in previous chapters, are young newcomers, both women and men. The native poor also include both sexes, but they do not fall into any specific age category, which might seem surprising, given the high proportion of elderly people among them. Yet as one welfare specialist, intimately acquainted with the community, explained, when a person became elderly in earlier times, he or she also became poverty-stricken; but recently the elderly are probably more financially secure than at any previous period in their lives. This is especially true for those people who sold their farms at the peak of the market. But it also is the case more generally due to social programs (pensions, OHIP, subsidized housing for seniors). There also is the factor of personal habit. Most of these elderly people have scrimped all their lives, and they continue to do so in retirement, so that a little money goes a long way.

One can, of course, still find impoverished elderly people in Paradise, such as one woman who roots through garbage containers for food. As for the younger natives, it is somewhat inaccurate to describe most of them as impoverished. They usually enjoy the invisible economic support of the extended family to help them through rough patches, such as unemployment. But in one important respect their lives differ from their parents. In the past, most lower-class people had their own homes. One man related how his parents had helped him out financially to get his first house, with his brothers contributing their labour. What saddened him was that it was beyond his capacity, in view of house prices today, to do the same for his own son. Like so many of the young newcomers, some young natives also seemed destined for a future spent in apartments, or worse: according to one housing specialist for the area, more and more poor people will simply move into trailer parks, and consider themselves fortunate.

Just as poverty has become less visible in the community, the same is true for wealth. As one man stated, 'When you're talking about wealth, well back then everybody knew for sure who was wealthy. Now you don't.' You can go to a party, another man pointed out, and the most sloppily-dressed person could be the richest. Nor, he added, could you draw any firm conclusions on the basis of residence. Some of the people in the beautiful new houses, he thought, hadn't got two cents to rub together; they were mortgaged to the hilt, holding on in the hope of making a killing when (and if) the market took off. According to an individual who claimed that poor people like himself in the past were totally dominated by the upper class: 'We're still not on the flat. We know who is rich, but they don't push it. They don't say, hey, I'm rich.' Nowhere was the reduced visibility of the wealthy more apparent than in relation to local politics. As one man put it, 'To have the power used to be very important for people with position. I don't think it is any more.' Several reasons were offered to explain why wealthy residents no longer run for council, including a lack of time and a lack of responsibility. According to one retired businessman, 'People with money today have better things to do with their time, such as making more money.'

There was also an important change in the criteria people used to rank each other, and to explain it I shall briefly draw on Weber's distinction between class and status. To comprehend Paradise's stratification system in the 1950s, both class as an objective measure of one's life chances determined by the market situation, and status as a measure of prestige and esteem, had to be entertained. Paradise people themselves placed a greater weight on status in those days, and much the same is true today in relation to the manner in which natives rank each other. Thus, a woman or man from the lower class who has come into some money still may find the middle class out of reach. Similarly, some families continue to enjoy high status despite having slipped in wealth. Subtle differences in status continue to be evoked by people who occupy the same class position. In economic terms, for example, there may be little to distinguish two upper-class individuals, yet one of them may claim to possess greater 'honour' on the basis of behaviour or family pedigree. Similarly, among the poorest people from the past there was constant jockeying for superiority. One woman, born on the street by the dump, confided smugly that her family had always been regarded as snooty by the neighbours. This same woman was almost beside herself with rage after being snubbed by an acquaintance, also from a poor family, who had returned for a visit to the community.

When the natives rank the newcomers, the criteria change: class, conceived in terms of the market situation, rather than status takes priority. This is essentially because the newcomers are an unknown quantity to most of the natives.[6] To evaluate a person's status, or, in Newby's terms (1977), to discern one's interactional as opposed to attributional status, requires subtle personal knowledge. Lacking such knowledge, the natives fall back on cruder criteria such as type of residence, automobile, and occupation, reflecting levels of economic power. When asked to rank the newcomers, the natives reacted in three ways. One was simply to express ignorance. The second was to assume they were mostly middle class; even many of those who said they lacked knowledge added that they thought the newcomers might be middle class. The third, which blurred the distinction between class and status, was to describe the newcomers as the dregs of the barrel. A typical comment was as follows: 'You got a low class of people. You could really notice it.' The man who spoke these words was a member of the fallen aristocracy, but such negative comments were equally prevalent among lower-class natives. As a woman who had complained bitterly about the unfair treatment suffered by her family at the hands of the former elite remarked, 'One can see more scum in town now.'

As for the newcomers, they placed the emphasis on class rather than status, both when evaluating themselves and the natives. When asked to rank fellow newcomers, sometimes they confessed ignorance; if they did venture an opinion, it usually was to label them middle class, conceived as a category of people with similar life chances and relations to the market. When asked to rank the natives, the most prevalent reaction was to say they just did not know. There were, however, two other reactions. One was to claim that all the natives fell into the lower-middle or lower classes, and again economic criteria rather than 'honour' prevailed. As one person asked rhetorically; 'Is there a true middle class here? You know, in terms of the middle class in the city?' Even those newcomers who had had a glimpse into the indigenous ranking system, where status thrived, often took a similar position. For example, a young couple who had become friends with an elderly woman who lived next door thought it was hilarious that she put on airs and presented herself as aristocratic. As they chuckled, her furniture looked like it came out of the Salvation Army (in actuality, the elderly woman's furniture would have caused an antique dealer to swoon). Their criteria were class-based in Weber's sense: occupation, education, and especially income, and the life chances that these reflected. The other reaction, even less generous, was a carbon copy of what some natives said about newcomers, even to the extent of once again blurring the distinction between class and status: they are low-class scum. In one person's words: 'I hate to use the term, but we've got white trash here. I sometimes think I've moved to the Ozarks. You'd swear they've been interbreeding.'

Returning now to class in the descriptive sense (corresponding to Krauss's stratum), I draw the obvious conclusion: Paradise in the 1980s was obviously not the same community as in the 1950s. Whether or not the changes were perceived as good or bad depended partly on a person's class position. Those in the aristocracy thought the community had disintegrated, and bitterly complained that they no longer received the recognition due to them. The newcomers were generally ignorant about their past accomplishments and family heritage. Even those who were perfectly aware of their stature – other natives in the classes below them – no longer automatically treated them with respect and deference. One member of the old elite, for example, met a young man in an apartment hallway, who passed by with only a brief greeting. She was furious: 'I felt like telling him that his grandmother used to clean my mother's house.'

People in the lower class also lamented the rampant changes that had fragmented the cohesion of the community. Referring fondly to the past, one man mused about how wonderful it had been when he had known everyone in the village: 'We had something there, aye?' Unlike the aristocracy, however, lower-class natives also saw some sun shining through the clouds. Their perspective can be summed up as follows: fragmentation equals ambiguity equals opportunity. What they meant was that with the disintegration of the sense of belonging went the normative rules and gossip that had kept them in their place. As one, man said about the past, 'People in my class would sit back and say, hey, we don't like it. But we wouldn't do anything. But now,' he added, 'people speak right up.'

According to Newby (1977:335), after middle-class newcomers invaded the East Anglian countryside in England, the previous class antagonisms between the ruling class (the squires) and the working class broke down, as they joined arms to oppose the invaders. Despite the wide gulf between natives and newcomers in Paradise, there has been very little evidence of a similar pact between the upper- and lower-class natives. The closest to it has been the emergence of a somewhat expanded upper class, as people formerly in the lower-upper and middle classes, especially among the elderly, have gathered together socially to play cards and take refreshments. Paradise people continue to identify with their class positions in the past, especially at the polar ends. Lower-class natives, rather than linking arms with those in the upper classes, have tended to derive pleasure from the discomfort of the old elite, brought on by the rampant changes in the community. But such class antagonism has taken an individualistic rather than collective form. In other words, social interaction is still not predicated on the basis of class consciousness. Even at the upper end of the scale, the relationships between the old elite and the new elite (the wealthy newcomers, mostly businessmen) are cordial rather than close, partly because they do not recognize the same criteria for success. As for lower-class natives, they have not embraced the newcomer poor as brothers and sisters struggling within the grips of capitalism, which indeed would have amounted to an expression of class consciousness and an appreciation of Marxian laws of history, linked to class interests. To the contrary, their more usual reaction has been to dismiss these newcomers as vermin that threaten the health of the community.

Politics

Election day in Western democracies, according to Marx, represents an opportunity for people to decide who will oppress them next (see Bottomore 1965:62, Selsam et al. 1970:348). That is an apt description of the Paradise scene where the positions of reeve and councillors, at least until the late 1950s, were monopolized by community elites. In 1959, however, a new era began. A former farmer became reeve, and every occupant of the position since (or the mayor's position after the community's status changed from village to town in 1978) has been modestly educated and drawn from the middle or lower-middle class. In 1970 a well-liked man whose father, trained in the medical field, had had one foot in the aristocracy, became reeve. He himself, however, had not gone beyond secondary school. Over the years he had been a successful farmer, a merchant, and a real estate agent – the occupations of the middle class. On only two other occasions have individuals who might be placed in the aristocracy attempted to reclaim the political leadership of the community. The most dramatic contest occurred in 1982 when a wealthy businessman ran for mayor against the incumbent, 'a good old boy,' who allegedly coveted the job largely because it was a source of income for him.[7] For different reasons the election in 1988 was almost as intriguing; for the first time in the community's history a woman became mayor, defeating a representative of the old guard.

Patricians versus Plebians

The election in 1982 was surrounded by scandal from the outset. The incumbent had been charged with three gun-related offences after confronting his mistress and her new lover, effectively making the point that the liaison did not have his full approval. The mayor, neither well educated nor sophisticated but recognized as a clever politician, had been born on a farm near Paradise, moving into the community in 1952. Over the years he had been a farmer, an employee in a bakery, a salesman for farm produce and for life insurance, and a truck driver. He was elected to council in 1963 and became the community's first mayor in 1978, having served the previous five years as reeve.

The man who opposed him had been born in England. In 1952 he moved to Canada with his family, and in 1968 he settled in Paradise. Trained as an engineer, he soon became a prominent and highly successful businessman, running local enterprises and investing wisely in real estate. Elected reeve in 1980, he became the acting mayor before the 1982 contest when the antics of the incumbent forced him to take a leave of absence. The results of the election seemed to be a foregone conclusion. The mayor's reputation had hit rock bottom. When he called on people at their homes, asking for their support at the polls, doors were slammed in his face. The challenger did not overtly make an issue of his opponent's personal problems, nor was that necessary; the behaviour of the mayor, and the damage that he had done to the town's reputation, was the topic of conversation of the day. Instead, he put himself forward as a competent entrepreneur, a man who understood business and who had the education and sophistication necessary to deal with provincial bureaucrats, precisely the type of person to guide the town through the next period of growth; then he sat back to compose his victory speech. When the results of the election were out, he was in shock: the mayor, although with only a margin of thirty-six votes, had won.

The mayor's re-election was due to three factors. First, there was a sympathy vote. His personal problems had been widely reported, even reaching the Toronto newspapers (one of his political enemies had gleefully contacted the outside media). The feeling among many people was that he had suffered enough. The man helped his own case by making little attempt to defend himself or excuse his actions. Instead he was contrite and apologetic, only asking forgiveness for the one great mistake in his life. Second, there was the insider-outsider dimension. The mayor was a native, a man who understood the people, and in turn was understandable. The challenger was a relative newcomer, not even born in Canada, let alone in rural Ontario. The third factor was most significant of all: social class. Although some people dismissed the mayor as 'a good old boy' and 'a bungling idiot,' what most people appreciated about him was that he was just an ordinary man, a person easy to talk to on the street or to approach in his office with a problem. In sharp contrast, his well-educated and wealthy challenger was considered aloof and aristocratic, obviously an intelligent and competent man, but one who gave the impression of being superior.

Certainly their individual styles and personalities contributed to these impressions. The mayor, a regular in the Legion, was prepared to socialize with all and sundry. Almost every morning he presided over 'the senate,' the tag pinned on a group of influential citizens who met for coffee in a restaurant. As the challenger himself remarked about the mayor, 'He was a better politician. He politicked all year round. I was outspoken. He sat on the fence. He socialized more locally. We socialized with a different group than he did. We socialized with the professional people. Not that I'm a snob.'

Despite this last remark, many people did think that he was a snob, and often attributed it to the fact that he was born in England. As one man stated, 'He was English. He was one of those guys who was friendly around election time, but that was all.' Even some of his supporters agreed that the man thought he was special, but they insisted that he had reason to do so. As one of them pointed out, the man was an exceptionally clever businessman, head and shoulders over most other people in the community. What was perhaps most impressive was the fact that people in the lower classes who got to know him well, despite his reputation as a snob, often became his strongest supporters. For example, a woman who had worked for him in one of his stores pointed out that he had never treated her an inferior; instead, he had been consistently considerate and kind. Another person who had lived in an apartment owned by the man had grown to admire him greatly: 'As a tenant, he could have made me feel inferior, but he didn't. He never belittled me, never looked down on me.' In her judgment, he would have made an outstanding mayor, and what cost him the election was nothing more or less than his ethnic background: 'A lot of people didn't like him. He's English, you know. There's racism everywhere.'

Despite the views expressed by Paradise people, the man's ethnic background was only the apparent cause of his failure at the polls; after all, a generation earlier it would have been a liability *not* to be British in origin (the incumbent's background was Scots and German). His failure had a deeper basis: the impression, shared by both his detractors and supporters, that he was a throwback to the old aristocracy. Evoking the memory of the famous mayor in the early 1950s who had ruled the community as his personal fiefdom, one man commented: 'He's that guy all over again. He's just like the old gang.' The challenger himself, who had never met his illustrious predecessor but was quite familiar with his story, confided: 'You talk about that man! Sometimes I think I'm him reincarnated.' On the eve of the election, the coup de grace was unintentionally delivered by the local newspaper, which came out in support of the challenger. The owner of the newspaper, who no longer lived in the community, was himself a member of the old aristocracy, and in the judgment of many people in Paradise the patricians were once again ganging up on them. As a former member of the council observed, people today don't like their leaders to be too intelligent or accomplished. By re-electing the incumbent, he chuckled, they laid that fear to rest.

Business Sense versus Clean Government

The election in 1988 was a replay of the one in 1982 in that it pitted a member of the establishment against an upstart from the lower-middle class who had made a living as a clerk and by doing odd jobs. There were, however, some important differences. The wealthier candidate did represent the old guard. He had been a local business-man most of his life, taking over a store previously run by his father. Yet the business was solid rather than spectacular, and neither he nor his father had ever been counted among the aristocracy. In this election, then, the gap between the class positions of the candidates was not quite as wide. Another difference was that both candidates in 1988 were natives, although the lower-middle-class individual had only taken up residence in the community in 1957.

The most significant difference was that this second person was a woman. Although she had been born on a farm in another part of Ontario, her husband's father had been raised in Paradise, and that is what had brought them to the community back in the 1950s. When they first moved to Paradise, they knew hardship first hand: 'We came here without too many pennies in our pockets.' Her husband, a carpenter, had health problems, and was unable to work regularly, and tragedy struck other members of her family. If these were meant as tests of character, she passed them with flying colours, buckling down and doing whatever was necessary to supplement the family's income:

'I did cleaning. I mowed lawns.' In 1974 she made her move into the limelight, becoming a councillor, then deputy reeve. In 1980, by which time the top position was mayor, she ran unsuccessfully for reeve. Two years later she put her name forward for the same position and won. In 1988, when the man who had unfortunately allowed his jealousy to overcome his better judgment had decided not to contest the top spot again, she made local history.

How did this woman from such a modest background manage to defeat an opponent whose family name prompted respect, and who himself enjoyed the reputation of being an astute and successful businessman? Part of the explanation, no doubt, was what she herself described as her 'people skills' – her capacity to relate to the voters and to make them feel good. The main reason, however, concerned the continued impact of the previous mayor on the town. After being reinstated to office in 1982, he was found guilty in court and sentenced to two months in jail. That was too much for most citizens, who suffered a sense of collective shame about their community. The establishment's candidate ran on a platform of solid business practices. This struck a responsive chord, because many residents held the opinion that the mayor should have a demonstrated capacity to manage the community's finances. But because he was associated with the old guard, he had two strikes against him from the outset. What people wanted more than anything else was to bury the ghost of the previous mayor, to wipe the political slate clean. To do that required a complete change. His opponent, ironically, *because* she was to a large extent unaccomplished, at least in the world of business, was regarded as the safer choice.

Cynicism

The new mayor's victory celebration was hardly over before the criticisms began: 'I think it's the poorest council we've ever had' ... 'The damn place is just drifting. No leadership' ... 'She's a wishy-washy mayor' ... 'She isn't very intelligent' ... 'This council here, well they're like this NDP government. They got in there but they don't know what they're doing'... 'Probably the worst. This council, it's pathetic.'

The remarks about the council often went deeper than the question of competence. There was a general cynicism about politics and the people who run for public office: 'Some of them are sweet talkers. But what do they do? They raise their own wages'... 'If you lie a lot, you're a good politician' ... 'They all take money under the table from the developers' ... 'I don't like chewing anybody's rear, but, like, what decent guy wants the job?'

Numerous citizens complained about the humble origins and modest accomplishments of the council members, and regretted that the council was not composed of successful businessmen. One man remarked that it used to be an honour to serve on council, but now people only did so because of the financial remuneration. Another man thought that a higher quality of people used to be elected when it was ego rather than money that had been the lure. One man remarked: 'We need someone with a little broader vision, a little more business background.' He had the perfect candidate in mind: himself. Actually, both this man and the two businessmen who had run for mayor in the 1982 and 1988 elections were exceptions. Whereas in the past, the expectation was that the leading businessmen would do a stint on council, in recent years the assumption has emerged that a council seat is bad for business. As several people explained, controversy and unpopularity always surround the council and inevitably spill over onto one's business affairs. Of the seven people elected to council in 1988, only two were businessmen. One of them, an insurance agent, was the brunt of constant bickering within the council, and the other, a real estate agent, had apparently decided not to run for re-election partly because of the negative impact on his business. The third councillor was a skilled tradesman, and the fourth a fireman. The mayor, as indicated earlier, had been a clerk. The reeve was a retired Protestant minister, and the deputy reeve (a relative of the reeve) was a former farmer. Three of the seven members of the council were newcomers, but the major division was not between newcomers and natives. Instead, it was between one councillor, a native, who vehemently opposed new housing developments in the town, and argued that all the council's energies should be devoted to attracting industry, and the rest of the council, including the mayor, who were in favour of further population growth, although they hoped that the industrial base would expand as well. From the perspective of the majority of councillors, their maverick colleague was conservative, rude, hotheaded, and naïve. Yet he was the one member of council who was consistently praised by Paradise residents.

It must be added that not everyone held the current council in disdain. One man ventured the opinion that 'there's not a single person on that council who's there to benefit themselves.' I suppose he was in a position to know the score, since he was a member of the council himself. Another man stated: 'The council we have are trying their best.' A third person argued: 'They obviously try. They try *too hard* to please everybody.' These comments, however, expressed the minority opinion. What was striking in Paradise was the deep cynicism about politics, not only on the local scene, but also on the national scene. Politicians, most people thought, are slippery and dishonest, looking for ways to line their own pockets. As one woman on welfare commented about federal MPs in Ottawa, 'I'd like to be at their house when they have a meal. To see what they eat and what they do with the leftovers.' A similar degree of hostility was aimed at the mayor in Paradise, and at most of the other members of the council. Even when citizens attempted to say positive things about the mayor, the words often gave the impression of a put-down. For example, she was described as a person who loved the ceremonial aspects of the job, the implication being that she lacked a capacity to deal with issues of substance. On several occasions people referred to her as 'the perfect transitional mayor.' That is, she was the right person to put some distance between the town and her gun-wielding predecessor, but she didn't have what it took for the long run.

Who Has Power?

During the 1950s the council exercised almost dictatorial powers over the populace. Its greatly reduced influence by the 1980s was neatly captured by one citizen: 'You don't have anybody with the authority to wipe out people's careers any more.' Few individuals were more aware of the council's limited authority than those who had been recently elected. As one councillor complained, he and his colleagues are allowed to issue a by-law controlling dogs, but when it comes to more important matters their hands are tied. Since the formal leaders of the community are no longer drawn from the elite, it might be assumed that an informal power structure composed of economic giants has emerged behind the scenes, and that it is these people who run the town. Yet this is not correct. One person, for example, said he used to know exactly who to approach privately when he needed someone to intercede on his behalf with the council. 'Nowadays,' he commented, 'you can't get things done that way.' In fact, the vast majority of people, when asked who has power today, inside or outside the council, had a uniform response: nobody.

The only exception, according to Paradise residents, concerned an unelected member of staff at the town hall who had lived in the community for three years. It was widely believed that he completely dominated the mayor, most of the councillors, and the clerk-treasurer. The amount of hostility towards him was enormous. As one man commented, 'I think he pulls the strings in council now. There's nobody with the guts to stop him.' An elderly woman seethed: 'He's a terrible man. He's trying to worm his way up the ladder in town hall.' Rumours, most of them ugly, abounded about his romantic relationships and his unauthorized use of public property, such as vehicles. As I indicated earlier, it is always possible to find somebody who despises the town hero or stands up for the town villain, and that was true in this case. One of the man's few supporters described him as the most qualified and effective employee in his job that the community had ever hired, and was worried that the gossip, which he believed was completely baseless, would drive him away. In his view, the man was not liked for four simple reasons: he was a newcomer, he was divorced, his mannerisms were abrupt and undiplomatic, and, perhaps most important of all, his extraordinarily piercing eyes made people uncomfortable. The town employee himself candidly admitted: 'I'm aggressive. I lobby inside closed doors. I'll talk to the councillors privately, and I'll get support that way.' But he insisted that he was only trying to do his job the best way he could. This man certainly had the ears of the members of council, but it would be stretching the point to describe him as a powerful figure behind the scenes. To the contrary, he was a highly visible cog in the wheels of the public administration.

If power was not in the hands of the council or an informal collection of economic notables behind the scenes, who held it? The answer, according to some astute residents, was the provincial politicians and bureaucrats. 'Queen's Park,' one man suggested, 'call the shots. We have very little say.' In the opinion of another resident: 'The OMB [Ontario Municipal Board], the system its rules and regulations, is the power.' Certainly the impact of the provincial and federal governments on small towns in Canada has increased dramatically over the last half-century. In 1930, for example (Dasgupta 1988:177), 80 per cent of municipal revenues were generated by local property taxes; by 1981 the proportion from this source had dropped to 33 per cent. In 1961 only 11 per cent of the revenues for communities like Paradise consisted of government grants; by 1981 such grants accounted for almost half of their revenues.

The reactions in small towns to the outside bureaucracy, according to Leung (1990), have ranged from regarding it as a mere nuisance (interfering with local council), to a whipping boy (powerful outsider imposing its will over the locals), a bogey man (used as a scapegoat by local politicians for unpopular decisions), a fool (outside experts wasting the local politician's time with abstract, unrealistic nonsense), and friend (someone with resources to distribute). Some residents of Paradise applauded the influence of the provincial authorities, arguing that they reduced the arbitrary exercise of power by unscrupulous local politicians. One man, for example, pointed out that if the reeve in the past had been opposed to someone's plans to build a new house, that house would never have got off the ground. Now, however, a person only has to complain to the OMB in order to see justice done. Yet the more prevalent reaction to the outside authorities was resentment. 'The government,' commented one man, 'call the shots. Because if you're going to get grants from the government, you're going to dance to their tune.' A member of the local council observed: 'We have become the buffer zone between the provincial government's regula-tions and the townspeople. It's almost like the Marshall Plan in the United States, who went into other countries, gave them funds, but then controlled them.'

A representative of the provincial Ministry of Municipal Affairs, sent to Dufferin County in order to conduct a study of possible boundary changes, experienced such resentment first hand: 'I think,' she remarked, 'it's this perception that Big Brother is watching over you.' Apparently the unelected local civil servants were particularly hostile: 'We've always found that staff are more protective of their turf than the politicians are. There's a complete mistrust,' she added, 'between the staff and the politicians.' It was not only the reaction of the staff and the politicians that had unnerved this woman, whose home was in Metro Toronto: Dufferin County turned out to be a cultural shock for her. She was amazed that the locals felt sorry for her because she lived in the city, thinking that the sympathy should be the other way around. She was also surprised at the amount of alcohol consumed, even during lunch-time, and wondered if she would not have made more progress had she been willing to follow the local custom. What really perturbed her was the fact that it had been the county officials who had requested the study of possible boundary changes. Yet they had done so, she flared, 'for all the wrong reasons,' such as being able to blame the ministry for changes which they wanted to make anyway, but which they knew would be unpopular with the electorate.

Although the usual attitude among residents of Paradise was that Big Brother held the strings, the above example demonstrates that manipulation sometimes went both ways. In this respect, it should be pointed out that the council elected in 1988, despite the many criticisms against it, had made a major and successful effort to tap virtually every government grant that was available.

In Paradise, then, there has been a shift from traditional authority to bureaucratic (or legal-rational) authority, with the latter tied to provincial and national institutions. At the same time there have been changes involving power. Status power and political power, as I argued in chapter 2, are always conditioned by class power, but the extent to which class power constitutes the independent variable can vary in time and place (indeed, as Marx recognized, the ideological super-structure, at least in the short run, can even achieve a life of its own, although there has never been any evidence of that state of affairs in Paradise). During the 1950s status power clearly was an important ideological element in the stratification system, and the same was true for political power; in fact, it essentially translated into authority. By the time the 1980s had rolled around, class power had largely been stripped of its ideological clothing, exposing the naked force of the market. The upshot has been to integrate local power into the broader context of state capitalism.

It should be made clear that while the wealthy residents of Paradise, who today occupy the upper echelon, no longer get their kicks by agreeing to serve on the local council, this does not mean that their power in society has faded. What has transpired is that they have become integrated, albeit unwittingly, into a more cosmopolitan system of stratification which has eroded the uniqueness of the small town. This leads to a final observation. The transformed class composition of the local council in Paradise might be interpreted as a victory for democracy, since the aristocracy no longer has a stranglehold on the council. The people in the upper classes, however, were never actually defeated by those in the middle and lower-middle classes. Instead, they came to the realization that local administrative authority and informal influence within the community no longer counted for much, and simply stepped aside.[8]

Still a Community?

Academic specialists have not found it easy to define 'community.' For guidance, I turned to Paradise people, asking them two questions: What is a community, and does Paradise still qualify? Some of the replies of the natives were as follows. 'A community,' spoke an elderly man, 'is when you talk to everybody. If you needed something your neighbour would be here. It's not a community any more because they [the newcomers] couldn't care less if you're well or sick, and they aren't here long enough to get to know them.' A middle-aged woman defined community in terms of physical boundaries and shared interests, stating, 'I think it's still a community, but not as strong. It's too fragmented now. It might be more two communities now – the older generation and the newcomers.' Another person remarked: 'It would be made up of a group of people who would call that area their home, and contribute to the benefit of the whole. There isn't that sense of community left.' Several people defined community as a place where there is mutual support in times of emergency: 'That to me is a community – if you can get help from people if you need it.' The general opinion was that in this sense Paradise was still a community; people pointed to a recent example of a couple who received money and household items from generous neighbours after their house burned down. Yet by this definition New York and Paris might qualify as communities if an emergency was severe enough. One young couple defined community as a place where everybody knew each other and came from the same background. Paradise, they thought, no longer is a community 'because there's too many different people, different countries, and from different places like Toronto. The bulk of the population no longer is long-standing.'

With a couple of exceptions, the consensus among the natives was that Paradise no longer qualified as a community. One of the exceptions consisted of people who had vested interests in the newcomers, such as the politicians who had put out the welcome mat and some business people with dollar signs in their eyes; these people plausibly argued that the increased population had resulted in many beneficial changes: new roads and schools, better shopping facilities, and even cultural outlets. The other exception concerned those citizens who were able to carry on with life as if the newcomers did not exist. For the most part, these were elderly people. They continued to meet in each other's homes for tea and cards; they went on bus excursions and one-day outings with friends and relatives by car to nearby towns; and they gathered together in the funeral homes and churches to mourn the passing of old acquaintances. Among these elderly people, who essentially ignored the newcomers, widows stood out. As one woman stated, 'Once I became a widow, it's a different life, I'm telling you. Since becoming a widow, I've gone to more teas and lunches than ever before.' Another woman observed: 'It seems as soon as a person becomes a widow, why, somebody invites her in, and we become a sort of social group.' In the minds of these people, little has changed in Paradise. Indeed, one widow in her eighties, who still cut her own grass and shovelled her sidewalk in the winter, complained that her social life was so full that she hardly had time to enjoy her one great passion – hockey night on television.

The newcomers, if anything, were even more articulate about what constitutes a community: 'Participation. Working in a joint effort to make the community better. Like the hub, the centre of things. I guess joining of all the people who live there'   'I guess a community is a microcosm of your family life' ... 'Community is where you are happy' ... 'To me, community is a group of people living in harmony together, helping one another, to the benefit of all' ... 'It relates to people interacting – friendships, relating ideas, helping each other' ... 'Being able to walk on your street and being able to say hello. Knowing the old people as well as the young people.'

There was a wider range of opinion among the newcomers about whether Paradise still qualified as a community. Those who had lived there ten to fifteen years or more were inclined to express the same opinion held by the natives. 'It used to be an old folks' home,' commented one man. 'Now it's got rowdy. It's sort of like Toronto.' A woman stated: 'It's not the quaint little town that we used to know. And that's why we moved here.' Not surprisingly, the newcomers who were financially secure and who had become integrated into the town were the most positive. As one of them remarked, 'I think the majority of people do work together. There's still community spirit.' In sharp contrast, a woman whose family was in the process of moving back to rented accommodation in the city commented about small towns in general: 'I don't think they're as nice as some people think they are.' In her judgment, Paradise was merely an unconnected series of residential areas posing as a community. Perhaps the most sensitive appraisal of all was made by a newcomer who expressed love for the town and vowed he would never leave (even though his wife had):

'Living in a small community is something like adopting a child. You shouldn't do it unless you are prepared to devote yourself to it, care for it, and enjoy it.'

By 1990, twenty years after the newcomers had begun to settle in Paradise, the wheel had turned full circle. Although the newcomers had arrived with high hopes, many of them eventually became disillusioned and moved elsewhere, often back to the urban centres where they had previously lived. The natives, for their part, initially reacted in shock to the invasion of outsiders and lamented the destruction of the community. In due time, however, they too revised their opinions. Paradise in 1990 may not be the same community that they had known a generation earlier, but for most of them there still was no better place in which to live. As so many of them remarked, even while complaining that they no longer knew people in the stores and that danger lurked on the streets: 'It's still home.'

Perfect Strangers: Ethnic Minorities

Chapter Eight

British Subjects and Aliens

'You'd never see *that* in the past.' These were the words of an elderly shopkeeper, whose customer, a black person, had just left the premises. There was a time, the merchant ruminated, when even the local Italian family was regarded as peculiar, but now the place is starting to resemble Toronto, with immigrants from every corner of the globe, including 'the coloureds and the Pakis.' In parts one and two, the focus was on natives and newcomers. Here, in part three, the focus switches to the other major category of people in the study: minorities. The minorities share with the second category the fact that most of them are recent inmigrants from the urban centres to the south.

The two major groups among the minorities are African Canadians and Asian Canadians. Although both groups have been subjected to a great deal of prejudice and discrimination, their reactions have been remarkably different. The African Canadians, some of whom traced their roots in Canada back several generations, complained bitterly about the racism around them. The Asian Canadians, most of whom were first-generation immigrants from India and Pakistan, gave the impression that racism did not exist. Similar paradoxes surrounded the other two groups among the minorities: the Jews and the French Canadians. According to the natives, the few Jews who had lived in the community over the decades had been highly regarded and royally treated; according to the Jews themselves, Paradise was a nasty little community, rife with anti-Semitism. Precisely the opposite contradiction applied to the handful of French-Canadian residents. In their minds, Paradise was a delightful community, brimming with hospitable and tolerant citizens; yet in the judgment of many of the natives and newcomers, French Canadians were not simply another ethnic group of European origin like Greeks, Germans, or Serbians. Instead, they were an inferior and dangerous 'race' intent on taking over and ruining the country. Finally, it was often assumed in Paradise that the more interaction a person has had with other ethnic groups, the greater the tolerance. Yet it was not the natives, but rather the newcomers, most of whom had previously lived and worked alongside a wide variety of ethnic groups in urban centres, who were inclined to embrace the deeper brand of racism.

Natives

Paradise had been settled almost entirely by people who traced their ethnic origins to Britain. In 1911 (Lustig 1990:114), 99 per cent of the inhabitants were British in origin, including 43 per cent from Northern Ireland.[1] The census of 1951 did not contain data on ethnicity for Paradise, but a rough estimate can be made. In that year, for example, 92 per cent of the population of Dufferin County as a whole was British in origin; the next largest ethnic groups were Dutch with 2.9 per cent and German with 1.4 per cent. A complementary source of information was my interviews with 122 natives, all of whom had lived in the community in the 1950s; 91.6 per cent of them were British in origin, and a further 5.6 per cent were partly British, making a total of 97 per cent.

During the first half of the twentieth century, a handful of Jewish families from Eastern Europe had settled in the community, as had a couple of Chinese families. In the 1950s there was an Italian family, a Norwegian family, and an Estonian family, plus a scattering of non-British families in the surrounding farm country. The overall picture of the area's ethnic composition, however, at least until the 1970s, was of unchanging homogeneity. Yet here we encounter another little paradox: the terminology for nationality, citizenship, and by implication ethnicity has been repeatedly modified in the community's official tax assessment records, suggesting an attempt to cope with a constantly shifting population. In the 1950s, for example, one of the categories on the assessment form was 'British Subject or Alien' (the source for the title of this chapter). Other terms such as 'Nationality' and simply 'Alien' were employed later to classify the population.

Assessment Rolls

The oldest assessment roll available in the local archives is for 1904. In that year there was no category for race, ethnicity, nationality or citizenship, although there was one for non-resident, with sixteen individuals indicated as absentee property owners. There also were categories for religion and occupation. Under the former, most people were indicated to be Anglicans, Presbyterians, and Methodists (this was long before church union took place). Under the latter, some people were listed as 'Laborer' and others as 'Gentleman.' Most of the 'Gentlemen' were sixty years of age or older, but age was not the sole criterion, because a few of them were in their thirties and forties.

The same assessment form was used in 1911, but nobody was shown as a non-resident, even though some of the people labelled as such in 1904 continued to be on the roll. It is possible that these people had moved to the community, thus changing their residential status. Yet by 1915 five of them were once more marked as non-residents. The implication is that there was a degree of arbitrariness in the records, reflecting the whims of the individual assessors, all of them residents of the village until the county assumed responsibility for the job in the early 1970s. This helps to explain the inconsistent manner in which Jews were recorded in the assessment rolls. In 1904, for example, two residents were designated under religion as Jews. Yet in 1911 this category was left blank for one of the Jews, while in 1915 the same man was once again indicated to be a Jew.

In 1917 a new category was added to the assessment form: 'British Subject or Alien.'[2] Although the category was left completely blank that year, in later years, such as 1924, everyone's status was indicated by the assessor. In 1924 there were no Jews on the assessment roll. This was curious, because in 1928 the names of Jews who had lived in the community as far back as 1915, and in one case 1911, appeared on the roll. In 1928 also, two families labelled Jews under religion were undesignated under the category of British subject or alien. Yet two other families also indicated to be Jews under the category of religion were labelled aliens. How can this be explained? According to two of the former town clerks, British subject or alien referred solely to citizenship, rather than to national or ethnic origin. The implication was that the two families indicated to be aliens were not Canadian citizens, and thus not British subjects. One of these families, however, had lived in the village since 1911, rendering that interpretation somewhat implausible. To make matters even more complicated, in 1945 this same family's status was left unmarked under British subject or alien. This does not mean, however, that the family had since taken out Canadian citizenship. Instead, by that year this category was left blank for all the Jewish families in the community. Two years later, their religious affiliation was treated in the same way. It was as if the assessors were at a loss to know how to handle the Jewish residents. The tendency was either to label them as aliens, or to ignore them.

In 1964 the term 'British Subject or Alien' was replaced by 'Nationality.' Yet under the new title people continued to be designated by the letters 'B' or 'A.' While virtually everyone was marked B, there were a couple of interesting exceptions. One concerned a couple whose origins were Chinese. The man was marked B, but his wife was designated A. The explanation, according to a former town clerk, was that the woman, from Hong Kong, was not a Canadian citizen. The second case, involving an Italian family, was more perplexing. The husband was indicated to be a British subject, but his wife was listed as an alien. Back in 1950, however, she too had been listed as a British subject. As far-fetched as it might seem, it is possible that some assessors interpreted citizenship partly on the basis of occupation and gender. Both men in the two cases just mentioned, for example, were indicated to be businessmen under the category of occupation; their spouses, however, were listed as housewives, despite the fact that each of them worked alongside their husbands in their stores.

In 1968 the term 'Nationality' was replaced by 'Alien.' An explanatory note on the assessment form indicated that under the Alien category, people were to be classified into three groups: Alien (A), Non-designated (N), and Citizen (C). Yet absolutely nobody's status was indicated by the assessor that year. In 1970, Alien was changed to 'ciz' (citizenship), and the old initials B and A resurfaced, but with quite different connotations. Whereas in the past almost every resident was labelled B, in 1970 only a half-dozen people were identified in this manner. Why were they singled out? It appears that B had begun to mean recent immigrants from Britain, rather than people who were Canadian citizens or British by ethnic origin. It is too whimsical, I suppose, to follow the same logic and suggest that A meant American citizenship. Yet one woman who had been labelled A in 1970 was actually an American by birth, and as a former town clerk frankly admitted, the decision to label an immigrant either a British subject or an alien was occasionally a matter of guesswork, rather than based on sound knowledge of their citizenship status.

In 1973 the category 'ciz' remained on the assessment roll, but was completely disregarded by the assessor. A year later the entire category was removed from the form. For the first time since 1916, then, there was no section on which to indicate ethnicity, nationality, or citizenship. The 1974 assessment form, from which the categories for religion and marital status had also been deleted, was still in use in 1991.

Newcomers

According to the 1986 census, the proportion of the Paradise population that was fully or partly British had dropped to 81.5 per cent (48 per cent of the former, 33.5 per cent of the latter). Almost the same proportion – 80 per cent – of the 107 newcomers whom I interviewed were British, or at least partly so, in ethnic background (63 per cent of the former, 17 per cent of the latter). To turn this around, by the 1980s one in five of the residents of the community, virtually all of them newcomers, had no ethnic roots in Britain. About one half of these people traced their origins to western Europe (excluding France), and the other half to eastern Europe. Although it is conventional to define 'white ethnics' as immigrants from eastern Europe, I also include western Europeans in this category, because in the Paradise context anyone who was not British was considered to be an ethnic, at least in the 1950s. By the 1980s the number of ethnics had expanded to the point where they no longer could be considered exceptional cases. It was then that the old version of 'real Canadians' – those whose origins were British – gave way to the broader category of 'white people,' embracing both the British and the white ethnics. This conceptual adjustment was no doubt spurred on by the contrast with the people of colour who had begun to settle in the area.

For the most part, the white ethnics have become integrated into Paradise and the surrounding area. However, when we examine individual cases there is considerable variation in terms of adjustment, which the following examples illustrate.

White Ethnics

I shall begin by comparing two men of Italian origin. The parents of the first man, referred to as British subjects in the 1924 assessment roll, operated a grocery store in the community before the Second World War. Although successful merchants, their ethnic background, plus the fact that they were Catholic, prevented them from becoming part of the aristocracy. The storekeeper's undiplomatic behaviour suggests that he never did aspire to join the ranks of the elite. According to one long-term resident, he sometimes would park a truckload of fresh produce in front of a store owned by a competitor, who did belong to the aristocracy, and offer bargain rates. Their three sons served overseas during the Second World War. Expressing admiration for them, an elderly man of high status commented: 'They fought alongside our own boys.' The implication was that they weren't really true-blue Canadians.

After the war, one of their sons, who had been a prisoner of war, took over the grocery store. Although he was always referred to as an Italian, his agreeable personality and sound management brought in the customers, and he prospered; in later years, he even served briefly on council. Today, in retirement, his identity has been transformed from that of an ethnic stranger to that of a bona fide local – one of the decreasing number of elderly natives in the community. People still refer to him by his Italian heritage, but it no longer has a pejorative connotation. By the 1980s one's non-British ethnicity had ceased to be noteworthy. Contributing to the man's acceptance was the fact that he did not make a fuss over his Catholic upbringing. Indeed, a few years ago he divorced his wife, also Italian in origin, and was remarried in a local restaurant by the unconventional retired Protestant minister described in the previous chapter.

The other Italian Canadian moved to Paradise in 1970 from Toronto, where he had been born. His father had been born in Italy, his mother, also of Italian descent, in Canada. For the first couple of years he commuted to work in the city but hated it. One of the lucky ones, he found a good job in Paradise. When he first settled in the community, he became more aware of his Italian heritage than ever before. People, he said, used to comment on his peculiar name, and he was constantly the brunt of ethnic jokes. The fact that he was a Catholic in a Protestant enclave, he stated, also made him appear a bit odd. For several years neither he nor his wife were invited to social events, and they found it difficult to make friends, even though they both worked in the community. He thought it was about five years before they were invited to their first wedding. Until then they weren't even welcome at funerals, although now they go to all of them. Helping them to become accepted, he stated, was his decision to join a local service club, plus the fact that within a few years he and his wife were only one of dozens of families representing a broad range of ethnic backgrounds. This man made a point of stressing that the experiences of his two children, who grew up in the community and regard it as home, have been completely different. They realize that their heritage is Italian, but nothing in their lives has suggested that it has any more importance than one's preference for Pepsi or Coca-Cola.

My next two cases involve men who migrated from the Baltics as children. Although similar in background, their receptions in and adjustments to rural Ontario have been very different. The first man came to Canada with his mother in 1951, joining his father who had arrived the previous year. Although his father had attended college in the country of his birth, the only work he could get in Canada was as a labourer. For a couple of years the couple lived in a small city, and then became sharecroppers on a farm near Paradise. Eventually they were able to purchase their own small farm, consisting, the man said, mainly of rocks and swamp.

The enduring memories of this man's childhood are ones of constant prejudice and humiliation: 'You didn't feel you belonged. Not from adults so much as from the children. I did a lot of fighting in elementary school. I didn't speak any English. I just sat at the back of the class.' What made things worse, he stated, was that his family had never really wanted to emigrate to Canada, or to any other country, it was the circumstances of the Second World War, especially the communist takeover of his natal country, that transformed their lives.

Again reminiscing about his childhood years on the farm, he commented: 'You knew who was from a different background. There was a feeling of communality with anyone who wasn't British.' Two other immigrant families from the Baltics operated farms a couple of miles away: 'These were the people we associated with. We helped each other. There was a tendency to trust, perhaps, or deal with people who were non-British.' As a child and young man, he confessed, he hated the British, by which he meant the vast bulk of the people who lived around him. At one point, however, he had an opportunity to live for a few months in Britain, and loved the experience: 'Now I'm an Anglophile.'

Although this man surmounted the poverty and prejudice of his childhood and graduated from university, he remains poignantly aware of his ethnicity. When he walks into a room, he claimed, he can tell immediately who is British, and whether anyone originates from the Baltic states. Although he has enjoyed a successful career in Paradise, he still considers himself an outsider, marginal to mainstream Canadian society. As in the case of the previous figure, he thinks that the experiences of his children have been remarkably different. They are conscious of their Baltic roots (their mother too originates from that part of the world), but it doesn't really count for much: 'The mix of ethnicity now,' he remarked, 'is so much more that you no longer care who is different.' The exceptions, he added, are people who stand out: the visible minorities.

The experience of growing up in a new country, dominated by people of British origin, was much more positive for my second case from the Baltics. This man's natal country had been successively invaded by the Germans and the Russians. In 1944 his father fled with the family to Germany, and in 1948 to Canada. They settled initially in northern Ontario, where his father, a university graduate, found work as a labourer. Life was not very pleasant for them. They had arrived in Canada with only the clothes on their backs, a couple of suitcases, and a few dollars. Dressed in their foreign garb, and living in a shack, they soon learned what it was like to be treated as inferior beings.

His father found work near Paradise within a couple of years. The family's reception into the small village was remarkably warm. Then about sixteen years old, the young man soon became a popular student in the school, especially among the sons and daughters from the higher social classes. The adult members of the elite themselves began to call regularly on his father at their little house a couple of miles outside the village. Several factors produced this happy outcome. First, the young man was athletic, clever, charming, handsome, and, at least on the surface, confident. Secondly, his father was not only a university graduate, but apparently also a remarkably interesting and genial person, with a good command of the English language. The educated and wealthy people in Paradise, including the doctors, ministers, and merchants, recognized him as one of their own, despite the setback in life that history had dealt him, and sought out his company. Thirdly, the members of this family were sufficiently flexible to change their ways in order to conform to their new environment. For example, although they were raised in the Greek Orthodox Church, they quickly became members of the United Church, and attended services on a regular basis. Finally, under some circumstances the exceptional case may enjoy novelty value, rather than being regarded as weird. It appears that this family, its reputation established by the learned and captivating father, was one of these cases.

Tragically, the good life in the new country was temporarily shaken: the man died a few years after moving to Paradise. With his death, the regular visits of the elite to his home ceased, but by then the family was well established in the community. His mother remarried, this time to a local man whose first wife had died young. Her son's ambition had been to become a policeman, but his father, whose experiences in eastern Europe had turned him off the police, had been adamantly opposed. He wanted his son to attend university, but there was not enough money. As a result, after completing grade twelve the young man found work in a large corporation, eventually rising to a high level in management. Although he no longer lived in Paradise, for many years he kept in close contact with old friends, and periodically returned to visit his mother and relatives of his wife, who was a Paradise native. Only in recent years has he finally lost touch with the community that had so generously embraced him.

My final two examples of white ethnics were born in neighbouring countries in eastern Europe, but that was about all they had in common. The one man deeply resented what he claimed to be the inhospitable environment of narrow-minded people who had made life miserable for him. The other man expressed a warm attachment to Paradise, and declared that it would be his home for ever. I shall deal first with the discontented individual. He emigrated to Canada around 1972 and married a woman from southern Europe. For several years he worked as a skilled tradesman in Toronto. By the time I met him, he had lived near Paradise for five years. For the first two years he commuted to work in Toronto, and thought the driving was going to kill him. Since he was determined not to live in the city, he bravely established his own small business in the countryside. As he pointed out, both he and his wife had been born in small villages in Europe and felt more comfortable in a similar setting.

Unfortunately, life has not been a bowl of cherries for them in the countryside. This is partly because they have had to struggle to keep their new business afloat. But the main reason, the man insisted, concerned prejudice and discrimination. As he stated: 'I found the locals don't accept you.' He pointed out that he hires locals, and buys materials for his operation from surrounding businessmen, but to no avail: 'They always look at us like we're garbage.' Time after time, he declared, the same individuals would come into his place of business and ask him once again where he was from. As he fumed, they didn't have enough guts to call him a foreigner to his face, but made the same point indirectly.

This man reported that his wife and two children had also been the victims of prejudice: 'My wife finds the people not very friendly. Very picky. Discriminative. They always have something bad to say to her, about being a foreigner.' He said his daughter used to come home in tears: 'I've had my child in school here – she's dark – when we moved here, called nigger.' He too has a dark skin, and complained angrily: 'I have in many instances been called Paki.' When I asked him to compare his experiences in the city and in the countryside in terms of the degree of prejudice, he didn't hesitate: 'I think it's a lot worse in the country.' To prove his point, and especially to demonstrate that his own case was not atypical, he talked about the many hunters who invade the back roads and swamps during the deer season. Regardless of their ethnic origin, the locals always call them 'wops.'

In this man's opinion, Canadians simply do not appreciate the contribution of immigrants like himself: 'If it wasn't for the foreigners they'd all starve.' He said that since he had been in Canada, he had never taken a cent in government handouts; on the contrary, he had created jobs for Canadians. Yet, he raged, Canadians always assume he had been on welfare. Talking about the effort he and his wife have put into their business, he remarked: 'I don't think a real Canadian-born person would have been able to carry it on.' Immigrants like himself, he went on to say, are little more than slaves. They arrive with nothing, work their heads off, and end up being treated like dirt. For almost twenty years he kept his nose to the grindstone, hoping things would improve. But in 1990 he made a trip back to his natal country, where he still has many relatives, liked what he saw, and decided to return there to live. As he pointed out, his country of birth was no longer under the yoke of the Soviet Union, and democracy had taken root. Moreover, he added, Canada's depressed economy had reduced its attractiveness for immigrants.

It is always difficult to separate institutional racism and personality, but in this particular case it is relevant to reveal that several people believed that the man's problems had been caused mainly by his prickly, volatile personality. Certainly, he was aggressive: 'I don't take shit from anyone.' A woman who had briefly worked for him said she never knew what mood he would be in on any given day; sometimes he was friendly and gentle, at other times aloof or hostile. A person who knew him quite well described him as 'loud-mouthed, nasty, and selfish.' This person was from the same country in eastern Europe, but his ethnic background and religion were different, making it possible that his evaluation echoed old rivalries in the homeland. In my own judgment, it was not a matter of choosing between prejudice and discrimination on the one hand and personality on the other in order to comprehend this man's unhappy experiences in rural Ontario: it was their combined impact that did the trick.

I turn now to the man from eastern Europe who had fallen in love with Paradise. Trained as an engineer in his natal country, he emigrated to Canada in 1957, preceded by a sister and an aunt. His first job was as a waiter in a restaurant in Toronto. Two years later he moved to northern Ontario in order to take up a job more closely related to his training. Within another couple of years he had married a woman from western Europe and returned to Toronto to establish his own business. In the late 1970s he bought a farm on the outskirts of Paradise. For several years he continued to run the business in the city, escaping to the farm on the weekends. But life in rural Ontario had seduced him, and he decided to move his family there. He loved the farm, especially ploughing, which he said is 'like therapy.' Yet he realized that he couldn't make a living from it. He sold the business in Toronto and established a new one in Paradise. What struck him immediately was just how different it was to be a businessman in a small town. In the city, he stated, his relations with his customers were narrow and specific: either the job he performed for them was satisfactory or it was not. But in Paradise, being a businessman involves 'your whole person, your faith, your character, your personal qualities.'

Success did not come automatically. Commenting on the reception from other businessmen, he stated: 'Here they put all kinds of obstacles for you to trip over.' They wanted newcomers to fail, he insisted, but thought that that was just their way of attempting to protect themselves. One merchant said to him: 'I'll give you two years and you'll be out of here.' That prediction did not materialize. Not only did he work hard, but he also made a major effort to get to know people. Although he had been brought up Greek Orthodox, he had converted to the United Church while living in Toronto and even became an elder. In Paradise he continued to attend church, albeit somewhat irregularly in more recent years. When he did attend, he observed, 'My business just about triples.' His bank manager urged him to join a service club, and he became active in other voluntary organizations as well, helping, for example, to organize the community soccer league. This man also became a regular member of 'the senate,' the informal group of prominent citizens who met for breakfast with the erstwhile mayor in a local restaurant. Contributing to his successful integration into small-town life was his attractive personal qualities. Unlike the previous character, he was consistently charming, suave, humorous, and self-deprecating. He also appeared to be highly competent. Several years ago he had realized that he could never work for anyone else, because inevitably his superiors became jealous. He was the type of person, indeed, who had to underrepresent his knowledge and capabilities in order to fit into the crowd. This seemed to make him even more attractive to those individuals who appreciated his superior gifts, and he was encouraged to run for the position of mayor.

It would appear that this man is a story-book representation of adjustment to rural society. Yet not all has been smooth sailing for him. After living in Paradise for several years, he came face to face with tragedy: one of his children was killed in a car accident. A long-range consequence was that he became alienated from his grief-stricken wife, who apparently had never enjoyed living in rural Ontario and insisted on returning to the city, away from the setting of the tragedy. As for her husband, the death of his child left him devastated. In his words, he was 'stripped bare, vacant, lifeless.' Much to his surprise, after a couple of years had passed his strength and will to live began to return, but not before he had had time to do a lot of thinking. His mind began to dwell on his homeland, or at least a romanticized version of it. He returned for a visit, and by doing so was jolted back to reality. He remembered that he had grown up in a house without electricity or a telephone, and that his mother had been killed on the doorstep during the Second World War. Unlike the reaction of the previous character, who also returned to the land of his birth, the trip merely confirmed his commitment to Canada.

His period of reflection, nevertheless, left him agitated about several small matters. When he had settled in Canada he had anglicized his name, but began to regret that he had done so: 'I look at it as a prostitution.' Although his businesses had been financial successes, he also began to lament that he had failed to follow his youthful dream to become a teacher – a profession, he thought, that would have given more meaning to his life. In spite of all the evidence to the contrary, this sensitive and gregarious man even started to have doubts that he had been accepted in the town that he had grown to love. But as time went on, he became more and more appreciative of the enormous outpouring of sympathy and support from friends and acquaintances. Paradise, in the end, had resuscitated this man, as small towns are supposed to do, and nobody was more aware of it than the man himself: 'This is home. When I leave here, they'll carry me out in a box.'

Minorities

The impression often conveyed by Paradise people was that Canadian cities have become overrun by visible minorities. What disturbed many of them was that the minorities had begun to spread out into the small towns and villages and rolling hills of the countryside. Yet in 1981, according to Dasgupta (1988:48–9), nine out of every ten Canadians were still of European descent. The smallest proportion of non-Europeans was located on farms, with the non-farm rural population falling between the farms and the urban centres in terms of ethnic heterogeneity. The census indicates that there were only five black, thirty Chinese, and thirty-five Jewish families in Paradise in 1986, and not a single family from India or Pakistan. Although those figures were no longer accurate by 1990, the fact is that the majority of the visible minority newcomers lived in the countryside around Paradise rather than in the town itself; none of them made a living from farming, although a couple were part-time farmers.[3]

The ethnic composition of the eighty-one minority members who were interviewed, all of them newcomers, was as follows: Asian Canadian thirty-six, African Canadian twenty-eight, Jewish three, French Canadian fourteen.[4] As indicated in table 10, the majority of the minorities, unlike the natives and newcomers, were born outside Canada. Indeed, if the French Canadians and Jews, all of whom were born in Canada, are excluded from the analysis, four out of five of the remaining minorities were born in other countries. Whereas about half of all newcomers had lived in the community less than six years, for the minorities the figure was about 60 per cent. Compared to the natives and newcomers, the minorities are significantly different in terms of religious affiliation, with 45 per cent of them non-Christians, and with a much higher attendance rate. Conversely, their participation in

TABLE 10
Characteristics of 81 Members of Minorities

Country of Birth			*Age*	
Canada	28 (35%)		50 years or older	27 (33%)
Other	52 (65%)		Less than 50 years	54 (67%)
Unknown	1			
			Marital Status	
Length of Residence			Single	11 (14%)
0–2 years	19 (23%)		Married	68 (85%)
2–5 years	29 (36%)		Divorced	1 (1%)
6–10 years	15 (18%)		Unknown	1
11–30 years	18 (22%)			
			Education	
Religion			Primary	4 (6%)
Protestant	18 (26%)		Secondary	40 (56%)
Catholic	20 (29%)		College or technical	8 (11%)
Sikh	15 (22%)		University	20 (28%)
Hindu	9 (13%)		Unknown	9
Muslim	2 (3%)			
Jewish	3 (4%)		*Occupation*	
Other	2 (3%)		Professional	6 (11%)
Unknown	12		White collar	27 (48%)
			Blue collar	23 (41%)
Frequency of Worship			Unknown	2
Regular	26 (47%)		Inapplicable	23
Occasional	13 (24%)			
Never	16 (29%)		*Self-Employed*	
Unknown	26		Yes	28 (50%)
			No	28 (50%)
Membership in Organizations			Unknown	2
None	54 (76%)		Inapplicable	23
One	14 (20%)			
Two or more	3 (4%)			
Unknown	10			

Note.

All percentages are calculated in terms of known and applicable cases. Inapplicable cases regarding occupation and self employment consist of individuals not in the workforce (2 unemployed, 9 student, 5 retired, 7 homemaker).

voluntary associations, at least local ones, was the lowest of the three groups, which is one measure of their lack of integration into rural society. The age profile of the minorities was virtually identical to that of the newcomers, with two thirds of them less than fifty years old. Like the natives and newcomers, the vast majority of the minorities were still in their first marriages. Among the African Canadians, two of the marriages were interracial, and a couple of the French Canadians had married English Canadians; although none of the Asian Canadians had European-origin spouses, in one family a son who lived in Toronto had married a woman of French heritage.

Although the minorities boasted the highest proportion of university graduates among the three groups, the majority of them Asian Canadians who had earned their degrees in their home countries, the proportion of both minorities and newcomers who had attended university, college, or technical school was identical – 39 per cent. About one person in two in each of these groups held down white collar jobs (in this category I include the owners and operators – usually the same people – of gas stations, motels, and variety stores). Compared to the newcomers, a somewhat higher proportion of the minorities (41 per cent versus 34 per cent) were locked into blue collar jobs, despite the identical post-secondary educational achievements of the two groups, reflecting the employment obstacles that confront minority members. Where the minorities differed significantly from the newcomers, and resembled the natives, was in the number of self employed: only one in every three of the newcomers versus one in every two of the minorities and the natives. Similarly, a much lower proportion of the minorities (26 per cent) than of the newcomers (63 per cent) were commuters (the figure for the natives was 16 per cent). Finally, the class composition of the minorities was much more homogeneous than in the case of the other two groups. My estimate is that about four out of five people among the minorities fell into the middle class, at least as measured by indices such as occupation and income. Education is a different matter, because the majority of the university graduates were employed in jobs that normally only required a secondary school diploma, but to some extent that was true for the newcomers as well.

This quantitative overview, of course, tells us very little about what it is like to live in rural Ontario if one is a member of a minority group. To achieve a deeper understanding, it is necessary to turn to qualitative materials, such as the case studies provided in the following chapter.

Chapter Nine

African and Asian Canadians

A fundamental question guides this chapter: Is racism in rural society more or less extensive than in urban society? Most of the African Canadians thought that rural society was the less hospitable environment, although there was a lack of consensus as to whether there actually was more racism in the countryside, or whether it simply showed up more, or was felt more. The vast majority of these people expressed a strong desire to interact with their neighbours, and when they were rejected they reacted with bitterness and sometimes with anger. The Asian Canadians, in contrast, were inclined to regard racism as natural and inevitable. From their perspective there was little difference between urban and rural society, although they reported a slightly greater number of confrontations in the former. Compared to the African Canadians, the Asian Canadians made much less effort to become integrated into rural society, and they were much more likely to react to racist incidents that did occur with a shrug of the shoulders.

African Canadians

Although Paradise natives in the 1980s were inclined to regard the few African Canadians in the area as an entirely new dimension in their part of rural Ontario, they were mistaken. About a century and a half ago, the first non-Aboriginal settlers several miles from Paradise, deeper into the countryside, had been blacks. Approximately 350 blacks – some of them fugitive slaves and others free women and men who had settled in the Niagara peninsula during the American Revolution – became homesteaders on fifty-acre lots along what was known as the

Old Durham Road. By the end of the nineteenth century there was little trace of these black pioneers. Some of them had travelled north to work at the Collingwood shipyards; others had moved to settlements in Simcoe County, their homesteads taken over by Irish and Scottish settlers. Those who had remained had become absorbed into the European-origin population through intermarriage.

In October 1990 the historical record, long concealed by a conspiracy of silence, was dramatically acknowledged. A ceremony, presided over by the lieutenant-governor of the province, Lincoln Alexander, was held on the grounds of a cemetery where some of the black settlers had been buried. The cemetery had been ploughed under in the 1930s, and crops had been planted on the site. It had taken the determined efforts of a handful of people, some of them African Canadians from Collingwood whose forebears were buried in the cemetery, others local whites, to recover buried and broken gravestones and reconstruct the cemetery. The ceremony itself floated in an atmosphere of goodwill. One of the public speakers, taking note of the fact that the volunteers who had worked so tirelessly to reclaim the cemetery had included blacks and whites, as did the crowd in attendance, lauded the racial cooperation that had made the event possible. An African Canadian who had travelled from Toronto to attend the ceremony commented that he could not help but wonder how many more black doctors and scientists there might have been in the country had race relations always been so enlightened.

Although euphoria was in the air, the emotion closer to the ground was somewhat different. Previous efforts had been made to reclaim the cemetery and recognize the historical role played by black pioneers, but the opposition had always been too stiff. As a Protestant minister who took part in the ceremony in 1990 remarked, 'Certainly there was an effort not to let this happen.' Among those who had successfully blocked previous attempts, apparently, was one of the minister's predecessors in the local church, who reportedly had said: 'Let well enough alone.' A retired farmer who had attended the ceremony commented that he could understand why 'the coloureds' were so eager to rebuild the cemetery, but he could not fathom the motives of his white neighbours who had contributed their time and labour. One local volunteer who had played a leading role was singled out for criticism. What's a man from 'a good British family,' sniffed an elderly woman, doing meddling in this sort of affair? Another woman, who described the man as a 'no good hippie,' stated that he had been a great disappointment to his family, and hung around with a sinister group of friends who 'wore long hair, sandals.' One of the man's neighbours claimed that he was the kind of person who was always on the outlook for something sensational in order to make people forget that he has never held down a regular job.

One of the reasons why some people had been determined to keep the lid on the record of the black settlement was the apprehension that they themselves might have black ancestors, and that their pasts would become common knowledge. While a few individuals proudly made public their black heritages, the reactions of other people were much more evasive. For example, when I asked a retired farmer if he had black forebears, his wife quickly answered: 'He doesn't really know.' A few minutes later she stepped out of the room to get more refreshments, and her husband spoke up: 'Of course, some of them, my folks, were darkies.' Later when I asked them if it had been a sound decision to reclaim the cemetery and honour the black pioneers, the woman exclaimed: 'No! Definitely no!' Again when she was out of the room, the man quietly stated: 'I think it was a good thing. The dark has a right to be recognized. I've got nothing against dark people.' The unveiling of the area's past for this simple and delightful elderly couple, for whom the expression 'the salt of the earth' might have been coined, had obviously added an unexpected complication to their lives. This was generously recognized by one of the African Canadians whose forebears rested in the cemetery. Although he was grateful that his efforts over the years had paid off, he expressed sympathy for those white people who might have to come to grips with the fact that their family trees contained blacks.

Moving back to Paradise and its immediate vicinity, we find virtually no record of black residents until recent years. One exception in the 1950s was a woman from Toronto who had been hired as a domestic when a local woman's health had failed. As one of the daughters in that family, who at the time had been a young girl, remarked, 'After a while, we didn't even realize she was black.' A more significant exception concerned a family that had settled near the community before the Second World War. The man, according to an elderly native, had been a sailor, originally from Britain, who had married a woman whom he had met during a voyage to Africa. He described the man as white and the woman as black. Another native remembered them somewhat differently: 'He was mulatto. She was straight nigger.' A third native claimed that after these people settled into their modest home outside Paradise, 'She was never seen again in public. When she died, the undertakers just took her away.'

This couple's son apparently had served in the army during the Second World War, but according to an elderly resident, who described him as a slippery character, not even the army could do anything with him, and he was given a dishonourable discharge. His own two sons – the third generation of the family in the Paradise area – attended elementary school in the community. Two teachers, now retired, who had taught them, disagreed on how they had been treated. One of the teachers could not recall any prejudice against them. The other teacher cryptically observed: 'Kids can be cruel.' A middle-aged man who had been in the same class throughout elementary school as one of the sailor's grandsons recalled that everyone called him 'Nigger.' But he claimed that he had never realized the significance of the nickname at the time. Like their father, these two individuals were remembered as unsavoury characters. One of them, according to an informant, married 'a half-breed Indian' and never amounted to anything, while his brother went into the coal business, and became a lay preacher. The story has it that he peddled a mixture of ordinary coal, coal that had already been half-burned, and stones painted black. When customers complained that their stoves didn't seem to throw much heat and asked what they should do, the crafty merchant, chuckled my informant, would advise: 'Pray, pray to God.'

The grandsons of the sailor and his African wife were remembered as having borderline black features, although there was little consensus about the nature of these features. A man who had been in school with them, and who said he had always called one of them 'Nig,' thought it was their thick lips that gave them a Negro appearance. Another former classmate disagreed: except for being a bit darker than normal, he stated, there was nothing unusual about them. One of the former teachers remembered 'a Negro look on their hair.' Today the children of one of these men – the fourth generation – remain in the community, but in terms of their physical features there is nothing to indicate their descent from the African woman who had settled in the area prior to the Second World War, and few people in the community make the connection any longer. One elderly man, a member of the old aristocracy, who did remember the family's history, remarked about their father: 'He had quite a Negro look about him. But his children,' he continued in a tone of mild astonishment, 'are fine looking white kids.'

The first major influx of Black Canadians into the Paradise area occurred in the early 1970s. This was the period when small farms were being swallowed by large farm operations, the owners of which were interested in the land, not the house. People from the city, including black families, attracted by the reasonable rents for the abandoned farmhouses, began to make the trek to rural Ontario. A man who at the time had been a teacher in Paradise recalled the day when 'a truck with about fourteen kids in back, half of them black, and the other half mulatto,' pulled up in front of the school. The black driver, who had apparently collected the kids from several different families, remarked jovially: 'I've come to integrate your school.'

By the 1980s almost all of the families, including the black ones, that had arrived a few years earlier had departed, partly because rents had steadily increased and it no longer was possible to find bargains. They were replaced by a new wave of migrants, and the African Canadians among them tended to be middle-class people who owned their own homes.

Life in Town

'I've never been called "nigger" in my life until I came here.' These were the bitter words of an African Canadian who lived in a prestigious subdivision on the edge of the community. The setting had been a local store, where the man and his wife had just placed an order at the counter. The young clerk, in relaying the order to another employee, had used the term 'nigger.' The stunned customer demanded: 'What did you say?' Apparently failing to understand the customer's annoyance, the clerk repeated his words, again including 'nigger.' As voices began to rise, the clerk's boss arrived on the scene, discovered in horror what had transpired, and apologized profusely to the angry man and woman. As they drove away from the store, the utter ridiculousness of the situation made them laugh so hard that they had to pull over onto the shoulder of the road. It was difficult to believe, remarked the man, that anyone in this day and age could be so utterly naive as the clerk, whom he thought was only recently off the farm. Ironically, this was not the only time that they were called nigger in Paradise. A few months later the offensive term slid out of the mouth of the self-appointed leader of a small religious sect in the area.

This couple, each of whose roots in Canada went back well over one hundred years, had grown up in the Niagara peninsula, close to a community described by the woman as 'a very racist little town. As soon as you got of age, you have to leave. No work for blacks.' For several years they lived in the vicinity of Toronto, where the man had enjoyed a successful career in the construction business. As they approached retirement age they decided they had had enough of city life. They built their own impressive house in the subdivision on the edge of Paradise, having been attracted by the reasonable cost of the land and the prospect of a better quality of life. Before I had met these people, I had been told that they had become so fed up with the racism that they had confronted in Paradise that they had decided to sell the house.[1] While they confirmed that they did indeed plan to put the house on the market, they denied that racism was behind the decision. As the woman remarked, 'I wouldn't sell to run away.' Her husband chimed in: 'Nobody will drive me out.' The reason they had decided to move on, they said, was simply that the house was too big, especially since none of their four children lived with them any longer.

When asked to compare their experiences in the country with those in Toronto, the man said: 'I tell you, there's more racism in the country than there is in the city.' Then he mused that perhaps it isn't the case of a greater degree of racism, but instead a more obvious reaction to 'coloured people' (his term) because they are such a novelty: 'I don't think they're more racist. It's just that it shows up more. Whatever comes in here that is different, like us, they're going to catch hell.' A contributing factor, he thought, was the parochialism of rural people: 'You know, there's people here that never've gone downtown to Toronto.' Referring to the subdivision in which they lived, the man remarked that nobody had put out the welcome mat for them. One neighbour in particular, a professional man, impressed them as a complete racist: 'They say he is one son of a bitch.' For a while one of their daughters lived with them in the new house. While shopping in a local store one day, a young man called her 'nigger' and told her to get to the back of the line. She reacted violently, and a fight broke out. Shortly after she moved to Toronto, vowing never to live in Paradise again. 'What really makes me mad about racism,' her mother declared, 'is this is my country, and the people who call me names have an accent! I'm a Canadian. I get very upset when people say "yeah, you're Canadian, but what *are* you?"' The implication, she said, is that a black person – even one whose forebears settled in the country in the middle of the last century – can't really be a Canadian.

This couple went on to talk about how they coped in a predominantly white society. The woman remarked: 'I think I'm better than them [white people]. I think I'm superior. I was brought up, you don't do that stuff. Have sex. Lower-class whites do that.' Her husband declared: 'Each individual black person's got it in them, we're *better* than them. That's your only weapon. The confidence I'm better. Listen, I *have* to be better.' Later he commented: 'You've got to be true black inside and out.' At that point, he and his wife burst out laughing. His family tree included blacks and whites, and not only did he have light-coloured skin but also blue eyes.

The woman pointed out that blacks and whites were mixed together in her family too. One of her brothers had married a white woman, and two of her own children had white spouses. The mother of her son's wife, she revealed, had attempted to prevent the marriage from taking place, but when the grandchildren came along she adored them. A lot of people, remarked the Paradise woman, chuckled over that woman's change of heart. Reflecting on the mixed marriages in her family tree, and her husband's, she asked rhetorically: 'How can I hate white people?' It was evident, however, that the birth of light-skinned children in such marriages held a certain degree of fascination for her. Taking down a photograph of one of her grandsons, she remarked that although he appears to be white, in her mind he is black, and added: 'When I pass a kid on the street who looks white, I know they're black kids.' She wasn't sure how she knew, but thought it was perhaps the eyes. One of her own daughters has a very light-coloured skin. On one occasion in elementary school in the city, she and her older sister, whose skin colour is dark, were being harassed by the other kids. When their mother discovered that the younger daughter thought the name-calling had only been aimed at her sister, she asked her what colour she was. The girl said she was white. Thereafter, the woman declared, she made certain her daughter knew she was black. Yet problems of identification poignantly followed this youngster to secondary school; apparently she preferred to associate with white students, and consequently was harassed by black students. While her parents lamented this example of what they termed 'reverse racism,' the man confessed a certain degree of sympathy towards it. His wife, in contrast, stated that she didn't have time to pay attention to prejudice, regardless of its nature: 'What's important is my family.' Indeed, she added, black hatred of whites is just as severe a problem in Canada as the opposite: 'Racism is racism, whether it's white against black, or black against white.'

Although this man and woman had expected a much friendlier

reception in rural Ontario, and had looked forward to getting to know their neighbours, what they did not seem to realize was that in the subdivision in which they lived hardly any visiting back and forth took place, regardless of people's ethnic backgrounds. For a variety of reasons, their interaction in the town itself was very limited. The man was semi-retired, and the woman worked part-time as an accountant in a small business in the countryside. While they did not belong to any local organizations, they were dedicated Christians. The Pentecostal church which they attended, however, was located several miles away. Perhaps had they been in business in the town, they would have become more integrated. In order to explore that possibility, I turn to an immigrant from the West Indies who had taken over a small enterprise that catered essentially to the elderly.

Within seconds of meeting this man, who had been working outside in the yard at the time, I felt reasonably confident that an account of his experiences in Canada would not be in high demand by tourism and immigration officials. When I offered my hand, he refused to shake it, remarking that his own hands were dirty. He did agree to talk to me in his office, and slowly the truculence faded as his story unfolded. For eighteen years he and his wife had lived in Toronto, where he had worked in construction and as a transport driver. His wife had contributed by taking in foster children. It had been a constant battle, he said, to keep their four children in the academic stream; the teachers assumed, he claimed, that black kids are stupid, material for the trades rather than the professions. To encourage his children, he did his best to expose them to black role models – educators like Marcus Garvey who had left their marks – and he repeatedly coached them that they had to perform at a superior level even in order to hold an ordinary job.

It was after they moved to rural Ontario, he revealed, that racism hit them squarely on the jaw. They had decided to make the move because his health had declined, and he wanted a slower pace of life. The business that he had taken over, however, was dependent on referrals from professionals in the health field; such referrals apparently were few and far between, and it was his strong belief that he had been boycotted because of his skin colour. He and his wife, he stated, were often verbally abused by some of their clients. One elderly man repeatedly called them 'nigger' and 'black bastard.' When this old man died, he attended the funeral, but was completely ignored by the relatives – the usual reaction, he observed.

Commenting on racism in the small town, he said: 'It's not subtle, but it's not outright. It's somewhere in between.' After reflecting for a moment, he added: 'I think you feel it stronger up here than in the city.' Elaborating, he confessed that he felt lonely and isolated in the town, whereas in the city, despite the problems that he and his family had encountered, at least he could visit fellow West Indians and have some human contact. To illustrate his limited interaction with the residents of the town, he talked about an elderly woman who had lived behind him. In poor health, she went to stay with relatives. Soon after she died, but it was not until three weeks later that the unhappy news reached him. He was shocked. As he explained, where he was born and raised, it would simply not be possible to be unaware of a neighbour's death. In his judgment, the only reason to live in a small town was to enjoy meaningful relationships with one's neighbours; the circumstances surrounding the elderly woman's death made him question the quality of life in Canada as a whole.

This man had only met three people willing to pass the time of day with him in the community. Two of them were themselves newcomers from Toronto – both Englishmen, he stated – but the most interesting one was a woman who had been born and raised in rural Ontario. This woman, who worked in a store, enjoyed talking to him about their different cultural backgrounds. Yet as open-minded as she was, she apparently reacted with fright one day when several blacks passing through the town stopped to shop in the store. It was a mark of the excellent rapport between this woman and the man from the West Indies that she frankly confessed her reaction, and her inability to understand it. Perhaps, he told her, it had something to do with the media focus on black violence.

After struggling with their small business for two years, this man and woman decided to sell it and move back to the West Indies. Despite the racism they had encountered in both rural and urban Canada, they thought that the years they had spent in their adopted country had been worthwhile. Their children – one of whom had graduated from university, and another from a community college – had been exposed to new opportunities, and it was the hope of their parents that they would remain in Canada. When his children were growing up, the man stated, he had discouraged any signs of reverse racism that they displayed, and in this respect he believed he had been successful. When they lived in the city, white kids were frequently in their home, and one of his sons had a white girlfriend. As the man remarked about his family as a whole, 'We are not racialists at all.' Despite the fact that he had never left my side during our first meeting, and therefore had no opportunity to wash away the alleged dirt, when we parted he warmly shook my hand.

Our next case concerns a single black woman in her early thirties who was the owner and operator of a specialty shop in Paradise. When I first met her in 1988 she vowed that she would never move back to Toronto, where she had spent most of her youth, but by 1990 she had done just that. What had happened to change her mind?

Born in England, she came to Canada with her parents and siblings when she was five years old. That was in the 1960s, and she was the only black child in her elementary school. She remembers running home terrified one day when the kids in school called her 'chocolate face' and threatened to boil her down and eat her. Not only was she black, but she also had an English accent, which earned her the nickname 'Limey.' Secondary school, she said, was not nearly as traumatic, partly because she had become acclimatized to Canadian society, and also because most of the racism in the school was between Canadians and Italians.

In the late 1970s her parents moved near Paradise. Her own formal education was completed by then, but her brothers attended the local secondary school. Although they apparently were popular with the other students, they found life in the country a little on the slow side and eventually found jobs in the city. Their sister was more taken with rural existence, and decided, with assistance from her parents, to purchase the store in Paradise. Almost from the beginning a number of problems, most of them racially inspired, she thought, began to emerge. An elderly woman, for example, entered the store, saw a black person behind the counter, and turned on her heels and walked out. That woman, she discovered, was from 'high society,' and she emphasized that the prejudice she encountered came from all levels of the class system. When she had first opened up for business, she had made a point of dropping into the other stores along the main street to introduce herself. Yet as the months went by, virtually none of these merchants returned her visit. A sympathetic junior police officer, she claimed, informed her in private that 'the hidden power people,' including some of the merchants, were determined to close her down.

At the end of two years she realized she wasn't going to make it: 'My business started going down. People just started boycotting my store.' She decided to put it up for sale. When her bank manager asked her why, she told him that it was mainly because she had faced so much prejudice and discrimination. His reaction was disbelief. In his judgment, Paradise people were remarkably tolerant. The same reaction was voiced by one of the older merchants. He insisted that the woman had had the support of the business community, and suggested that her venture had failed because of three reasons: she was in the wrong business – there simply was insufficient demand for her product; her store was in a poor location – too far up the street; and she did not keep regular business hours (ironically, neither did he). Although this man's explanation was plausible, it was a fact that some people did prefer to drive a few miles away to another community where the same type of specialty shop was located. Whether they did so for reasons other than an unwillingness to deal with a black person is beyond my knowledge, but one thing is clear: it was not the behaviour or personality of the African Canadian that kept them away. She was consistently pleasant and friendly, and absolutely not a racist herself. Her best friend in the community, in fact, was a middle-aged woman whose ethnic roots were British.

During her brief period in business this woman had been the subject of a great deal of gossip, some of it, she realized, prompted by her status as a single woman: 'People watch me. They seem to know every move I make. I hate small towns. Because of the talk.' Complicating matters was the religious factor. She was a committed Christian, Pentecostal in persuasion, and regularly joined a small group of African Canadians in worship. Sometimes services were held in a room in an elementary school, sometimes in her apartment above the store, and occasionally at her parent's house. While none of this prompted anything more than mild curiosity from the locals, her alleged connection with two other religious groups was regarded as more sinister. One was the 'no-name' church referred to in an earlier chapter which doubled as a drop-in centre for alcoholics and drug addicts – the pet project of a woman who was regarded as weird by Paradise people. Although the African Canadian denied that she belonged to that church, the fact that her own store was situated next door and that she had attended a couple of services had been enough for people to conclude otherwise. She had also worshipped briefly in a small church in the countryside that had been established by a black pastor from the United States. The gossip suggested that strange things were occurring in this church. The pastor, according to the Paradise woman, did have some peculiar ideas about how his flock should dress, but that was the extent of it. Eventually the church was burned down by two local youths, and the pastor moved on to greener pastures, leaving behind unpaid electricity bills and a landlord looking for the rent. Although the woman had ceased attending services at this church several months before it was destroyed, her reputation nevertheless was affected. As one Paradise native remarked, people were only too willing to believe that all blacks are strange and untrustworthy.

This woman's problems did not end with her decision to sell the store. One day, for example, a potential purchaser entered the premises, inquired about the price, and was sufficiently interested to ask to see the owner. When the black woman replied that she was speaking to the owner, the visitor thanked her for her time and walked out. This made her wonder if she was going to have as much difficulty selling the store as she had running it. By 1990 the store had been rented, and she had moved to Toronto.

Life in the Countryside

When I asked an African Canadian whose home was located on a few acres of land in the countryside to compare race relations in the city and the country, he commented: 'I don't think it's better in the country. The only thing is that you can avoid your neighbour better.' This man, in his mid-forties, had emigrated with his wife to Canada from the West Indies about twenty years ago. For most of those years they lived near Toronto, where he worked as a skilled tradesman; he also was a pastor for an essentially black congregation (apparently only one white family attended regularly) in a church located in the countryside a few miles away. His wife, when I met her, had returned to university to complete her degree. They had three children, the oldest of which had left home.

The experience of this middle-class couple in urban Canada had not always been pleasant. One of their next-door neighbours had been so hostile that he refused even to greet them when they encountered one other outside their houses. According to this mild-mannered African Canadian, his workplace near the city also left a lot to be desired. While he enjoyed good relationships with some of his co-workers, his manager, he claimed, was a complete racist, and always bypassed him for promotion, or when there were opportunities to enrol in courses to upgrade his qualifications.

In 1986, with the hope of finding a better quality of life, including more meaningful interaction with their neighbours, they moved to their new home in the rolling hills near Paradise. 'When we first came up,' he stated, 'we made a big barbecue, and invited all the neighbours.' Their first disappointment was that only one of these neighbours ever invited them back. Five years later he and his wife still felt almost as isolated as they had when they moved there. Perhaps, he mused, he should be more content, because at least people wave at him when they pass by in the car, rather than ignoring him as sometimes happened in the city. 'My neighbour to the south,' he remarked, 'was a little quiet at first. They're not the social type. In fact,' he added, 'I can almost count the number of times that we've stood up together to talk.' The children in another family nearby, whose parents were university graduates, were the same age as his own, and one was the same sex, but they never played together, and had never been in each other's house. One day his daughters watched the neighbouring kids bounce a basketball on their driveway, and walked over to ask if they could play. The answer was no. Of course, it is always possible that the members of this other family were motivated by a keen sense of privacy rather than prejudice, but the fact that not even the children interacted is suggestive.

These immigrants from the West Indies had also run into a few problems with township officials concerning building permits and taxes, and wondered if they were being treated unfairly because of their ethnicity. What disappointed them most of all was that the friendships that they had anticipated had failed to materialize. When it was pointed out to them that social life in rural Ontario has changed, with visiting among neighbours reduced to a minimum, partly because so many people, like themselves, were commuters, the man retorted that that was precisely his point: the value placed on privacy provided a cover for racially inclined individuals.

Precisely the same interpretation was made by another man who had emigrated from the West Indies. He and his wife had lived on a farm a few miles from Paradise for more than ten years. Although they kept a few cattle, chickens, and ducks, their main source of income was the man's job with a company located on the outskirts of Toronto. What has surprised them about life in the country has been the essential isolation of individual households. Visiting back and forth, they revealed, is almost non-existent. It is this absence of interaction, they argued, that allows people to hide their racism. Actually, the man

observed, there is a basic contradiction in rural life. On those occasions when his cows had got out onto the road, complete strangers had
stopped to help round them up. Yet one's own neighbours react as if
one has two heads when one drops in unexpectedly for a visit. The
woman in this family, a dedicated Christian, believed that the only way
to defeat racism was with love and kindness. For a half dozen years
they were given the cold shoulder by one neighbour, a retired civil
servant, who openly expressed his disdain for black people. But they
continued to greet him cordially, and offered their assistance when it
was needed. Eventually the ice thawed, and this neighbour became a
friend and ally. Such a happy outcome was not repeated with another
couple who lived nearby. These elderly people, who had farmed in the
area all their lives, apparently took their hatred of black people to
their graves.

By 1990 the middle-aged man and woman from the West Indies were
having second thoughts about rural life. This was not because of racism, although in their judgment the country was no more hospitable
than the city. Instead, it was because their children had all grown up
and left home, and they no longer were certain that they wanted to
spend the rest of their lives, especially the winters, in the Ontario
countryside. When the man's company relocated in the United States
after free trade became a reality, and he lost his job, he and his wife
decided that it might be time to think about returning to the West
Indies.

One African Canadian who lived on a farm in the area did express
contentment with the lack of interaction with the neighbours, but his
situation contained some special features. In the late 1980s he was
fired from his position as a technician in a large public organization
in Paradise, and his case was placed under review by the Ontario
Human Rights Commission. The grounds for his release, according to
the organization's chief administrator, were straightforward and more
than sufficient: the man was incompetent at his job; he worked overtime unnecessarily in order to claim double pay; he physically molested
both male and female clients; and he was mentally unstable. According
to the man himself, all his problems were racially generated. For
several years, he said, he had happily worked in the organization, but
everything changed when a new administrator, whom he claimed was
a racist, arrived on the scene. The man who fired him was yet another
administrator, who, according to the black employee, could not stom-
ach the thought that a black man earned a decent salary. People in

town who were aware of the confrontation were divided about which version to believe. One long-time merchant dismissed it as a typical case of black people screaming racism in order to conceal incompetence. A woman, also a native of the community, who had had an opportunity to watch the African Canadian perform on the job, insisted that he was 'a terrific technician.' Virtually every black person who knew about the confrontation thought that it was a clear case of racism, and some of them suggested that the fact that the man's wife was white was part of the problem. The technician, about forty years old and educated in the United States, admitted that he did experience a mild nervous breakdown, but blamed it on the stress created by the administrator, who, he claimed, always criticized his performance, and attempted to destroy his reputation. It is understandable, then, that when this man returned to his farm a few miles from Paradise after work, he was contented simply to relax in the company of his family, and, when he had time, to putter around in the fields or in the bush.

School

Black teenagers gave a mixed report about their experiences in the local schools. Two of them apparently had been popular, partly because they were athletic, and a third youth's charm had won him many friends. Not all of them were so fortunate. One student who was determined to attend university was placed against her will in the general rather than the advanced course of studies. Her parents, who emphasized that it was the teachers rather than the students who gave their daughter a hard time, attempted to have her switched to the advanced program, but to no avail. As a result, they removed her from the school and enrolled her in an institution closer to the city. Inasmuch as she excelled in the advanced program in the new school, her parents concluded that they had been correct to interpret her problems in Paradise as racially motivated.

Another student, who came from a poorer family, and in fact was living on her own, did not have the advantage of middle-class parents to help fight her battles. One of her parents was white, and her own skin colour was light, which led people to sometimes mistake her for Italian. In her own mind, she very definitely was black. In fact, she revealed: 'I used to hate white people, even though my mother was white.' When she was a child, she added, she had never regarded her mother as a white person. She frankly stated that she had also hated Chinese and East Indians, but as she grew older, realized she had been wrong, and insisted that she now treated everyone in the same manner.

In this young woman's judgment, Paradise is a very racist little community. To illustrate, she said that her two brothers, who have dark skins, are regularly taunted and have not been able to locate steady employment. One of her friends, British and French in background, claimed that when she entered a local restaurant with her black boyfriend, she was greeted with these words: 'Where's the leash for your nigger?' These two young women themselves were not devoid of prejudice. They described the man who had made this statement as an uneducated country bumpkin, and one of them remarked: 'He walks into the restaurant with his boots covered with pigshit. He's your stereotypical farmer.' As for the school, the teenager in question stated: 'I find it to be very racist.' She made it clear that she was not only referring to the student body: 'Well, the teachers are very prejudiced too.' One teacher in particular, she claimed, was an absolute racist. What was significant was that this same teacher's name was repeated by several other African Canadians.

The principal of the school offered quite a different perspective. As far as she could judge, she said, the school was free of racism, both among the students and the staff. When I showed her a letter to the editor of the local newspaper that had been written anonymously a couple of months earlier by a visible-minority student, complaining bitterly about the racism in the school, surprisingly she expressed a complete lack of knowledge about it. One of the teachers in the school was considerably more aware of the situation. Discussing the attitudes of the students, he stated: 'There have been racist incidents. There's been name-calling in class about the Pakis and Sikhs. Maybe somebody yelling "Chink."' He made it clear that he did not tolerate such comments in his own classroom. He also contended that race and ethnicity were not the basis for group formation in the school. The exception, he said, was the Dutch Reformed kids, but he thought they stuck together because of the religious rather than the ethnic bond. While he believed that a couple of his colleagues were intolerant, judging by the comments that they made in the staffroom, that was not his impression of most of them: 'I'd rate them as much more tolerant than the general public.'

This brings us to the case of the teacher who was consistently fingered by blacks as a racist.[2] This man, like the principal, contended that there was absolutely no racism in the school. 'We do have a division in our school population,' he said, 'between the general and advanced.' The kids in the general program of studies, he explained, do not participate in anything, including sports. In this man's view, social class too was irrelevant within the student body: 'There's certainly no grouping, or different treatment, on that basis.' Yet as he talked, some interesting contradictions began to emerge. Like a few other people, he was inclined to equate low intelligence with poverty, and to explain both in terms of incest. Referring to the impoverished region near Paradise which in an earlier chapter was labelled 'Hillbilly Ontario,' he remarked: ' A lot of kids from there are mentally handicapped because of inbreeding.'

The teacher drew a distinction between Asian and African Canadians (plus Native people), and expressed a clear preference for the former: 'A Filipino family came in this year. They made a positive contribution. They're talented. They're good in sports.' He described recent Korean immigrants in the town as 'a good family.' Indian kids (by which he meant Native people) and black kids, he observed, present the same problem: 'They don't integrate.' Both blacks and Indians, he continued, are militant, semi-paranoid, usually come from weak families, and 'aren't education-oriented like the Orientals.' At one point he commented: 'I don't think the black kids get any hassle.' He implied, indeed, that the problem was quite the reverse: 'Those big, strong black boys tend to be physically imposing.'

As this man revealed his attitudes about a wide range of issues, and provided information about his relatively parochial background, I began to visualize a familiar figure: the authoritarian personality. Commenting on the lack of respect teachers are given today by students, he made it clear that he himself never had problems concerning discipline in the classroom. It is possible that what some African Canadians have interpreted as a racist orientation was nothing more than an expression of the man's forceful personality and his insistence on rigid control in the classroom.

A Success Story

From what we have seen so far, it made little difference whether the African Canadians came from families that had been pioneers in the nation or recent immigrants, whether they were in business locally or commuters, whether they worked or were retired, whether they were men or women and elderly or young, and whether they lived in town or out in the country – the results were the same: widespread racism, or at least the perception of such racism. There were, however, some exceptions. One concerns a middle-aged couple – the man from the West Indies, the woman from England – who moved to the outskirts of Paradise around 1985. The man ran his own business, while his wife was employed in a government organization. Both of them insisted that they had rarely encountered racism anywhere in Canada, including the Paradise region, and expressed happiness with their lives in rural Ontario.

Prior to moving to Paradise, they had lived in another town in Dufferin County, and there they did have an unpleasant experience. One of their neighbours left little doubt about what she thought about interracial marriage, and was nasty to their children. Their solution was to write a letter to the editor of the local newspaper, complaining in general about intolerant, narrow-minded residents. That the message was aimed at one neighbour in particular was apparently common knowledge; guilty of giving the community a bad reputation, this woman found herself without friends, and within a year she and her family had moved to another town.

When the man from the West Indies and his wife settled outside Paradise a few years later, they did encounter the normal opposition to newcomers who attempt to establish businesses in the area. 'I used to have people say you'll never make it here,' said the man. But make it they did. Although only in their early fifties, they were semi-retired by 1990, with property in different parts of the province, plus a few acres in the West Indies. Unlike the previous African Canadians who have been described, this family had no complaint about being given the cold shoulder by neighbours. This does not mean that they had been warmly embraced. The reality, instead, was that they did not have any friends in the area, nor, they said, did they want any. In the woman's words, 'We're very private people. We really don't neighbour a lot.' Although they did not belong to any local organizations, the woman attended church on a regular basis, but it was located in a community several miles from Paradise. Their lifestyle, she commented, has allowed them to avoid the one thing about rural life that drives her mad: gossip. This hard-working and successful couple, it might be observed, have made a powerful discovery: if one does not need other

people, one's vulnerability to the negative aspects of human interaction is remarkably reduced.

Asian Canadians

Unlike the African-Canadian pioneers who had homesteaded several
miles away from Paradise during the previous century, there were few
Asian Canadians in the area before the 1970s. Prior to the Second
World War there was a Chinese laundry in the community, as well as
a Chinese restaurant, owned by two families in succession. The people
who operated the restaurant in the 1950s were remembered with
fondness and respect by elderly residents. One man, who had owned
a store next to the restaurant, described them as 'great citizens.' Apparently one of his daughters had been a close friend of the daughter
in the other family and was a guest so often in the restaurant that she
even had her own chopsticks. This does not mean that these Chinese
Canadians were highly integrated into the life of the community. In
fact, as one person remarked about the male head of the family, 'I
never saw that man outside the restaurant.'

While there were two Chinese restaurants in the town in the 1980s,
the vast majority of people from Asia who had moved to the area in
recent years were immigrants from India and Pakistan, and most of
them were involved in three types of business: gas stations, motels, and
variety stores.

GAS STATIONS

On one occasion when I was visiting a gas station owned by local
whites, a man drove up to the pumps, got out, and exclaimed (presumably with considerable hyperbole): 'This is the eleventh place I've
tried tonight. If this place had changed hands, and somebody with a
cloth on his head walked out, I'd give up.' That man's attitude pretty
well sums up the reaction to the Indian and Pakistani Canadians who
had bought service stations, which makes it understandable why so
many of their businesses failed. Prejudice and discrimination, however,
cannot have been the only factors dictating success or failure because,
as the saying goes, a constant cannot explain variation – in this instance, the fact that some of these gas stations were highly successful
operations. The additional factors, as the following case studies illus-

trate, include the past reputation and location of the gas stations and, equally important, the behaviour of the people who operated them.

My first example concerns a Sikh about forty-five years old who had emigrated to Canada in the 1970s. For several years this man, who had the equivalent of about a grade ten education, worked in a factory near Toronto. After rising to the position of supervisor, he found himself without a job: 'They let me go, because they wanted to promote a white guy. And he don't know nothing.' The same thing, he claimed, happened in two other jobs. Eventually he bought a variety store, and with his wife employed as a nurse in a hospital in Toronto, the family prospered. Several of his friends had gone into the gas station business, and he decided to do the same. He sold the variety store and rented a service station near Paradise that had been closed for several months, with the option of purchase. He attempted to hire local help, but claimed that he could not find anyone willing to work for him: 'I'm sorry to say it: these white people don't want to work.' He himself put in about fifteen hours on the job every day, rising at 5 a.m. and closing the station at 9 p.m.

Business was brisk enough at first, mainly because local people, curious to see who had taken over the station, stopped to buy gas. Eventually this source dried up, and he was left mostly with the trade of people in transit. It was sometimes apparent, according to the man, that neither the locals nor the travellers were very pleased to see a person of his ethnic background handling the gas pump: 'People don't tell you that to your face. But you can feel it. They don't like it when I own this business.' Yet these signs of prejudice, when they were evident, did not bother him very much. His attitude was that racism is natural, and therefore it was not worthwhile getting upset about it: 'It's everywhere. Even back home too. Nobody can stop that. It's the nature.' This interpretation of racism seemed to pervade all aspects of his life. He explained that he never talks to his children about racism. They may be subjected to name-calling in school, he commented, but if so he did not want to know about it. His rationale, again, was that racism is universal and inevitable, and his children simply have to learn to cope with it.

When this man first settled in Canada, he did attempt to make friends with what he termed 'Canadians,' by which he meant people of European origin: 'I had a couple of friends from work. I invite them home a couple of times, and they see how we live and don't like it. You can tell.' At this point, it appeared that he was referring to the attitudes of his visitors towards the odour of Indian cuisine, but he explained: 'It wasn't the food. Food-wise, they love it. They were jealous.' The reason, he stated, was that he lived in a lovely house, with new and attractive furniture, and had all the standard amenities such as a microwave oven and a video cassette recorder. His visitors apparently voiced their surprise that an immigrant could have accumulated so much, and were unimpressed when he pointed out how hard he and his wife had worked. As a result of the envious reaction of these guests, he concluded that he had been mistaken to think that it was possible to make friends with white people, and never again invited 'Canadians' into his home.

He had heard about Philip Rushton, the psychology professor at the University of Western Ontario, and had a crude understanding of his argument: namely, that Orientals are more intelligent than whites, who in turn are more intelligent than blacks. When asked if he thought Rushton was correct, he replied: 'Maybe he is.' Then he added: 'The dumb people isn't going to like it.' About the identity of the 'dumb people' he left no doubt: black people. He also speculated that the uproar about Rushton, and the effort to keep him out of the classroom, had little to do with the professor's remarks about black people. Instead, it was a result of Rushton's thesis that Orientals are smarter than whites; as he observed wryly, 'White people don't like that.'

This man made it perfectly clear that he was living in Canada solely because of the greater economic prospects, especially for his children: 'That's the main purpose behind it. If I go back home, I can live like a king. I still have a house there.' Influenced by his attitude that racism is just a normal part of life, on the whole he was satisfied with what he had accomplished since emigrating to Canada. Although he did not have any white friends, four of his brothers lived in and around Toronto, and he visited them on weekends. As for the experiment in country living, it did not work out. Despite his hard work, business never did pick up, and the main reason was clear. The previous owners, also immigrants from India, had apparently lacked the capital with which to carry the business until it became established. Even more damaging was the fact that they did not keep regular hours, or provide efficient and friendly service when they were open. By the time the current operator arrived on the scene, the gas station had been closed for several months; despite his valiant efforts to win back customers who had grown accustomed to buying their gas elsewhere, he was unable to overcome the stigma that had become associated with the station. Within a year he had decided not to exercise the option to purchase the station, and had returned to the city.

In some cases, businesses went under as a result of the combined impact of discrimination and poor location. For example, a family from India bought an attractive service station located on the main street of a village near Paradise. The business had previously been owned by local people and apparently had been viable. For about six months the new owners went through the motions of opening the station in the morning and closing it in the evening, wondering where all the customers had gone. Eventually they accepted the obvious: they had been boycotted. Many of the residents of the village had begun to drive a few miles down the highway to a gas station owned by local people. Had the Indian family's station been located on the highway, rather than in the village, they would at least have had access to the trade of travellers. As it was, within a year they had put the business for sale.

Some of the Asian Canadians who owned service stations, faced with the hard reality that they were being boycotted, tried a different strategy: while they remained the owners, they kept in the background and hired local people to operate the stations. Not even this ploy, however, guaranteed success. Two young local men who took over one service station proved to be irresponsible. They failed to keep regular hours, were discourteous to customers, and drank heavily on the job. Yet even when the local operator was dependable, the results were often little different. In 1989, for example, an immigrant from Pakistan bought a gas station with an excellent location on a busy highway. Since he was totally involved with another business in Toronto, he hired a fellow countryman to run the station. Almost overnight business plunged. The desperate owner then engaged the services of a man who had grown up on a nearby farm. Although this individual was hard-working and well liked, the business showed only a modest improvement. As he explained, a lot of people still refused to buy gas from him because the station had previously been in the hands of 'Pakis.' Some of them were aware that the Pakistani Canadian was still in charge behind the scenes, and made it clear that they would get their gas elsewhere until a white man bought the business.

The local man hired to run the service station, a high school dropout, confessed that he used to share his neighbours' attitudes towards people from Pakistan, but working for the man from Toronto had been an eye-opener. He had learned to admire the owner, whom he described as a shrewd businessman, but honest, fair, and decent, and he regretted the prejudice and discrimination harboured by the people among whom he grew up. Such a change of heart was not evident in the case of another local man employed to help operate a gas station which was also owned by an immigrant from Pakistan. In his words: 'I don't care for Pakis myself.' He went on to state that he would work for them, 'but not for the same money; I want more,' implying that he was well paid in his current job.

The location and past reputation of service stations were not the only factors conditioning the degree of success or failure. Just as important was the behaviour of the owners and operators. An African Canadian, for example, stated that when a family from India took over a station a few miles from his home, he purposefully gave them his business in order to help them out. Yet he would never know if the station would be opened or closed; when the attendants were on duty, they were curt and sloppy. After a few months, he began to avoid the gas station, which was eventually put up for sale and purchased by another family from India.

I learned about five service stations owned by Asian Canadians that went bankrupt at least partly because of poor management, or at least the perception of poor management: given the prejudice and discrimination in the area, the fact that the owners and operators were dark-skinned 'foreigners' was sometimes sufficient grounds for people to conclude that the businesses weren't being run efficiently. In two cases, however, there was little doubt that management problems did exist; the people in charge drank regularly on the job, and sometimes didn't even bother to unlock the doors. A third case, in which the owner's behaviour and personality were the subject of gossip, was somewhat more complicated. This man, a Sikh who had immigrated from India in the 1970s, had driven a taxi in Metro Toronto for several years. In the late 1980s he bought a service station near Paradise. Immigrants, he remarked, were getting smarter; they were no longer satisfied to toil in menial jobs while their bosses get rich. In the city he had worn a turban, but in order to enhance his acceptance in rural Ontario he decided to remove it during working hours. Despite this concession to local sensibilities, and the excellent location of his business on a well-travelled highway, he gradually moved closer and closer to bankruptcy. In his case, part of the problem was that he had invested in two other businesses as well, but with the downswing in the economy it became evident that he had spread his finances too thinly. The other part of the problem was his unenviable reputation among the local farmers and the nearby villagers. Not only was it said that he was a little too fond of the bottle, but he was also described as unpleasant and quarrelsome. One elderly farmer remarked that he seemed to have a superior attitude, treating his customers with disrespect. In my own judgment, this evaluation of the man's character was somewhat unjustified. It was correct that he often seemed aloof and distracted when interacting with customers, but that may have reflected the financial pressure that he was under, plus his guarded personality. On several occasions, in fact, I observed that both he and his wife were warm and considerate towards the elderly natives who occasionally hung around the small store connected to the service station.

When a service station develops a bad reputation, it is extremely difficult for new owners, regardless of their efforts and behaviour, to turn the business around. The following two cases were exceptions. In the late 1980s a Hindu about forty years old who had lived and worked on the edge of Toronto for several years, sometimes driving a taxi and at other times employed by a small firm involved in construction, decided the time had come to take the big gamble and establish his own business. He bought a gas station near Paradise which had gone steadily downhill under the inadequate management of the previous owner, also an immigrant from India; the business had actually been boarded up for several months. It was touch and go for almost a year whether he would make it. Not only did he have to overcome the past reputation of the station, but he also ran into his share of obstacles. He vividly recalled the hostile reaction of one woman who had pulled in for a refill, and cursed him up and down for the simple reason that he was not a 'Canadian,' but it was typical of him to observe that maybe she was nasty to everyone. A farmer said to him: 'People like you, you'll never make it.' Sometimes the comments were more humorous. An elderly man who stopped for gas demanded: 'You're from what country?' When the owner indicated India, the customer observed that he must be at least partly civilized, thanks to the British colonial presence. Occasionally customers just stared at him without uttering a word. What he found curious was that this was the reaction sometimes of people who originated from his own part of the world. A particularly vicious rumour, launched shortly after he had opened for business, was that he added water to his gas. Yet the most threatening confrontation involved two men from his homeland who operated their own gas station nearby. Shortly after he had taken over the business, they arrived on his doorstep and suggested that it would be safer for his health if he found another way to make a living. A little while later their own gas station went bankrupt. As the man remarked, it was ironical that he had been threatened by fellow Indians rather than by Canadians. It just went to show, he added, that the most violent people in the world are East Indians, Chinese, and Italians. Americans and 'the English,' he thought, would never stoop to such vile tactics.

Despite these various obstacles, the man persevered, and within a year he was the proud owner of a remarkably improved business. This was partly a result of efficient management. The station was open regularly from early morning to late evening, and service was prompt and courteous. But there was more than that to the story. Over a two-year period I had an opportunity to observe this man's interaction with his customers. At the beginning local people were curious, wary, and occasionally hostile. Yet as the months passed, more and more of them began to drop into the little coffee shop, just to pass the time of day. What had produced the change in their attitudes? It was primarily the attractive personal qualities of the owner. Joking around, talking in colloquialisms, swearing with the best of them, it almost seemed that he had been born just down the road; at least, one would have thought, he must have come from a similar rural background. In fact, he was raised in one of the largest cities in India. Although not well educated or sophisticated (his wife was a university graduate), he was intelligent and witty, and was soon recognized as a man of enjoyable company. This case, indeed, reflects the salutary effect of education in the broadest sense: the locals had gone through a learning process which undermined their prejudgments.

I do not mean to paint this man as a saint. He confessed that he used to gamble a bit too much, and was known to take a drink or two. He also held some rather contradictory attitudes about matters racial. He sympathized with 'coloureds,' by which he meant blacks, and remarked: 'I think the Jews have suffered more than the coloured people.' Yet he also was not reluctant to refer to some of the locals as mentally retarded, and he argued, tongue in cheek, that the Canadian government should send him a monthly cheque for employing a young local person, thus keeping him off welfare. Like a previous character who was described, he also thought racism was not only inevitable but also natural. Nothing, he declared, would ever change it.

Although this man's example clearly demonstrates that one's behaviour and personal qualities can condition the degree of one's success or failure, the limitations of the argument should be kept in mind. In previous chapters, it was shown that the interactional status of a poor person might be higher than that of a wealthy person; however, nobody ever assumed that a pleasant personality changed the hard reality of the rich man's superior class position and power. Similarly, the behaviour of Asian Canadians in the gas station business, whether attractive or repulsive, was overshadowed by their ascribed statuses as non-white minorities. Thus, despite the relaxed and amicable relationships that the man from India enjoyed with local people, when the working day was spent and it was time to eat supper or perhaps sip a couple of beers with friends, the locals went their own ways. Now was it a one-way street. Although the owner of the gas station possessed a remarkable capacity to communicate with the local people, he made it clear that when he shut down the pumps at the end of the day, the interaction ceased. His companions then became friends from India down the road and his brother and his wife's cousins who lived towards the city. Perhaps, he once observed, things will be different for his children; as for himself, despite his demonstrated capacity to bridge cultures, he could never really escape from the conviction that the natural basis of social interaction was race.

The other exceptional case concerns a Sikh family that purchased the poorly managed gas station that the African Canadian had reluctantly decided to avoid. The new owners, consisting of an older couple, their children, the spouses of their children, and their grandchildren, lived on a nearby farm. While the daily operation of the station was in the hands of one of the sons, assisted by his brother's wife, other members of the family who commuted to jobs in the Toronto area were expected to take turns relieving them when they arrived back in the evening.

I had heard from some local whites that hardly anyone bought gas at this station, but my observations indicated otherwise: business, in fact, was booming. As the young man in charge explained, people were wary at first, wondering if the new owners would be as inept as the previous ones. But he kept regular hours – from 5 a.m. to 11 p.m. – was courteous with everyone, and made a major effort to make friends with the local people. He also provided credit to regular customers ('I give the credit to the white peoples. I give a limit – like $20'), and like some other Asian Canadians, he sold his gas for slightly less than his competitors. In many respects he had the same capacity to communicate with the locals as had the man in the previous case.

He often greeted customers by their first names, and sometimes casually and unselfconsciously put his arm around them as they walked into the store. His sister-in-law possessed the same touch. On one occasion as I watched her chatting and joking with a young local woman, the impression was that of close friends who had grown up next door to each other. As a middle-aged man from the area observed, the difference between these people and the previous owners was like night and day. He had begun, he said, to think that all people from India were dirty and unreliable, but the new owners had proved him wrong.

When the young man who operated the gas station was asked if he had confronted any prejudice, he remarked: 'Some crazy people, they don't like foreigners. I tell them we are all foreigners in this country.' Occasionally, he added, a customer will berate him for taking over a business that should be run by 'Canadians,' and accuse him of receiving hand-outs from the government. He also stated that some of the local people who owned a nearby gas station had been less than friendly, but put that down to jealousy rather than racism, reflecting the growing popularity of his own gas station.

Despite the undoubted capacity of this man and his sister-in-law to get along with the locals, they too separated their working and their private lives. When not on the job, their interaction was with their extended family and with friends from India who lived nearby. Surprisingly, this young man, who also ventured the opinion that it was natural to stick with one's own kind, had never once visited the little village a mile or so from the gas station. His behaviour, while apparently adequate for the gas station business, was not likely to get him invited into the homes of his neighbours. Yet perhaps there was hope. One evening when I stopped at the gas station, pandemonium had erupted. Several Asian men and women were running around amidst curious customers. The cause was soon apparent. There, on wobbly legs, trying to serve gas, and loudly berating everyone who tried to help him, was our genial young gas attendant, drunk as a skunk. As I watched the unfolding drama, I could not help but wonder, in view of the area's reputation for hard-drinking men, whether his condition would be held for or against him.

MOTELS

In 1991 a former native of Paradise, on a sentimental voyage to the land of her youth, checked into a local motel and fell into a state of mild shock: the owners of the motel were Sikhs from India. As she made clear, the people in the world she most despises and fears are the Sikhs. This woman was much too gracious to make her feelings explicit, and if her hosts detected anything peculiar about her reaction to them, they kept it to themselves.

The motel in question had actually been owned by a Moslem family from Pakistan when I began my research in 1988. Within a year they had sold it to the family from India and had returned to Pakistan for an extended holiday. The people who bought it were well-educated (both the wife and husband had university degrees), hard-working, and ambitious. The husband continued to work and live in Toronto, where they owned two houses, returning to the motel on weekends when he was free (he also worked part-time in real estate). Helping his wife to run the motel was her sister-in-law and, while he was unemployed for several months, her younger brother.

The woman from Pakistan who had previously operated the motel had complained that the people of Paradise always stared at her, something that did not happen in the city. Her successor's experiences were similar. In Toronto, where she and her husband had lived for several years, she had worn her native garb to work. She continued to do so on first arrival outside Paradise, but switched to Western dress because of the reaction of the locals. When they took over the motel there were a few problems with people who capitalized on their lack of experience and skipped off without paying. Although they soon learned to make certain that their clients possessed sufficient funds, they also proved that they could be generous when the circumstances warranted it. For example, they allowed a young unemployed man to stay for a couple of weeks without paying while he looked for work, on the condition that he would do so when he was able. This man, true to his word, found a job and eventually settled the debt.

As far as prejudice and discrimination are concerned, the owners of the motel had no major complaints. The woman said that occasionally it was obvious that a client did not appreciate her national origin, but she just ignored the implied racism. Their two children have encountered some difficulties, but nothing too serious. For several weeks a youngster regularly telephoned the motel and berated the children with foul language and racist terminology. Their mother eventually discovered the caller's identity – a schoolmate of her children – and put an end to the nonsense. Occasionally she would learn that her son had been involved in a fight at the school, but he was always reluctant to discuss the matter, and she was never sure whether it involved racism or was simply normal schoolyard antics. Certainly, her own children fared better in the school than those in another Sikh family, whose parents could not afford to buy them decent clothes (and, according to a woman who was also originally from India, were too uneducated to know how to dress their children). In contrast, the woman at the motel not only had sufficient money to purchase attractive clothes for her children, but had the good sense to allow them to choose their own clothes so that they would fit in with the other kids at school.

This woman, who dismissed the stares of locals as innocuous curiosity, stated that on those rare occasions when she had experienced what appeared to be racism, the setting had been the urban centres to the south, rather than the Paradise area. For example, on one day after moving to the motel she travelled to Toronto to shop, taking the opportunity to wear her native clothes. Several white youths accosted her on the street and began to shout 'Paki, Paki.' As she smiled thinly, they didn't even realize she was from India. Her brother's experiences were similar. A few months after moving to the motel, he stayed overnight in Toronto with a friend from India. When he came out of the house in the morning, he discovered that his tires had been slashed. But as he pointed out, there was no certainty that the vandalism was racially inspired, because how could anyone have known that the car was owned by a person from his ethnic background?

While the experiences of these people would suggest that rural Ontario has been more hospitable than urban Ontario, it must be made clear that their interaction with the locals in and around Paradise had been severely limited. This was partly a result of the business itself: most of their clients were strangers passing through, or construction workers temporarily residing in the area. It also was a result of choice: the owners of the motel, although hospitable to their clients, and warm and friendly with those among them who stayed for lengthy periods and who expressed an interest in getting to know them, almost never entered the town of Paradise. Except for another family from India nearby, they had no close friends in the area. Whenever the woman had free time, she joined her husband in the city, where they socialized, shopped, and worshipped. Like many other immigrants, their long-range plans did not necessarily include Canada. Canada had provided an opportunity, with hard work, to become economically secure, and to establish their children in an industrialized nation. While the couple intended to return to India on retirement, where they still owned property, it was their hope that their children would remain and prosper in Canada, the land of their birth.[3]

The experiences and attitudes of the owners of other motels were essentially the same. A Hindu couple who had bought a motel expressed nothing but appreciation for the opportunity to make a living and raise their children in Canada, a country which they had found to be remarkably tolerant. The man had formerly worked his way up to a supervisory position in a factory elsewhere in Ontario. Later he and his wife owned and operated a supermarket in a small town, where their children played baseball and he belonged to a service club. By the time this couple went into the motel business, two of their children had been graduated from Canadian universities. Sophisticated, adaptable, worldly, and hard-working, what was surprising, given the degree to which they said they had become integrated into settings where they had lived previously, was their essential isolation in the Paradise area. They only interacted on a regular basis with one family, also recent immigrants from India. What made the difference, presumably, was that their children had grown up and left home, and thus no longer brought them into contact with other families, plus the fact that the motel business catered mainly to transients and outsiders.

In another motel, the owner possessed a professional degree from an Indian university. Although it perturbed him that his credentials were not recognized in Canada, which forced him to turn to a career in business, he had no complaints about his reception in rural Ontario. The locals, he stated, certainly were inclined to stare at him as he walked along the street, but that was mere curiosity, he thought, prompted by his skin colour and newcomer status. What made this man somewhat different than the other motel owners from Asia was his greater presence and interaction among the locals, to the extent that an influential member of a service club was considering nominating him for membership. In this immigrant's case, two things were different. First, connected to the motel was a large restaurant. Secondly, the motel, unlike the ones referred to earlier, was located within the town itself. Both factors helped to make the man a familiar figure in the town, and brought him into daily contact with the locals.

VARIETY STORES

My first example consists of a Hindu couple, both of them university graduates, who emigrated to Canada about twenty years ago. They lived in Toronto for several years, where they owned a specialty shop, and moved to Paradise in the late 1980s after seeing an advertisement for the sale of a variety store. Their two children went through a period of adjustment, but they excelled in school (one of them currently attends university), and apparently became popular. Although both the man and the woman said they had rarely encountered prejudice in Canada, and never in Paradise, they also revealed that they did not have any friends in town. The reason, they explained, was that they didn't have time: the store was open from early morning until late evening. Yet they did find time periodically to visit old friends in the city, and to keep up their contacts in the East Indian community.

The picture these people painted of benign race relations in small-town Ontario was echoed by the owners and operators of other variety stores. Although one of these stores was a hang-out for long-haired local youths, the Korean Canadian who ran the business for his uncle professed not to be concerned. He insisted that he liked them, and certainly his rapport with them was excellent. He joked back and forth with them, and on one occasion when several customers had crowded into the store, one of the young men with dangling locks went behind the counter and helped out. Even when the store operator was forced to push several of the adolescents who had been drinking too much out onto the street one evening, there had been sufficient mutual respect to avoid an ugly confrontation. The man who operated the store, about thirty years old and a university graduate, was not thrilled about the prospect of spending the remainder of his life in rural Ontario. But it was boredom rather than prejudice that made him long for the bright lights of the city. The owner of a third variety store, also originally from Korea and a university graduate, expressed more contentment with life in the small town, possibly because he was a decade older. Respected as an excellent businessman, he had been wooed by a service club to become a member. Like most other Asian Canadians who had moved to the region, however, he preferred to confine his interaction specifically to business matters. He did belong to a voluntary organization, but it was located in the city, and its purpose was to serve the Korean-Canadian community.

It is apparent that the degree of prejudice towards visible-minority newcomers gradually diminished as we moved from the cases of the gas stations to the motel business and finally to the variety stores. Why should that be so? One possible explanation is that the owners or operators in all of the variety stores were university graduates, which may have enhanced their reputations among the locals, and made them more knowledgeable about how to communicate across cultural divides. Yet most of the motel owners also were university graduates; besides, it was improbable that many of the locals even knew who among the Asian Canadians possessed university degrees. Another reason might concern the personal qualities and behaviour of the people who operated the variety stores. In the three examples that were provided, the individuals were pleasant, diligent, and sober; these same qualities, however, were prominent among most of the motel owners, and among many of the gas station operators as well. While the impact of education, personality, and behaviour cannot be dismissed entirely, two additional, and possibly more profound, explanations for the different degrees of prejudice exist. One concerns the amount of interaction between the Asian Canadians and the local population. There may have been less hostility on the part of the locals towards the owners of the motels compared to the owners of the gas stations because the former's business consisted primarily of outsiders and transients; the locals simply did not come in contact with them; in contrast, they had to buy their gas somewhere, and it was becoming increasingly more difficult to do so in a station owned by local people. Of course, that does not explain why the people in the variety stores, who also had regular interaction with local customers, appeared to experience the least prejudice of all. At this juncture we must introduce the second explanation: sheer economics. Both the gas stations and the motels were regarded by locals as important, lucrative businesses. The variety stores, in contrast, were seen as low-prestige affairs, where one counted in pennies rather than in dollars – the proper place, some people thought, for the Third World immigrants.

Conclusion

If we ignore the territorial dimension of community, and define it solely in terms of a sense of belonging, then the Asian Canadians who were dispersed around Paradise constituted a community.[4] Certainly, national origin (whether from India, Pakistan, or elsewhere) and religion (whether Hindu, Moslem, Sikh, or otherwise) had an impact on relationships and sometimes divided people, but no more so than did social class in the Paradise of the 1950s; besides, the divided community is the norm rather than the exception. The Asian Canadians were connected to each other by an informal network of communication, the efficiency of which I experienced first hand: sometimes I would stop at a gas station or motel primed to explain that I was conducting research in the area, only to be informed by the owners that they had been expecting me. That never happened among the African Canadians. While black families living in close proximity usually knew each other, and may even have been aware of others in the area, there was no black community per se. This essential difference between the Asian and African Canadians can be explained partly by the fact that the former were concentrated in three types of high profile local businesses, whereas the majority of the latter were commuters. In other words, the African Canadians were much less sociologically visible both to each other and to the surrounding population.

The community status of the Asians – or perhaps more accurately, given the narrow sense of the definition employed here, their quasi-community status – helps to solve three little puzzles. First, why did the Asian Canadians, unlike the African Canadians, make little effort to become integrated into local society? Secondly, why did the African Canadians, unlike the Asian Canadians, think that racism in rural society was widespread? Thirdly, why did the Asian Canadians assume that racism is natural and inevitable, while everything about the reactions of the African Canadians implied that they thought otherwise? The African Canadians, lacking even a quasi-community, were essentially isolated and vulnerable. As normal human beings, they craved contact with others, and when their overtures to their neighbours were rejected, they drew firm conclusions about the level of racism in rural society. The Asian Canadians, as will be demonstrated in chapter 11, were not regarded any more positively than the African Canadians by local people. But because they rarely attempted to socialize outside their community, they did not test the degree of prejudice and discrimination that existed.

Finally, the assumption among Asian Canadians that racism is natural was in many respects a boundary mechanism. It rationalized their lack of effort to make friends among the local people, while simultaneously strengthening their dependency on their own community. One might observe, indeed, that there was nothing 'natural' about the assertion that racism is natural. One of the ironies of the contemporary world is that as industrialization and global communications have increased, primordial ties of ethnicity have not decreased. Indeed, as

Cohen (1969) has argued with respect to the Hausa community among the Yoruba in southern Nigeria, ethnic consciousness may actually be a product of modernization. The Asian Canadians living in rural Ontario expressed themselves in terms of race rather than ethnicity, partly because they were visible minorities in a predominately European-origin society, and partly in order to employ the language of the times.

Chapter Ten

Jews and French Canadians

What is remarkable about anti-Semitism and racism is their capacity to flourish even in settings where their targets are almost non-existent. The proportion of the Canadian rural population that was Jewish in 1981 (Dasgupta 1988:151–2) was a mere 0.1 per cent; in Canada as a whole that year, Jews made up only 1.2 per cent of the population. From 1904 to 1951, according to the assessment records, only eight Jewish families had lived in Paradise. At the turn of the century, they were country peddlers, travelling by cart from farm to farm, selling clothing and pots and pans; as recently as the Second World War a peddler still operated in the area, although he owned a home in Toronto. Another family in the early part of the century had a tailoring shop in Paradise, and over a period of several decades the same clothing store was operated by three families in succession. By the early 1950s most of these families had moved elsewhere, and it was not until the period of reverse migration during the 1970s and 1980s that the town's population once again contained a modest number of Jews (thirty-five of them in 1986, according to Statistics Canada).

As for the French Canadians, the census does not provide data on ethnicity in Paradise in the 1950s, and there was no record of them in the assessment rolls. The 1951 census does indicate that .9 per cent of the population of Dufferin County as a whole was French. Although this would translate into eleven people in Paradise, based on its population size, informants could only remember one French-speaking resident in the town at that time. This was a middle-aged bachelor, originally from Quebec, who worked as a bookkeeper at a sawmill. He apparently had been an avid fan of the Montreal Canadiens, and one person, then a boy, remembers how amazed he had been when he found out that the bookkeeper listened to French broadcasts of the hockey games. This man's profile in the village had been low, but not necessarily because of prejudice. He apparently was not in good health, and did not even emerge from his apartment to buy groceries; instead he paid young people 25 cents to do his shopping once a week. By the mid 1950s another French Canadian, born in northern Ontario, had moved to Paradise with her husband, who became one of the community's most successful merchants. Just as the number of Jews in the town increased with the population turnaround during the past two decades, so did the number of French Canadians; indeed, according to Statistics Canada, there was exactly the same number of French Canadians as Jews in the town in 1986.[1]

Despite the relative absence of Jews and French Canadians in Paradise, people held strong, but opposite, opinions about them. They were inclined to praise the Jews who had lived in the community during the first half of the century as fine citizens, but to condemn French Canadians in general as dangerous interlopers. What is intriguing is that the Jews themselves who had grown up in Paradise, at least the ones whom I met, remember a life of insults and isolation, while the French Canadians acted as if they had been hired as the town's public relations agents.

Anti-Semitism

The vast majority of middle-aged and elderly natives of Paradise clearly remembered the Jewish families of the past, and insisted there had been absolutely no anti-Semitism in the village. 'Lovely people,' commented one woman. 'The Jews and Italians,' remarked another women, were treated 'like Canadians.' A former merchant pointed out that one of the Jews who had gone on to become prominent in academic and political circles had been invited back to speak at the school's commencement ceremonies. Another merchant described the peddler who still operated in the area during the Second World War as a unique and delightful man. The peddler, he said, frequently dropped into his shop with a bottle of sweet wine concealed in a rubber boot. What was amazing, stated the merchant, is that after they shared the contents of the bottle, this roughly dressed and apparently uncouth man would sometimes break out in the most lovely operatic arias.

Yet not all the evidence indicated that Paradise had been a haven for Jews. It will be recalled from chapter 8 that the manner in which Jews had been recorded in the assessment rolls – sometimes being labelled aliens, sometimes simply being ignored – suggested that the assessors did not know what to do with them. Some of the remarks of the elderly residents, while meant to underline the degree to which the Jews had been accepted in the community, unintentionally conveyed a different impression. For example, a man who had had regular contact with several of the Jewish children in the local school insisted that they had been treated like everyone else, and had been completely accepted by the other students. Yet this same man remarked that Jews are not a forgiving people; he was especially upset that they would not drop the subject of Nazi atrocities, and he expressed support for James Keegstra, the former teacher and mayor in Eckville, Alberta, remarking that he had been railroaded by the Jews.[2]

An elderly merchant, after insisting that the Jews in the village had been highly respected, went on to describe them as tricky businessmen. The only time that a customer had an advantage over them, he explained, was early in the morning, and that was because they thought it was an auspicious sign to make a sale to the first customer of the day, and thus were prepared to offer bargain prices. One of the most prominent and wealthy merchants in the 1950s declared that there had been no anti-Semitism in the community at that period. Yet almost in the same breath he remarked about the poverty-stricken families with low reputations that had lived on the street next to the dump: 'They might as well have been Jews.'

Occasionally the remarks of people about the former Jewish residents were more forthright. One man, who expressed admiration for the owner of the Chinese restaurant in the 1950s, thought that the Jews, in contrast, had made 'poor citizens.' A woman who had been in the same class in elementary school as one of the Jewish children insisted that he and his brother had been picked on by some of the teachers. She remembered on occasion when these boys had brought specially prepared bread or cake to school to share with their classmates in celebration of a Jewish holy day, only to be mocked by one of the teachers. Another woman remarked about the Jews whom she had grown up with: 'They were terribly run-on. Terribly.' What was interesting about this woman was that while she admired the Jews, she expressed distaste for the Asian and African Canadians who had recently moved to the area, and dismissed French Canadians as 'a low race of people.'

Perhaps the most intriguing reaction to the Jews was that of a retired businessman who stated bluntly that he had no love for Jews, but his personal experiences with them had made him have second thoughts. He had served overseas during the Second World War, and remarked: 'I wasn't very fond of Jews after the War.' His attitude started to change after getting to know two men whom he never suspected of being Jews. The former businessman and soldier owned some farm land, and confessed an absolute love for ploughing: 'When the birds are singing, and the bells ringing, and it's spring, and the smell of the earth, there's nothing nicer.' Apparently one of the men he had met through business also had a hobby farm, and asked the Paradise resident to teach him how to plough. Together they planted some corn, but shortly afterwards the other man was on his deathbed with cancer. Only then did the Paradise native discover that his new friend was a Jew. He was horrified, because he had often told him that he had no use for Jews. The same thing, he said, had happened in relation to another man he had befriended. This Paradise merchant, smart and sensitive, seemed to learn from these poignant experiences. He concluded: 'There's good and bad people among all races.' Yet later he commented that he couldn't stand Sikhs.[3]

The final source of information that allows us to evaluate the claim that Paradise was remarkably free of anti-Semitism is the most revealing of all: the testimonies of Jews who formerly lived in the community. Some of these families had emigrated to the United States, and others had moved to Toronto where their children, now close to retirement age, still lived. The two men whom I met in Toronto were brothers. Their parents, immigrants from Poland, had settled in Paradise in 1913, where they had made a meagre living in a tailoring shop. By the outbreak of the Second World War, both sons had left the community to embark on what turned out to be successful careers. A decade later, their parents too had relocated in Toronto.

From various sources I had heard that while the one brother had warm memories of the community, the other loathed it. Certainly the latter man's own account of life in Paradise, where he was born and raised, supported these rumours. Despite being a gifted athlete, excelling in basketball and tennis, he was not accepted by his peers. He claimed that at school he was called a dirty Jew by the other kids almost every day, and was constantly involved in fights. He also said that he had no close friends, not even through his sports activities, and never once was invited into the home of any of his school mates.

Indeed, only one family, next-door neighbours, ever welcomed his family into their house. His mother did have one close friend in the town: the unmarried sister of one of the most powerful businessmen. That woman's brother, still alive in 1990, stated that his family had not discouraged the relationship because the Jewish woman was so isolated and lonely. The latter's son, however, recalled the strains in the friendship due to the influential businessman's opposition.

Anticipating quite a different story from the other brother, I was surprised when he said: 'I can tell you, anti-Semitism there gave me an inferiority complex.' Pointing to his nose, he remarked wryly that it wasn't that shape when he was born. Although studious rather than athletic like his brother, he too had had his share of fist fights in response to the taunts of dirty Jew. But what really left scars, he observed, was the fact of being excluded from school excursions and from the get-togethers in the homes of his fellow students. Yet it was this same anti-Semitism that made him determined to succeed in life, to excel over his peers. He studied hard, and managed, despite the poverty of his parents, to attend university, eventually entering one of the professions.

There was, to be sure, another side to the story. Raised in an Orthodox Jewish family, they observed dietary regulations. Orthodox Jews travelling through the community were in the practice of taking their meals with the family. The two brothers explained that their parents did not want them to eat in the homes of their school mates because the food was not kosher, and would never have agreed for them to date Gentile girls (both eventually married Jewish women). One of the brothers thought that a Reformed Jewish family that had lived in Paradise had been more accepted, and from what I have learned that was true. The male head of that family was even elected to council, and a number of the older residents of Paradise made a point of saying that he was the only Jew who had ever contributed anything to the community.

While part of the isolation of the two brothers may well have been a product of their Orthodox Jewish heritage, that factor surely does not explain the hostile environment in which they were born and raised. Of course, from the point of view of the majority of people who remembered the Jewish families, Paradise had been anything but hostile towards them. Indeed, when the parents of these two brothers departed from Paradise in 1951, they were given a send-off party, including gifts of money and a watch. The obvious interpretation is that Paradise people were justified to claim that they were not anti-Semites. A less obvious interpretation is that when prejudice is ingrained into the prevailing attitudes of the times, when its typicality renders it invisible, collective delusion is always a possibility.

What is intriguing, in the end, is the polar opposite manner in which two young Jewish boys growing up in such a community reacted. The athletic brother, direct and aggressive, has turned his back on Paradise. He never visits the community, and has virtually no contact with the people with whom he grew up. The other brother, more placid and self-effacing, has retained his contacts with the community. He returned for a school reunion held about a decade ago, and was pleased that so many people seemed happy to see him. Nostalgia, for this man, clearly had its place. Showing me some old photographs taken in the community, he remarked that it was natural to keep up contact, for after all Paradise was where he was born and raised. As I listened to these men, both with similar memories of ill-treatment, the significance of personality once again asserted itself. The reaction of the more forceful brother was to thumb his nose at the people who had rejected him. The reaction of the other brother has been quite different. He had a need to be liked, to be accepted. The anti-Semitism that he had faced as a youngster may well have motivated him to excel. But, in a sense, he wanted to do *better* than his childhood school mates in order to show that he was as *good* as them, worthy of respect if not friendship.

As we approach the twenty-first century, has the anti-Semitism of the past in small towns like Paradise given way to a more enlightened era? Two of the most prominent Jews in 1990 were professional men who actually lived in other communities. Their religious and ethnic identity seemed of little importance to the residents of Paradise. As one man remarked, 'You never hear anybody saying they're Jewish.' He himself was ignorant of that fact until his wife pointed it out when I was interviewing them. One of the two professionals said that his patients, for the most part, do not seem to realize he is a Jew, reflected by the number of Christmas cards that he receives.

Nevertheless, anti-Semitic expressions are not entirely absent from the community even in the present. An immigrant from eastern Europe remarked that anti-Semitism is very prevalent in that part of the world. Although he described himself as a supporter of Israel, he confessed that his feelings about Jews were ambiguous: 'On a personal basis, it's very mixed. Individually, meeting Jews, it's okay. But as a group, I don't know. They're different. From my parents, I see they're different.' Another man from eastern Europe, a manager in a large corporation, said that while he himself has nothing against Jews, one of his relatives thinks they are 'evil, dirty, slimy.' As he continued in this vein with considerable animation, I had the peculiar feeling that he was talking about himself. Indeed, some of his friends described him as a virulent racist and anti-Semite.

Immigrants from eastern Europe are not the only people who still hold Jews in low regard. A former politician in Paradise, ruminating on his successful efforts to keep a local businessman from going bankrupt, commented: 'Well, if he had been some kind of Jew from Toronto, we would have let him sink. But he was a local boy.' In a similar vein, a businessman explained the allegedly shady business practices of another individual with the remark that he had had too much contact with Jewish lawyers in the city. Finally, there is the case of a Jew who applied to join a local service club. This man, who remarked that he is very proud of being Jewish and never tries to hide the fact, was quite aware that vestiges of anti-Semitism lingered in the area. It disturbed him that so many people use the expression 'they Jewed me.' Nevertheless, he did not think that anti-Semitism explained why he was not accepted in the service club. He had been involved in an attempt to prevent a gun club from opening and assumed that had made him some enemies; besides, he remarked, he wasn't sure if all that male-bonding in the service club was in his style. This man was apparently wrong about the role played by his ethnicity. Two members of the service club revealed that he was denied entry entirely because he was a Jew. Of course, he was never told that directly. As one of the members explained, 'His application just was never processed.' The other member, who confirmed that that had been the tactic, expressed dismay and anger that such a thing could happen today. Ironically, he himself had quite ambivalent views about Jews. In explaining why he had strongly supported the application of the Jewish man, he commented: 'I have to admire Jews, because all Jews are leeches. You know, manipulators.'

Anti-French Canadian

It would be a gross understatement merely to describe the attitudes of Paradise people towards French Canadians as intolerant. Not only did

the vast majority of them express support for the English-only movement that had emerged in some towns and cities in the province, but
some of them believed that French Canadians were involved in a
massive conspiracy to take over the country, and a few of them classified French Canadians as a separate (and inferior) race.[4]

A prominent businessman explained how disgusted he had been on
an occasion when he had telephoned a government bureau in Ottawa.
The person who had answered had spoken in French. Although she
had immediately switched to English, the damage, as far as the businessman was concerned, had been done: 'Oh, I was boiling mad.' That
little episode, he continued, just proved what he had always suspected:
the entire government has fallen into the hands of the French. An
elderly woman, retired from the farm, made the same point more
dramatically: 'I do think they're invading.' A much younger woman
who had recently moved to Paradise claimed that French Canadians
had a devious plan to gain control of the country: 'I think they start
on the small communities. Away up north, like Kapuskasing. I look at
the French Canadians as trying to be an octopus.' This woman was
exceptionally bitter towards French Canadians, and it is instructive to
consider her case at more length. Although she was born in Canada,
her parents were immigrants from southern and eastern Europe. She
grew up in an area of Toronto containing white and black people. The
two groups, she stated, lived in separate worlds, rarely interacting. In
her opinion, black people are a dangerous race, prone to violence and
lacking self-control: 'What scares me is you turn on the TV and what
you see's violence. And it's blacks.' In contrast, she expressed a great
attraction towards Japanese Canadians, some of whom she had met
through a relative's job: 'I'd love to have my street filled with Japanese
and Orientals. They're quiet and very polite.'

She defined French Canadians as a separate race, and ranked them
even lower than she had ranked blacks, adding: 'I don't think of them
as Canadians. Because they're so emotional.' Real Canadians, she
thought, were apathetic and unemotional. She described herself as
apathetic: 'I don't listen to the news. I'm your typical apathetic Canadian.' Ironically, however, she revealed that she is extremely emotional:
'I get hot to trot about French Canadians.' Several Paradise people
claimed that French Canadians thought they were a superior race,
which probably was a reflection of their own self-concepts, and this
woman was no exception. When it was suggested to her that many
French-speaking people in Canada felt suppressed, which has given

rise to independence sentiments, she roared: 'Let them have Quebec! Go! Secede!'

This woman defined race in terms of skin colour, and said there are three races – 'black, white and yellow.' Immediately she realized that she had a problem. How could she define French Canadians as a separate race, she ruminated, if skin colour was the measuring rod? Furthermore, what about the Japanese whom she admired? 'Because of the skin colour,' she reluctantly deduced, they are part of the yellow race. As she grappled with the problem, the solution suddenly came to her. Skin colour is not the only criterion. Equally important is the emotional dimension. Because of their great self-control, the Japanese, she concluded, are semi-white people. Because French Canadians, like African Canadians, are unable to control their emotions they are not part of the white race.

Rarely, she confessed, had she interacted with French Canadians, although she did meet one person in Paradise. After sharing a room in a hospital with her when they both were in labour, all her preconceptions were confirmed. The woman, she claimed, had absolutely no interest in her baby, and her husband was a drunk. Repeating her distrust of and hostility towards French Canadians and blacks, she apologized for being a racist, said she knows it is wrong, but cannot help it.

This woman was not the only resident of Paradise to define French Canadians as a separate race. A man who had been born near Paradise explained that the world's population could be divided into the following races: 'Blacks, whites, Red Indian, Chinese.' Then he added: 'Actually, I would call the French a race.' Since he too had used skin colour as the sole criterion, he recognized that there was a flaw in the scheme of classification, but resolved it by stating that it is language that makes the French a separate race. Some individuals were more flexible. For example, a woman on welfare traced the familiar route by first defining race in terms of skin colour and then including French Canadians among her list of separate races. But after reflecting for a couple of minutes, she commented: 'Actually, they have to be white people.'

Occasionally individuals voiced their opposition to the English-only movement. Two immigrants from Britain, for example, expressed how surprised they had been at the amount of prejudice in the country against French Canadians, and thought it was unfortunate that some communities had decided to declare themselves English-only. A young teacher remarked: 'I'd love to be bilingual.' Although in her judgment the English-only movement was financially rather than racially motivated, she still thought it was detrimental to the interests of the country. Most people, however, including this woman's husband, not only supported the communities which had opted for English, but also were undismayed at the possibility of Quebec secession. In her husband's words, 'I'd like to be bilingual, but I don't want bilingualism pushed down my throat.' Although he hoped Quebec would not secede, he said it wouldn't surprise him if it did, because 'French Canadians act like small children.'

A young couple, penniless and unemployed, stated that they did not support the English-only movement, but thought that all Canadians should speak English in public. A lower-middle-class individual remarked about Meech Lake: 'I'm out to lunch on it. I don't even know what they're talking about.' But he did agree with those communities that had declared themselves English-only: 'Well, that's about the same as Quebec did. When Quebec did it, that was fine. But it raised a stink when the English did it.' A woman in the same class level declared: 'It makes me angry that we're more or less forced to speak in French, but in Quebec they won't allow kids to speak English. It seems the French are putting themselves too much above everybody else.' A middle-class man, college educated, remarked: 'I'm not particularly anti-French, though we bend over backwards too much for them.' A middle-class woman, when asked to comment on the English-only movement, replied: 'Yes, I believe in that. It's costing us more money to buy soup because of the French on it.' An upper-class woman remarked about Quebec: 'They're a distinct society in their own right, but so are the English.' She thought that a civil war between French and English Canada was inevitable, and hoped that Quebec would secede: 'They're going to be the ones that suffer if they separate from us.'

The various people whose negative attitudes towards Quebec and French Canadians have just been related were either British in origin, or at least from western Europe. Similar sentiments, however, were prevalent among people from other parts of the globe. A couple who had emigrated from eastern Europe, for example, claimed that whenever they fly to Europe with Air Canada, if the members of the cabin crew are French Canadian and discover they don't speak the language, they are treated like scum and given third-rate service. 'They think they are superior,' fumed the man. This couple strongly supported the English-only movement, but want a step further: all residence of Quebec, they argued, should be forced by law to speak English in public.

The woman softened her comments by adding: 'I don't know any French Canadians. Maybe if I knew them, I'd change my mind.' No such waffling was evident in the case of another person, whose forebears included both African Canadians and French Canadians. He made it clear that if he had to choose to live with black people or French-speaking people, it would be definitely be the former, because he hates French people so much.

This last case brings us to a very peculiar phenomenon: the tendency for some people whose heritage is partly French to be strongly prejudiced against French Canadians. On one occasion I met three young people together who had French forebears. Only one of them expressed pride in her heritage. The second individual declared that he couldn't stand it when he heard people talking French. When he visited Montreal a couple of years ago, his impression, he said, was that he had landed in a different country. He himself could not speak French, and it maddened him that he was unable to understand the road signs. The third individual stated that he despised 'the French more than any other race.' An elderly woman, one of whose parents was French, was all in favour of those communities which had declared themselves English-only. She expressed pleasure that Meech Lake had failed, and remarked that Quebec would soon demand further privileges, and was bent on taking over the entire country. None of these people were fluent in French any longer, if they ever had been, but similar sentiments were expressed even by some people who did speak the language. A mild case concerns a wealthy couple who spent their winters in Florida. The Americans, they observed, become quite annoyed when people from Quebec spoke French in public. Despite the fact that both the woman's parents were French Canadians, she agreed with her husband that it was ignorant for French Canadians to use their own language. A more dramatic example involved a young man whose parents had moved from New Brunswick to Ontario before he was born. His wife, who was not French, had remarked about French Canadians: 'I don't think it's right for them to say "we're better than you."' Rather than defending his ethnic heritage, the man himself, who said he no longer is completely fluent in French despite being brought up by French-speaking parents, declared that he had absolutely no sympathy with the people of Quebec, especially those who sought to create an independent state: 'Let them starve. That's what I think.'

Turning now to the French Canadians who had migrated to Paradise during the 1970s and 1980s, we are immediately confronted by a stag-

gering contradiction: although they portrayed the community as remarkably hospitable and tolerant, the majority of their neighbours (at
least those who were interviewed) were at least mildly prejudiced
against French Canadians in general. It would almost seem that the
two parties had never actually met each other, and that was pretty
close to the truth. Scarcely any of the Paradise residents, including
those who expressed the deepest hostility, were aware of the presence
of French Canadians in the community. The latter moved in an extremely small social circle. Their invisibility became apparent when
attempts were made to contact them. The 1986 census indicated that
thirty-five of them had lived in Paradise that year. Yet inquiries at the
town hall less than five years later proved fruitless: nobody could think
of a single French-speaking individual in the community. My next stop
was at the post office, with the same result. A postal clerk suggested
that I talk to an elderly man who was highly respected as the local
historian. This man had never met or heard of a single French Canadian in town. Growing desperate, I inquired at the town library. The
woman in charge could not recall any French-speaking people who
used the facility, but her assistant thought that a French woman
worked in a nearby office. At that office I learned that the woman had
left the community a few weeks previously. French she was, said the
secretary, but 'she didn't look French.' On the main street a short
time later I heard two young women speaking French. It turned out,
however, that they were technicians who commuted to the town twice
a week to work in a dentist's office. Thumbing through the telephone
directory, I came across a French name and rang the number, only to
be told by the amused resident that his forebears were indeed French,
but they had settled in Ontario almost a century ago, and nobody in
his family had spoken French for several generations. One of the
merchants then gave me a hot tip: a man in his service club was
French. In his case too, however, the only French thing about him was
his name.

Finally, on a hunch, I walked into the Legion and struck gold.
Immediately I was introduced to a French Canadian from New Brunswick. It was at the Legion, over the next two weeks, where I met several of the fourteen French Canadians who figure in this study. Most of
them were from New Brunswick or Quebec, had no more than a
couple of years of secondary school education, worked in the construction industry as labourers, roofers or carpenters, and occupied the
lower-middle or middle class. In almost every case, their spouses were

also French Canadians. All of them could speak English, in some cases without a trace of a French accent. Ironically, some of them were no longer fluent in French, especially those whose families had been in southern Ontario for a couple of generations or more. They claimed that they only spoke their natal language when everyone present could do so. As I observed, people often greeted each other in French, but immediately switched to English.

Without exception, the French Canadians whom I met in and outside the Legion, both women and men, insisted that they had never been the victims of prejudice and discrimination in Paradise. These were not empty words, at least as far as the Legion was concerned. Although they were inclined to sit together at the same table, they were often joined by English Canadians, and mingled freely at other tables. Before I had made contact with the members of the Legion, I had been led to believe by some residents of Paradise that it was a hotbed of racism in general. As one man had declared, if a 'Paki or a Sikh with a turban' dared enter the premises, they would be tossed out on their ears. Yet an African Canadian from a town a few miles away apparently was a regular visitor to the Legion, and 'three Pakis,' as a woman put it, often dropped in for a beer. She added with a laugh that they had the good sense to leave their turbans at home. The only evidence to the contrary that I observed concerned an Asian Canadian in his thirties, whose parents owned a local business. He had come in search of a poker game, but was given a cold shoulder and soon disappeared. It turned out that he was not well liked. One man angrily called him a hotshot. This did not mean, he explained, that the other person was always a winner. It meant that his play was erratic; he would bet on anything, destroy the implicit logic of the game, and generate frustration and hostility among the other players.

Finally, and possibly most significant of all in view of the repeated accusation that the French were after nothing less than total control of the country, without a single exception the French Canadians whom I met were adamantly opposed to aspirations in Quebec to become an independent nation. As one of them exclaimed, 'I'm a Canadian. All that separation stuff is bullshit.' Another man, with a twinkle in his eyes as he looked at me, said the only ones who wanted separation for Quebec were the politicians and the university crowd.

One of the men whom I met was born in New Brunswick about 1950. His family had moved to Ontario when he was twelve years old. At the time he could not speak a word of English, but now speaks the language without a trace of a French accent. His wife, also from New Brunswick, is fluent in English, but no longer in French. This woman's stepfather was an African Canadian. She described him as a good man, and stated that it upset her when she heard people making negative comments about blacks. She worked in a domestic position for an organization located near Paradise. Her husband was self-employed in the construction business. They lived in a trailer park a few miles from the community. Although five other families also lived permanently in the trailer park, most of the owners were summer residents.

This man remarked that he was completely opposed to Quebec's independence movement, and added that he couldn't stand it when bilingual people in that province refused to speak English in the company of unilingual people. When he visits Quebec he sometimes purposefully uses English in a store or a restaurant. If the clerk or waiter berates him in French, or treats him as a second-class citizen, he explodes in the same language, accusing them of being ignorant and narrow-minded. Referring to the manner in which Paradise people have responded to him, he commented: 'I get along with everybody. If they don't like Frenchmen, I guess they don't let us know.' One measure of his identification with English Canada is that both he and his wife record themselves as English in the census (two other French Canadians stated that they did likewise). This man's partner in the construction business, an older man whose origins were British, treated the younger man almost as if he was his son. Not only did they work together, but they also socialized with each other. During my second meeting with them, they were planning to join a few pals from the Legion for what they described as a typical Friday evening: some take-out food, a few beers, and a game of poker.

Although I met most of the French Canadians in the Legion, there were exceptions. One of them was a twenty-seven-year-old individual from northern Quebec. When he quit school at the age of sixteen and went to live with a brother in Ontario, he could not speak English. In the decade since then, he has become bilingual, working mostly in construction, although when I met him he had been unemployed for several months. Four of his sisters and two of his brothers have remained in his home area in Quebec. Another brother and sister live in communities near Paradise, and he visits them regularly. He is the only sibling who did not marry a French Canadian. His wife was born into one of the notorious families that lived on the street in Paradise next to the dump, although her father has flourished in business, and in objective terms has climbed towards the middle of the class system (his status in the community, however, remains partly defined by his family's past reputation). This young woman, who expressed a deep allegiance to Paradise, could only speak a half dozen words of French. When her husband's mother visited them in Paradise (his father, who had worked in a sawmill, had died when he was three years old), they had to communicate in sign language, but apparently got along well.

The young man from Quebec makes a visit back home a couple of times a year, but said he could never live there again, because he has become accustomed to a different lifestyle: 'I like it here, so I do. If I moved anywhere, it'd be up north, in the country. I'd like to have a farm, a couple of cows. I like farming.' As for Quebec independence, he commented: 'I'm not for it, really. As far as I'm concerned, it's a mistake.' If Quebec did secede, he added, he was almost certain that none of his brothers and sisters would remain there.

This man stated that he had never felt discriminated against in Paradise. It must be made clear, however, that he lives an extremely isolated life. Except for playing hockey and broom ball in the winter, he has virtually no contact with residents beyond his immediate family. Being unemployed, he does not even meet people through work. He said he rarely leaves the house, preferring to watch television, while hoping that some sort of job will finally turn up. Surprisingly, he has never met any of the other French Canadians in town (he does not belong to the Legion). Although those French Canadians who do frequent the Legion have more contact with Paradise people, it still is severely limited, which is why the vast majority of residents in the town are not even aware that French Canadians lived among them. In this respect, the French Canadians have a great deal in common with the Asian Canadians. Both groups have little to complain about prejudice and discrimination because their isolation provides them with a shield.

Paradise is quite different than Alexandria, the Ontario community recently described by Rayside (1991). In Alexandria in 1986 more than half of the population was French, with only about one-quarter British in origin. While five out of every six French Canadians there were bilingual, only one in every three English Canadians were fluent in both languages; English was the working language, despite the French majority, and was used almost exclusively in service and recreational clubs. The self-image of people in Alexandria apparently was one of harmony between the two language groups, but Rayside points out that they actually occupied largely separate worlds. Paradise has anything but a French-speaking majority, but the image of separate worlds is equally applicable there. Yet Paradise, in terms of anti-French Canadian sentiments, was no different, in my judgment, than the other towns and villages that surround it.

In his classic study of French Canada, Miner (1963:31), drawing from a physical anthropology that now is obsolete, described two racial groups in St. Denis: blue-eyed Normans and dark Mediterranean Gascons. According to Miner, there was no antipathy between these two 'races,' nor were social relations organized in terms of them. Miner did contend that race has 'ethnic' significance in relation to the division between Catholic French Canadians and Protestant English Canadians. What is noteworthy about Paradise is that such ethnic significance seems to flourish even when only one of the parties promotes it.

Suppressed Ethnic Identities

Some people, especially those who were only partly French, attempted to dissociate themselves from their French Canadian backgrounds, and a few of them even harboured what amounted to prejudice against their own heritages. This peculiar brand of self-abrogation was also evident in relation to two other categories of people: those whose origins were at least partly German or partly Aboriginal.[5] During the Second World War, stated one woman, her family had kept very quiet about its 'German blood.' Even after the war, some people thought it was judicious to conceal their ethnic backgrounds. A man whose lower-class family moved to Paradise from Toronto in 1948 said that he and his siblings were always warned by their parents not to reveal that their father's parents were German. Another man, whose mother and father were German although he himself had been born in Canada, and who also took up residence in Paradise in 1948, had been engaged in a running battle with town officials for more than a quarter of a century. The council, according to this lower-middle-class man, was determined to put him out of business (he had his own small machine shop), and the underlying reason, he insisted, was his German heritage, which he had not been able to conceal. Although he even claimed that over the years he had received several letters castigating his ethnic background, his accusations did not appear to be entirely plausible. His principal enemy on the council – the man who became the community's first mayor in 1978 after previously serving as reeve – was himself partly German.

Although the mayor had been raised in a poor farm family, his years in public office had lifted his reputation towards the middle class, and the possibility existed that it was the combination of one's German heritage and one's membership in the lower classes that prompted animosity, at least in the period following the war. Thus a third man who also moved to Paradise in 1948 remarked that his German heritage had never been relevant in the community. This man, however, had been a highly successful merchant whose cronies came from the aristocracy.

As for the present, the occasional disparaging remarks about arrogant Germans still can be heard, but for the most part people of German origin have simply faded into the multi-ethnic fabric that has replaced the British one. For example, a woman revealed that when she had lived on the outskirts of Toronto as a girl in the 1950s, it had not been unusual to be called names because her parents were immigrants from Germany. Today, at her home near Paradise, her young children leaf through German-language books, and periodically she makes a trip with them to her parents' homeland, providing them with a sense of their roots (their father's ethnic background was British). The days when her German heritage counted against her, she observed, belong to the past.

Although about a dozen people whose ethnic backgrounds contained Aboriginals were interviewed, not a single one of them made that fact explicit; usually it slipped out towards the end of the interviews, implying that it was of little significance. Furthermore, none of these people defined themselves as Aboriginals; instead, they identified with the other part of their ethnicity, which was usually British and sometimes French, or a combination of both. Only one person, a young man in his twenties, expressed pride in the fact that one of his grandparents had been Aboriginal, although in his mind too he was British. The majority of these people belonged to the lower and lower-middle classes, but three of them were solidly middle class, and a fourth was upper class. Unlike the people with German heritages, social class did not modify the significance of their ethnicity. The people in the higher classes were as reticent about their ethnic backgrounds as were those in the lower classes.[6]

Elderly British-origin residents sometimes would remark that one of the lower-class men from the past had married 'a squaw' or 'a half-breed.' As for the present, the attitudes in Paradise towards Aboriginal people were twofold. On the one hand, there was considerable sympathy, especially in relation to the recent Oka crisis, where an armed confrontation occurred between Natives and the Quebec police and the army. As one woman put it, 'The Indian people are having a raw deal all the way round.' Another woman remarked: 'I think it is disgusting the way we treat our Indians.' On the other hand, some residents described Aboriginal people as indolent drunkards, living the good life on welfare. One man, referring to the Oka crisis, stated: 'I sympathize with them, but I don't agree with their methods. After all, we do have a legal system.' In another person's words: 'I think the Natives have made their point, but carried it too far.' Most Paradise residents, it appeared, guided by the romantic image of the noble savage, were happy to support Aboriginal people when it cost them nothing to do so. But when the latter began to assert themselves and displayed a willingness to move beyond speeches to armed combat, the normal reaction to minorities in such circumstances emerged: they are trying to change things too fast by unacceptable means.

Tolerant People

In the process of presenting small-town Ontario through the eyes of the African, Asian, Jewish, and French Canadians, and revealing the perceptions about them held by the natives and newcomers – an exercise which will be continued in more depth in the next chapter – the impression may have been given that virtually everyone in Paradise was prejudiced. That simply is not correct. While intolerant individuals did outnumber tolerant ones, examples of the latter could be found at all levels of the stratification system among both natives and newcomers.

Consider the case of an elderly woman who was born in England in 1900, moving to Canada with her family in 1907, where she eventually became an elementary school teacher. Her husband, whom she had married in 1924, was a farmer, but his poor health forced them to sell the farm and move into Paradise in 1948 (he died in 1974). This woman, ninety years old when I interviewed her, retained a keen interest in international affairs. '*Maclean's* magazine,' she remarked, 'is excellent on the world news.' She personally remembered the Russian Revolution of 1917, and expressed admiration for Gorbachev. At the same time she was highly critical of American military adventures in places like Panama, and remarked that she sometimes thought it was the Americans who posed a threat to world peace.

She regretted some of the changes that had occurred in Paradise, such as the dwindling attendance in the churches and the reduced profile of organizations such as the IODE and the Women's Institute, and she was not pleased that she only knows a few people in town now. Nevertheless, she thought Paradise remained a genuine community ('Among friends, we still get together in the evenings'), and expressed a remarkable degree of tolerance and compassion about a wide range of issues. When strong opposition to the plan to convert the town's old school into subsidized apartments developed, she stood up at a public meeting and declared that everyone should have a place to live, including the less fortunate. Whereas many people laughed behind the back of the former mayor who had gone after his mistress's new boyfriend with a shotgun while under the influence of alcohol, this compassionate woman encouraged his rehabilitation, and even complained to the editor of the local newspaper for splashing the mayor's story all over its pages. The only unkind comment she uttered concerned the class system. She was unwilling to accept the norm that people of wealth are somehow superior to poor people. Thus, when a woman from the upper class, who always had put on airs and demanded deference, lost her fortune and became an alcoholic, the elderly resident found it difficult not to conclude that justice had prevailed.

'The church,' stated the elderly woman, 'has always been my first love.' Raised initially in the Salvation Army, she switched to Methodist, and became a member of the United Church after church union. A few years ago, accompanied by some other residents of Paradise, she took the trip that she had been dreaming about for decades: a tour of the Holy Land. Referring to the United Church, she observed: 'The problem now is homosexuality.' About this issue, too, she was sympathetic: 'I can't draw myself to be the judge. We're all God's children.'

This woman was reasonably knowledgeable about South Africa, and expressed admiration for Nelson Mandela, the celebrated black leader who had been in prison there for many years. She regretted the intolerance that she had detected among some of her acquaintances towards the African and Asian newcomers in Paradise, and remarked that there was enough room for everyone. Ruminating about all the changes that have taken place around her, she stated: 'I can't draw my skirts around me; we have to live and let live. I guess times can't stand still.' Intolerance, it is often argued (Henry 1978 and Rosenberg 1986), is especially pronounced among two categories of people: those who are elderly, and those who are quite religious. This woman is a salutary reminder that such generalizations can be dangerous.

My example of exceptionally tolerant newcomers is a married couple in their early fifties, both college educated, who were born in England and brought up Anglican, although neither of them attends church now. They moved to a twenty-five-acre farm near Paradise primarily to enjoy a better quality of life. The woman stated: 'We were tired of the city, tired of the rat race, and buildings on buildings.' Her husband added that they wanted to be able to listen to the birds, and have a dog and farm animals (each of their twenty-five ducks has a name!) They were perfectly aware of the animosity of the farmers towards newcomers, and their sympathy was with the local people. Many of the weekenders, commented the woman, 'are filthy rich, and flaunt their wealth. I do find, honestly, that some of the Toronto people, the weekenders, come up here and talk down to the locals.' In sharp contrast, this middle-class couple had become remarkably well-integrated into rural society. They knew almost all of the farmers who lived around them and expressed an interest in learning about rural life. The farmers, in turn, described this couple as exceptionally fine people. Yet their acceptance, the woman cautioned, had been far from automatic: 'I think people weigh you up. You're not accepted at the beginning by any stretch of the imagination.' Her husband observed: 'One of the misnomers of living in the country is people are so much more friendly.' Newcomers, he said, have to make an effort to dislodge the initial mistrust: 'People hold back; they were assessing us.' One also has to adapt to the local mentality, stated his wife. Country people, she explained, aren't as aggressive as city people: 'They never tell you what to do, even if you're making a mess.'

Not all has been plain sailing for this couple. After living on the farm for more than a year, they put up a gate on the driveway in order to keep their animals in, only to discover that the visits from their neighbours stopped. Eventually they realized that the neighbours interpreted the gate to mean that they wanted to be left alone, so they took it down. During the hunting season they have had some minor confrontations with hunters who have strolled onto their property, but for the most part their relationships with the nearby farmers were guided by warmth and mutual respect.

From their years of living in Toronto, these people stated, they were aware that African Canadians faced tremendous racism. What particularly upset them was their impression that such racism even pervaded the school system. After relating some racist and anti-Semitic incidents initiated by well-educated people in a large organization where she formerly was employed in the city, the woman declared: 'I detest racism.' The countryside, they commented, is not necessarily any better. Referring to a gas station nearby, the woman remarked: 'A lot of people don't use them anymore. Why? They're Pakis.' (Actually, the family she had in mind was from India.) The same thing, she said, happened at another gas station down the road: 'They had to put these other people, white people, in there because nobody was buying gas.'

Contributing to this couple's acceptance in rural Ontario, no doubt, has been the fact that they have been able to spend most of their time on the farm. The woman was retired and her husband, who was self-employed and worked out of a studio at home, only had to travel to the city once or twice a week. Not to be overlooked, however, was their geniality, lack of snobbery, fairness, and flexibility, plus their genuine interest in the people around them – the same qualities that rendered them tolerant towards members of minorities.

Chapter Eleven

Patterns of Prejudice

We begin with two widely held assumptions in Paradise. The first is that the more there is contact among people of different racial and ethnic backgrounds, the less the prejudice. It follows therefore that rural people are more intolerant than urban people. This assumption was often articulated by newcomers, who thought that the elderly residents of Paradise would be especially inclined towards racism; occasionally Paradise natives would state the same thing about their friends and acquaintances. As for the African Canadians, more often than not their first reactions were to argue that racism was even more widespread in the country than in the city, although some of them qualified their remarks with the comment that maybe they just felt it more because of their novelty value and their isolation. The Asian Canadians were inclined to be neutral on the subject; from their perspective, there was little to differentiate urban and rural society.

Public opinion notwithstanding, this assumption, as indicated in table 11, is quite misleading.[1] Not only were newcomers in general more prejudiced than natives (61 per cent versus 50 per cent), but there was a glaring difference in relation to those among them who were highly prejudiced. Indeed, more than one newcomer in four could be described in this manner, while less than one native in twenty expressed a deep form of racism.

The second assumption is that the higher the social-class and educational level, the less the prejudice. This assumption was often expressed by both natives and newcomers in the middle, lower-upper, and upper classes (those below them, not surprisingly, were essentially mute about the issue). The Asian Canadians also tended to assume that poorly educated, lower-class people are the most intolerant, but

TABLE 11
Levels of Tolerance of Natives and Newcomers

	Natives	Newcomers
Highly prejudiced	3 (3%)[1]	22 (28%)
Somewhat prejudiced	45 (47%)	26 (33%)
Neutral[2]	20 (21%)	14 (18%)
Somewhat tolerant	21 (22%)	10 (13%)
Highly tolerant	7 (7%)	6 (8%)
Unknown or ambiguous	26	29
	122 100%	107 100%

Notes:
1 All percentages are calculated in terms of known cases.
2 'Neutral' consists of individuals who did not appear to be either tolerant or prejudiced.

not all African Canadians agreed; some of them, through experience, had arrived at the conclusion that their well-educated neighbours in the middle class and above it were just as racially oriented as the rest of the population.

This assumption too is misleading. With one exception, racial prejudice was not necessarily less among people in the higher classes. The real difference was in the form that it took. Among the lower classes, prejudice often was expressed in terms of economic competition, with people complaining that Third World immigrants were the cause of their unemployment or low wages. Among the higher classes, it was more probable that prejudice was expressed in biological terms, evoking the notion not only that distinct racial types in the physiological sense existed, but also that that explained the lack of integration of Asian and African Canadians into mainstream society.

Before illustrating these contrasting expressions of racism with case material, I should emphasize that there were two significant differences between the natives and the newcomers, the first of which constitutes the exceptional case alluded to above. Whereas tolerant individuals among the natives could be found at all levels of the class system, those among the newcomers coalesced in the upper classes. Part of the explanation was that these newcomers, professionally and financially secure, did not meet the visible minorities as economic competitors, as happened among those in the lower classes. But this cannot be the entire story, because the same was true for the native elite. Another pertinent factor was the age gap between the native and newcomer upper classes, with the former on the average being much older. Then, too, there were the different criteria for high-class membership in each group. The natives achieved elite status primarily by virtue of their wealth and family reputation. Wealth was also critical for the newcomers, but family reputation was overshadowed by the criterion of education. While advanced education by no means guaranteed tolerance, nevertheless, as the case of the newcomers in the higher classes suggests, it could not be dismissed as irrelevant.

The second important difference concerned the aspiring-middle class among the newcomers. The people whom I have placed in this analytic category were inclined to be more intolerant than any other people in the community, newcomers and natives included. The explanation, I shall suggest, concerns their aggressive and daring pursuit of middle-class status, which rendered them hard-hearted to anyone whom they thought might stand in their way, and jealous of the demonstrated success of others.

Native Perspective

When a young man living on welfare was asked if there was any racial prejudice in Paradise, he replied: 'Oh, there's plenty of it in this town.' He proceeded to talk about the black woman who had owned the specialty shop in the community: 'She had to close down her business. Because she's black, and nobody would buy anything. I know a few people would drive all the way to Brampton because they wouldn't buy off a dirty black woman.' After expressing sympathy for the woman, he remarked: 'I'm not a racist at all. I worked in a plant full of East Indians. They were fantastic. They'd always help you.' His wife embraced similar liberal sentiments about visible minorities, and the overall impression was that this poorly educated, lower-class couple (one of them had quit school in grade six, the other in grade nine) was remarkably tolerant. But then a different message emerged. 'I feel they're taking our jobs, and our housing,' stated the young woman, 'and they're filling up our daycares; they have so many children.' She also thought that immigrants from the Third World had an unfair economic advantage because two or three families crowd together in the same house. After listening to his wife, the man, who had been unemployed for several months, reiterated his sympathy towards visible minorities, but declared: 'When it comes to the fact they're taking our jobs, I don't like it.'

Another person on welfare, a single parent, began by voicing her strong opposition to the policy of permitting Sikhs in the RCMP to wear turbans: 'I don't say no to Pakistan people or Negroes trying to get in there. But keep it in one uniform and one uniform only. You don't take your religion to work.' When asked whether Sikh kids should be permitted to wear the kirpan (ceremonial dagger) in school, her reaction was equally clear: 'No! That's more or less like having an open season.' Actually, there was nothing exceptional about her opinions in relation to the turban and the kirpan. Virtually everyone, the intolerant *and* the tolerant, were opposed to them, and in general her viewpoint about racial matters was quite liberal. African Canadians, she thought, were unfairly portrayed on television as violent thugs and drug addicts. She also was sympathetic to the plight of Aboriginal people. When asked why a disproportionate number of them are in prison, she remarked: 'Same as a lot of Negro people. There's prejudice there.' The prejudice that this woman did express had an economic connotation: 'I've heard they get government assistance to do a lot of these things – the gas stations and these things. When they can walk in a buy a gas station and a new home, where do they get the money? The government.' She said that she wouldn't mind the Pakistanis if they worked in factories like everybody else. What worried her was that they were taking over the best jobs, and would soon be running the country if the current rate of immigration continued: 'What I mean, we're becoming the race – I mean, the foreigners; we white people.'

My next case, a fifty-year old lower-middle-class woman, was unique in that one of her closest friends in Paradise was an African Canadian. British in background, she was born and raised in Paradise, where she completed grade nine. For a few years she lived with her husband and children in southern United States. Before finally resettling in Paradise, she spent a few years in Toronto where she got to know and like several Jews. She was one of the people in Paradise who admired the black technician whose case was under review by the Ontario Human Rights Commission after being fired from his job, and she was highly critical of Paradise people because of their ill-treatment of the African Canadian who was forced to close down her specialty shop.

All this is what might be expected from an individual whose close friend was a black woman. As she continued to talk about race relations, however, her image began to change. In the United States, she explained, she had lived in an all-white area, but as a result of busing, the local school which her children had attended had been 40 per cent black, and racial clashes had been frequent and violent: 'Having lived there, I can see people becoming that way [racist].' A few weeks before I met her, she had taken a trip to Toronto: 'I kept thinking, where are the white people? I felt like a foreigner in my own country.' She was particularly displeased about the number of Asian-origin people she had seen: 'I have something about Pakistanis. I'm getting a little pissed off about the ones wearing turbans; you know, in the Mounties, and the daggers.' She hated to hear immigrants speaking their own languages: 'This is Canada. Isn't the English language the language of the country?' She also had little sympathy for the Aboriginal people, stating that they belonged in jail because of their laziness and immoral behaviour; and surprisingly, in view of the fact that one of her close friends was an African Canadian, she remarked that it upset her that so many blacks used racism as an excuse for not succeeding in life: 'So what if you're black? If you really want it [success], it's there. Maybe the possibilities aren't great if you're black or Indian, but still it's up to you.'

What was apparent among many Paradise people is that it only took a single unpleasant experience with a minority person for them to conclude that an entire ethnic group was despicable. The converse, as this woman's case illustrates, was not necessarily true. When she got to know a black person on an individual basis she was exceptionally tolerant, but that did not make her a fan of black people in general or of other visible minorities.

Not all lower-class or lower-middle-class people, as the last example showed, expressed their prejudices in terms of economic competition. Often it was the prospect of the country being overrun by visible minorities speaking strange languages that disturbed them. One man remarked: 'Some people, boy, if you mention a Paki or a black – boy!' He insisted that he himself had no respect for racists, but added: 'I realize what you call the old English descent is going to be extinct. We're letting too many coloureds in. They'll soon tell *us* what to do! I feel that if this country is good enough to let them in here, why don't they speak English? I mean in public.' While most people prefaced their comments by stating they were not racists, the occasional individual was more direct. Thus, one lower-middle-class woman declared: 'I'm a racist, you know, and so is he [her son]. But he can't say it.' Her son, she explained, was employed in a high-profile organiza-tion and was forced to keep his views about visible minorities to him-self. The woman was equally ill-disposed towards Asian and African Canadians: 'Those Sikhs. They're the snottiest.' Referring to blacks, she remarked: 'They cause all the trouble. And I think anybody who listens to them is just as bad.' Although she had never met a Sikh, she had met a black person: 'I had an Avon dame, but she didn't last long. Great big black woman.' She apparently made it clear to the Avon dealer that black people were not welcome in her house.

As we reach the level of the middle class, we begin to encounter biological rather than economic interpretations of racism. Blacks and whites, claimed a merchant, simply cannot live side by side because they think and act differently, and no amount of education will bring about a change, since the differences are 'natural.' Blacks, he thought, are especially prone to violence. In Toronto, he fumed, the police are in a no-win situation. If they rough up a black man, there's all hell to pay; but if black people attack a white person, nobody cares. England, he stated, provides the perfect example of the incompatibility between the two races. Around Liverpool, which he visited a few years ago, a white person doesn't dare walk outside at night because of the threat from blacks. England, as a country, he continued, is finished, because its political leaders did not have enough guts to cut off immigration from the former colonies. In this man's judgment, Canada is travelling along the same suicidal route.

Quite often people assumed that they were describing biological differences between races, but in fact were confusing biology and culture. For example, one person, solidly in the middle class, after claiming that blacks and whites constitute different races, illustrated her argument by referring to the clothes black people wear, and their food and 'low value on life.' This elderly woman, who kept referring to the RCMP as the North West Mounted Police, expressed a special hatred towards Sikhs. Like many other people, her prejudices were based on a single negative experience. She had met her first Sikh during a holiday to the Caribbean, 'an arrogant and nasty man' who shared a table with her at dinner. By the end of the holiday, she remarked with satisfaction, she and the others at the table had put him in his place, refusing to speak to him or to acknowledge him when he spoke, reducing him to a non-entity. Ever since then, she confessed, she has despised Sikhs.

The tendency to generalize from a single example also was evident in the case of a self-employed middle-class man in his late thirties who had attended college for two years. A few years ago he had done some repairs at a country home owned by an immigrant from India, who accused him of stealing a piece of equipment from the property. The enraged Paradise entrepreneur blasted the owner of the house for being too arrogant and stupid to realize that he had only removed the item in question to his workshop in order to repair it. The East Indian's reaction was to call the Paradise man a racist. That really made the latter's blood boil. He denied the charge, and said that he told the other man: 'A jerk is a jerk no matter what his colour, and you are a jerk.' Thereafter, commented the Paradise native, he had been wary of East Indians.

The Paradise man, while extremely conservative, was not in my judgment a racist. His case is significant, because it illustrates that people can be right of centre on the political spectrum without being sympathizers of the Ku Klux Klan. He was very supportive of Aboriginal people: 'We screwed the Indians. The Indians never surrendered.' Third World immigrants were a different matter. He thought that they should not be allowed to speak their own languages in public, and he accused the government of providing them with jobs while 'Canadians' starved. Like others, he opposed any concessions to visible minorities in organizations such as the RCMP: 'I'm totally against Mounties wearing turbans. I'm pro-Canada. I don't like to see Canada broken down into cultures.' What really upset him was to hear immigrants complain about racism: 'If someone doesn't like Canada they can get the hell out.' He thought Rushton, the psychology professor at the University of Western Ontario, was ridiculous to argue that blacks are less intelligent than whites, and certainly he did not agree that whites are less intelligent than Orientals. Yet he strongly supported Keegstra's right to think and teach what he wants – not because he necessarily agreed with Keegstra that Jews and blacks are inferior creatures who pose a threat to Western Christian civilization, but instead because he believed that freedom of speech is the cornerstone of democracy. My interview with this man had taken place shortly after Iraq had invaded Kuwait. In his opinion, there was a simple solution to that act of aggression: 'The Iraq people should be presented with an ultimatum: either they hang Hussein or the United States and other countries will annihilate the country.' That comment pretty well sums up this man's conservative political position. In his own words: 'I'm a basic redneck.'

Unlike people in the lower classes, who habitually referred to Asian

Canadians as 'Pakis' and 'turbans,' and made little attempt to obfus-
cate their prejudices, people in the higher classes were usually more
circumspect with respect to the language employed to describe visible
minorities, and more subtle in their opinions. For example, one lower-
upper-class man politely referred to visible minorities by their country
of origin, and used the conventional physical anthropological terms of
Negroid, Mongoloid, and Caucasoid. When this sophisticated man,
who was a university graduate, was asked to state his opinions about
racial matters, he often played the role of the objective observer and
reported what he assumed to be the attitudes of Paradise people in
general. Thus he stated: 'The kirpan business – I think people around
here would be *very* upset if they started wearing them in schools here.'
He pointed out that the Italian and Dutch people who had settled in
the area in recent years had been accepted by the local population,
but warned: 'If you start getting people with turbans, and black people, watch out!' There were already signs, he stated, that such people
couldn't be integrated into the rural population. Part of the problem,
he thought, was simply that there was a great deal of racism in Paradise. The other part of the problem concerned biology. While this
man had no doubt that distinctive racial types in the biological sense
existed, he did not believe that they could be ranked on a scale of
superiority and inferiority. Negroids, he explained, excelled in sports,
but Orientals had their own advantages: 'We've got Oriental people in
some of the variety stores, and they seem to be fitting in well. But they
seem to have an ear for languages and learn English fast.' Each race,
he thought, possessed its own unique strengths, and while that made
any attempt to rank them futile, it also, in his judgment, partly accounted for the lack of racial integration in society.

My final case among the natives of Paradise concerns a retired
upper-class individual who had briefly attended university half a century ago. He still read voraciously, and held strong opinions, some of
them quite liberal, on a wide range of issues. He thought that Colonel
Gaddafi, the leader of Libya, was a victim of American imperialism,
and he expressed his opposition to political parties that promote
elitism at the expense of working-class people. At the same time,
however, he remarked that the greatest error in modern history has
been the promotion of human rights; that policy, he argued, distorts
society by negating individual merit in order to respond to group
interests; besides, in his opinion human responsibilities rather than
human rights should be emphasized.

This man was quite familiar with Rushton's arguments, and revealed that even before he had heard of the psychology professor he had assumed that Orientals were the most intelligent race. It is deplorable, he remarked, that blacks are genetically deprived – the least intelligent race of all – but the facts are the facts. If Western political leaders had any integrity, he continued, they would face up to reality and not allow South Africa to be taken over by the black population, for the benefit of blacks themselves.

Newcomer Perspective

The same tendency that was evident among the natives for racism to be expressed in terms of economic competition at the lower end of the class system existed among the newcomers. One young couple, desperately poor, without sufficient funds to feed their two children, stated that they had nothing against 'foreigners.' The woman thought that the black people whom she had met at work when they lived in the city were quite nice, and her husband said 'they don't bother me.' When they began to discuss the job market, however, the tune changed. It was because of all the foreigners, they thought, that they could not find employment and had to depend on welfare cheques to survive. Another lower-class individual said he has worked with West Indians 'and they're pretty good.' He was less certain about East Indians: 'I get mad at them and call them things I shouldn't. But I don't mean it.' Although this man was grateful that he had a job, he thought he was being paid less than he should be because the Third World immigrants were willing to work for low wages, and had depressed the level of remuneration for unskilled workers such as himself.

The same opinion was expressed by a third lower-class couple. They strongly believed that 'the turbans' were not only taking jobs away from them, but also that they were being covertly supported by governmental funds: 'They come over here by the boat loads. They get houses. It seems that the government gives them everything. You never see a Vietnamese in a rusted car. I don't think it's fair, myself.' Unlike the previous two families, this man and woman had nothing positive to say about Third World immigrants even apart from the economic realm.

A lower-middle-class woman who worked as a waitress complained that the Third World immigrants had an unfair advantage: 'When they first come over, the government puts them on welfare, and sets them up in business.' She lamented that she and her husband, an unemployed construction worker, would never in their lives be able to afford a house of their own, and asked rhetorically how the Sikhs and Pakistanis become so wealthy: 'You know how they do it? The government. And they live together. I know a family, there were fifteen members living in one house. Canadians aren't having the children they used to because they can't afford it. But the minorities are.' This woman referred sarcastically to Brampton and Agincourt, two large communities near Toronto, as Bramladesh and Asiancourt, and commented bitterly: 'It's us Canadians that are becoming the minorities.'

Middle-class newcomers, like their counterparts among the natives, were inclined to express their prejudices in biological rather than economic terms. Consider, for example, a mild-mannered individual with a college diploma who had moved to Paradise from the outskirts of Toronto in the late 1980s. Describing his years in the city, he commented: 'There used to be a thing when a moving van came in, you'd go out and see if they were Chinese, or a white man.' Raised in Toronto, his classmates had included African and Chinese Canadians, and the area where he had lived before moving to Paradise was popular among visible minorities: 'In winter, they'd hibernate. You'd just never see them.' Their bodies, he continued, were obviously not suited to a cold climate. This man contended that it was natural for different races to want to be with their own kind, and he frankly revealed that he felt more comfortable in Paradise because there were only a few members of visible minorities.

He was quite familiar with Rushton's arguments, and disagreed completely with the efforts to keep the psychology professor out of the classroom: 'Like, who is to say he's wrong, really?' At one point he remarked: 'The people in some of these Third World countries are so backward.' In his mind, that just proved that they consisted of inferior races. Although this would appear to be a peculiar deduction from a college-educated individual, it was far from atypical. Another middle-class man who was a university graduate, after stating that he was strongly opposed to any form of racism, and believed that was true of Paradise people in general, observed that 'other races' don't value life highly: 'In India, kids are dying in the street, and they live with it, you know.'

Occasionally the man whom I have described as mild-mannered attributed the problems that he thought were caused by visible minorities to cultural differences. For example, it was his strong belief that Canada was disintegrating in large part because the Third World immigrants retained their own languages and cultures, rather than assimilating: 'I guess that's the difference between Canada and the States. When you go to the States, you pledge your allegiance to the American flag. But when I go here somewhere, and we sing the national anthem, I'm not sure of the words any more.'

'It always bothers me,' commented the man, 'when a person from another country says, "oh, it's so bad here".' What really angered him, however, was his perception that Third World people were much more prone to violence, and that they were responsible for a dramatic escalation of crime in Canada. Once again, this was a sentiment expressed by several middle-class people. In another man's words: 'You don't find a group of Anglo-Saxons getting together at a party and knifing each other.' As for the individual whom I have been discussing, he remarked: 'I don't go along with East Indians coming here with turbans and that dagger in the classroom. It's a weapon.' If he had his way, he declared, any such immigrants who committed a crime, even if they had become Canadian citizens, would be automatically deported to their countries of origin.

The impression often conveyed by the media and government spokespeople is that racists are poorly socialized, uneducated louts, or deviant individuals unrepresentative of society in general. This man's example is therefore instructive. Despite his intolerance, he was by almost every other measure a sterling citizen. The same thing can be said about virtually everyone else described in this chapter, including those who fell into the lower class. Intolerance among average citizens, it would appear, is not exceptional.

The main differences between the natives and the newcomers concerned the aspiring-middle class on the one hand, and the lower-upper and upper classes on the other. The people in the former tended to be the most racist of all the citizens of Paradise, while those in the latter were the most tolerant.

My first case within the aspiring-middle class concerns a young woman who made no attempt to conceal her racist orientation. There were two reasons, she said, why she and her husband decided to leave the city and settle in small-town Ontario. The main one was cheap housing (they bought a lovely new home, and with both of them employed, were able to handle the mortgage payments). A motive almost as important, she stated, was the desire to live in an all-white environment: 'That is one thing that I like about it here – none of those people [blacks and Asians].' She reserved most of her animosity for people from Pakistan: 'Pakistanians, I don't get along with them. I think they're a dirty race. I've had to work with some of them. I can't stand to work with someone that smells.' Referring to the controversy involving the kirpan in schools, she fumed: 'I think that's outrageous. If they can have that, I'll give my kid a switchblade. What difference does it make?' A few years ago she had been shocked to learn that her mother's new doctor was a woman from Pakistan; ironically, when she herself went into the hospital to have her first child, she found herself in a similar situation. Her husband, pointing to the doctor who was going to deliver the baby, asked: 'Darling, do you realize what race this lady is?' Much to her surprise, she found that the doctor, an immigrant from India rather than Pakistan, was 'okay.'

This young woman was somewhat more favourably disposed towards other visible minorities: 'I actually had a few black friends I'm really fond of. But to me, I found them lazy.' She also had worked in the city with Chinese Canadians: 'Chinese are not too bad; some of them are pretty friendly.' Although she had never heard of Rushton, she thought Chinese people were quite intelligent, blacks much less so, and 'Pakis would definitely be the least.' Although this person was unusually candid about her racial prejudices, that did not prevent her from resenting complaints from members of minorities: 'The thing that makes me sick is that every time there's a problem, they scream discrimination.' The final irony concerns her own skin colour. Because she is quite dark, in the summer she develops a deep tan: 'I had a lady say once, "you could pass for a Paki."'

This woman was not well educated (she left school after completing grade nine), but it would be an error to conclude that that explains her racist orientation. Consider, for example, the case of a man who had attended university for a couple of years. Both he and his wife, who had gone part way through secondary school, openly stated that they had moved from the outskirts of Toronto to rural Ontario for one fundamental reason: they were determined to get away from black people. Referring to the African Canadians in the area where they had lived, the woman remarked: 'We're by no means prejudiced people. But it was a main concern.' She claimed that blacks had turned that area into a war zone overnight, with gang wars and stabbings in the malls. Her husband chimed in: 'The plaza was full of blacks. I don't know how these people did it. They had mansions. All black people!

You know, the crime rate down there, that bothered me. That was my number one concern. You know, I'm not a prejudiced person. But you can judge a kind of people by their actions.' This man, who expressed a keen interest in genetics, evolution and physical anthropology, went on to conclude: 'The type of people they are, they're different. They're not like us.'

What finally made them decide to move out of the area was their belief that their son's safety at school was in jeopardy: 'The blacks, they changed the high school. Like I said, I'm not a prejudiced person. I work with black people, with Indians. I judge a person as an individual. But what happened, you know, the crime and that. I had black kids walking down the front lawns. When they came to my car, they walked over the top of it.' He also claimed that black youths habitually urinated on his car 'like dogs.'

Asian-origin people, in his judgment, were only moderately more acceptable: 'I've worked with a fair number of Indians. I find them a funny kind of people. They're an arrogant people.' He thought it had something to do with the caste system: 'Back in India, a lot of people who've moved over here were upper caste, sort of.' Talking about a nearby gas station that had been taken over by a family from India, he said: 'Nobody went there. They only lasted six months.' The same thing, he claimed, affected business in the variety stores run by Koreans and Vietnamese: 'Up here, they aren't secure, because people just won't go and frequent their store.' From his perspective, the reluctance of local people to support establishments run by visible minorities was one of the most attractive features of rural Ontario. This young couple is a perfect example of what was said before: people soft on racism aren't necessarily ogres. To the contrary, they both were pleasant, gracious, humorous, and hard-working; it was only when the topic turned to racism that they began to foam at the mouth.

Few people in the aspiring-middle class were as prejudiced against visible minorities as this couple, or as forthright in their views. More typical was a man in his early thirties who had grown up in Toronto, completing grade twelve; his wife also was raised in the city, and began her working career when she was seventeen years old. When he was 'young and immature,' the man stated, he had been full of hatred, and had run around with a gang of whites which had been 'somewhat racist.' His wife interjected that he used to be a complete racist. The man confessed that he had associated for a while with a white supremacist group, but had never actually become a member. He made a point of stating that he and his wife had not moved to Paradise in order to escape from visible minorities, and claimed that he actually had come to his senses as he had grown older and no longer was a racist. His conversion, he explained, can be traced to his job in a factory on the outskirts of Toronto to which he now commutes. He estimated that about 75 per cent of the employees were black, plus 'some Greeks and East Indians.' Working alongside these black people, he made an important discovery: 'They're normal people.'

When the question of which race was the least intelligent was raised, however, it became clear that his change of heart was not quite 100 per cent. Immediately his wife warned him: 'Now, you can't say blacks. That's not fair.' He retorted: 'No, I think blacks, no question.' His wife appeared to be considerably less prejudiced: 'I think a lot of people put blacks down.' She was pleased that at least a few visible-minority kids attended her son's school, remarking that otherwise he would grow up with an incredibly narrow perspective.

Yet this woman too was not immune to the racist bug. She confessed that she was not very fond of 'Pakis.' Before moving to Paradise, she had been a sales clerk in a store in the city: 'I had a couple of bad experiences with Pakistan women.' Even her support for blacks was fragile. When her husband insisted that blacks are the least intelligent race, she stated: 'Actually, he has a point.' She quickly added that environment had something to do with it. Her husband would have none of that argument, but did concede that the low intelligence of blacks is partly caused by 'their bad attitudes.' Once more his wife concurred: 'They do have a lazy attitude.'

In earlier chapters it was pointed out that newcomers in the aspiring-middle class often lived on the precipice of economic disaster. Usually they purchased impressive new homes that stretched their incomes to the breaking point; frequently their dreams burst and they were forced to slink back to rented accommodation in the city. When that happened to individuals who had left the city at least partly in order to live in a predominantly white environment, the trauma was doubled.

Consider the case of one young couple who found themselves precisely in that situation. The second most important reason for moving to Paradise, they said, was to bring their children up in an area devoid of visible minorities (the main reason was affordable housing). Malton, a community near Toronto which they referred to as 'Paki Palace,' has been completely taken over by Third World people, they claimed, and they were relieved that they had been able to escape to the country-side. As in so many other cases, however, they hated the commuting life, and found that even with both of them employed as unskilled workers in the city, they could not handle the monthly mortgage payments on their home. The prospect of living once again in the city next to people from the Third World, especially those from Pakistan, did not overjoy them. Not only would life be more dangerous for his family, commented the man, but in addition they would still be existing on the edge of poverty, because 'the Pakis,' who squeeze 'about fifteen people into a house,' don't need as much money. They will work for low wages, he explained, thus making it tough for white working people like himself, all the while screaming racism at the least provocation.

I only met one couple who were enthusiastic about returning to the multi-ethnic setting of the city. Both of these individuals were university graduates, and they fell into the middle class. Born and raised in Toronto, they had gradually become sick and tired of all the ethnic groups and their 'noisy, messy ways.' The woman remarked. 'We didn't want to bring our children up in this ethnic, working-class neighbourhood.' She and her husband made it clear that the desire to escape from all the ethnics was almost equal in importance to the low cost of housing in their decision to settle in Paradise, and their initial impressions were not disappointing: 'When we moved here,' spoke the man, 'we noticed a real change about the multicultural thing. There weren't any blacks in the school yard. I have to admit there was a certain comfort in that.' Yet after living for a couple of years in rural Ontario, they underwent a complete reversal in attitude. They began to long for the raucous interaction of the various ethnic groups in the area where they had previously lived, and the intrigue and chaos of Kensington Market. In the woman's words, 'But then the ethnic thing became after all the thing that we missed.' It was ironical, added her husband, that they had had to move away from a multi-ethnic environment in order to appreciate the degree to which it enriched their lives.

The tendency for the most racially oriented people to come from the aspiring-middle class possibly was related to their aggressiveness. More than those from other parts of the stratification system, they were risk-takers, betting on their capacity, despite the lack of funds, to fight and claw their way into the middle class. These people could not afford to be generous to anybody who might even remotely thwart their ambitions, including members of visible minorities whom they thought might compete with them for jobs or even depress their wages. A similar logic helps to explain why those in the lower-upper and upper classes were the most tolerant of all. Most of them were wealthy businessmen, or university-educated professionals. For these people the visible minorities represented customers and clients, not competitors.

By no means were all newcomers who occupied the upper classes devoid of prejudice. One man, for example, made it clear that he would not employ an African or Asian Canadian in his small factory. Another person complained that visible minorities always seemed to use racism as an excuse when things didn't go their way. 'I'm not a racist,' he stated. 'At least I don't think I'm a racist. I just think they're carrying things too far.' He blamed the country's politicians for lacking the guts to deny entry to Third World immigrants, and for bowing like cowards to their demands once they settled here, and angrily concluded that 'now it's probably too late.' Most of the lower-upper and upper-class newcomers, however, while very conservative – indeed, determinably right of centre on many political and social issues – were reasonably tolerant, with one glaring exception. Like the majority of people in Paradise, they had little love for French Canadians.

White Ethnic Perspective

In view of the prejudice and discrimination that white ethnics sometimes face, it might be thought that they would be more sympathetic than people of British origin to members of visible minorities. That was often not the case. One immigrant from eastern Europe candidly stated that she had moved away from Toronto because she could not stand black people. In another immigrant's words, 'The picture of Canada before I came here was a Mountie on a horse.' He could hardly believe that Sikhs in the RCMP were permitted to wear turbans. Immigrants, himself included, he added, had an obligation to shed their cultural upbringing and become real Canadians: 'I don't believe in multiculturalism. When you come to Canada, that's it. You're a Canadian.' This man, a commuter, worked alongside people from India and Pakistan, and was not thrilled by the experience: 'I tell you, we hate it. Those people, they don't have any idea of sanitation.' The Canadian government in his opinion made a major blunder in allowing Pakistanis and East Indians into the country. On the other hand, he remarked that 'a nice coloured family' moved into a house across from his own, but only stayed six months because their bodies were incapable of enduring the winters.

This man and his wife had heard of Rushton, but could not remember his arguments. After I explained the basics, he commented: 'Well, Asian kids are very intelligent, the way they study. I'll say he's 60 per cent right. Maybe he found something in a gene that proves his idea.' It is perfectly evident, he added, that genes rather than environment are the basis of intelligence, and he had no doubt which race was the least intelligent: blacks. His wife was less certain. When she had first arrived in Canada, she had worked in a factory with people of 'several different races and colours,' and remembered that some of them seemed just as intelligent as whites.

'I can't stand people being openly racist. But then I know there's a racist streak in me. If I go through Detroit, I don't want to associate with blacks.' These were the words of another man from eastern Europe who had just provided a detailed account of the massive prejudice and discrimination he had faced as a boy growing up in rural Ontario. Unlike the previous man and woman, who only had completed a couple of years in secondary school, he was a university graduate, and was quite well informed about Rushton's thesis: 'I would say there might be some truth in it. My perception is much of the crime in Toronto is connected with Jamaicans.' The media and the government, he believed, acted in cahoots to conceal that connection, because of their left wing orientations. As this well-educated man reflected on what he was saying to me, he almost seemed to be embarrassed. There was a time, he revealed, when he regarded himself as a socialist, and believed in the essential sameness and equality of all human beings. 'I guess,' he concluded, 'I'm getting more intolerant with age.'

Visible Minority Perspective

Did racism flow in the other direction – from the visible minorities towards the white majority? Although more often than not the African Canadians were aloof and on guard when I first met them, without a single exception they mellowed after I explained that I was conducting research on rural life. Some of them were quite bitter that their attempts to make friends among their neighbours had failed, but the very fact that they had made the effort would seem to indicate an absence of a racist orientation. Most of the African Canadians whom I interviewed were adults. While I sometimes met their young children, I did not encounter many of the older offspring who had left home, usually for the city, to begin their careers. Occasionally, a man and woman hinted that their son or daughter took a much harder line than they did towards intolerance, to the point where they had themselves almost become racists.

The great difference between the African and Asian Canadians was the latter's resignation that racism cannot be avoided because it is natural, and the virtual lack of any attempt to make close friends with white people. This approach to social interaction, as I indicated in chapter 9, was partly a defensive mechanism, and partly a function of the quasi-community that existed among the Asian-origin immigrants. The fact is that when people of European origin displayed an interest in interacting with the owners of the gas stations, motels, and variety stores, the apparent 'natural' barrier in the minds of the Asian Canadians crumbled and acquaintanceships developed. Recall, as well, the admirable capacity of some of the Asian Canadians to communicate with the locals. Yet it was precisely in relation to these success stories that a distinction in the quality of interaction between Asian and African Canadians and the white majority was apparent. Occasionally one encountered deep friendships between blacks and whites. The Asian Canadians, in contrast, while sometimes friendly with the locals, almost always imposed a limit on the depth of interaction.

Shared suffering is by no means sufficient to guarantee common bonds, and thus the African and Asian Canadians usually had little to do with each other. Sometimes a person from India or Pakistan would express sympathy towards 'the coloured people,' and on one occasion I observed a black man – who thought that people of colour (African, Asian, and otherwise) should join together for mutual protection – attempting to communicate with a woman from India, who seemed perplexed by his presence. Although she later made it clear that she did not think unkindly about black people, she wondered what in the world the man thought they had in common. Sometimes attitudes between African and Asian Canadians were less generous. One African Canadian, a university graduate, ventured the opinion that East Indians and Pakistanis were unable to integrate into Canadian society. The obstacle, he thought, was culture, not biology: people from these two countries did not seem to have the high level of sanitation standards that are expected in Canada. That unflattering appraisal was returned full force by an Asian Canadian, who also was a university graduate. The stereotypes about black people, he insisted, are accurate. Blacks have no respect for the law; they openly use and sell drugs and the operators of small businesses such as variety stores in cities like Toronto live in constant fear of attack from violent black youths.

There was no black community as such in the Paradise area, mainly because individual families were scattered throughout the countryside, and unlike the Asian Canadians did not gravitate into similar occupations such as the gas station business, but instead made the daily trip to the urban centres in the south to work at a wide range of jobs. In other words, the African-Canadian families were relatively invisible to each other. While this was the basic cause of their fragmentation, there was an additional factor. Relationships between immigrants from the West Indies and native blacks, many of whom traced their roots in Canada back a century or more, did not always appear to be cordial. In this respect, there was nothing unusual about southern Ontario. Such strains have historically been present among African-origin people in Canada, reflecting a degree of complexity within the black population that is not always appreciated.

The Asian community (or quasi-community) on the surface appeared to be much more cohesive and harmonious. This must be immediately qualified. By the Asian community I mean primarily people from India and Pakistan, not people from other parts of Asia such as Korea, Vietnam, and Hong Kong. Moreover, while immigrants from Pakistan could be found in the Paradise region, they were not as numerous as people from India, and therefore the Asian community consisted primarily of Sikhs and Hindus. What was interesting was that friendships were not necessarily based on shared religious beliefs. An owner of a gas station, himself a Hindu, declared, 'I don't care who's Hindu, who's Sikh.' These were not idle words. On several occasions I had an opportunity to observe warm interaction between this man and a Sikh family nearby. As he explained, the relationship worked because they always avoided the topic of religion. Religion, he declared, was the one subject that he refused to discuss with anyone, and it was not until after my third meeting with him that he relented, at which time he revealed that one of his close relatives had married a Sikh. In another case involving Sikh owners of a motel, their only regular visitors were members of a Hindu family who operated a gas station next to them. The Hindu man explained that they could be friends because neither of them tried to push his religion on the other.

The relative insignificance of religion as a basis of social interaction did not always extend to Moslems. A Sikh man, explaining why he did not have any Moslem friends, said it was simply because he had never gotten to know any of them well – even the families that lived a few miles from his motel. A Hindu man, who was acquainted with a few Moslems, remarked that it was common for Hindus and Sikhs to associate with each other, but neither took much pleasure in relating to Moslems. The reason, he claimed, is that Moslems are too fanatical. He thought that there was something in Islam to the effect that if a Moslem converts a non-believer, he or she will go straight to Heaven. It is curious, the man stated, that when he visits Moslems, they always talk about Allah and never offer an alcoholic beverage; but when Moslems enter his home, they happily drink his scotch.

While relationships between Sikhs and Hindus in the Paradise region were generally amicable, there were occasional exceptions. For example, a Hindu couple insisted to me that Sikhs were the worst immigrants in the country because they were all fanatics. Immigrants, they believed, had an obligation to downplay their natal culture in order to integrate into Canadian society. Sikhs, in their opinion, have been guilty of doing exactly the opposite. They thought that it was ridiculous for Sikhs to wear the kirpan in school, and insisted that they did not do that in India; as for the policy of permitting Sikhs in the RCMP to wear turbans, that had been brought about, they observed, by the typical Sikh practice of intimidation. These people also declared that in India there was absolutely no discrimination against Sikhs, leaving the impression, at least based on their attitudes, that the opposite might be closer to the truth.

While religion therefore was not quite as irrelevant for social interaction as some Asian Canadians professed, other factors, especially social class differences and individual behaviour, carried more weight. Well-educated and financially secure people tended to seek each other out, just as they did in the rest of rural society.[2] Individuals who were hard-pressed for cash, and those who were considered unsophisticated, crude, quarrelsome and immoral, were avoided. These people – again a replica of the rest of society – did not form friendships among themselves; instead they lived relatively isolated lives, punctuated by periodic attempts to interact with their 'betters.'

A Sikh woman, for example, whose family was middle class, explained why she was always in the company of a Hindu family down the road, while she never visited another Sikh family in the same vicinity. The latter people, she said, were uneducated and ignorant, while the former people were university graduates like herself. Her point was that religion did not count when it came to choosing friends or even interacting with strangers. On one occasion a Sikh arrived at her motel, stated that he planned to remain in the area for a couple of weeks on business, and virtually demanded a special rate. Although she was not impressed by his aggressive behaviour, she acquiesced to her husband's dictate to give him what he wanted. When the traveller moved into his room, he proved to be quarrelsome and obnoxious, and she revoked the special rate. The moral, she stated, is that there is good and bad in every race and religion, including her own.

Racial Classification

Paradise residents appeared to be nineteenth-century physical anthropologists at heart. Virtually without exception, the intolerant *and* the tolerant assumed that race is a meaningful biological concept in the phenotypical sense, and most of them were quite prepared to present a list of races and to rank them on a scale of superiority and inferiority. Even those people in the lower classes whose prejudices contained an economic rather than a biological connotation had little doubt that the world's population could be divided according to observable racial types. At the same time, Paradise people were remarkably confused about the nature of race, often mixing together biology, nationality, culture, language, behaviour, and even dress. The number of races that they identified ranged from two to almost a dozen. The criteria also varied widely, although the basic one was skin colour. In terms of ranking, most natives and newcomers placed blacks at the bottom, as did some of the Asian Canadians, but several individuals thought people from India and Pakistan belonged there, and occasionally that position was reserved for French Canadians.

A few examples, beginning with the lower classes among both the natives and newcomers, will serve as illustration. An elderly man presented the following list of races: 'African, Chinese, Korean, Australian, North American Indian, Eskimo, Yankee, Negroid, Spaniard and German.' He did not realize that he had confused race and nationality (or that he had included both African and Negroid), and went on to say that one can tell a person's race by the language she or he speaks. His wife interjected: 'There's the black, the Oriental, and the whites. You can tell by the looks.' After listening to her, he changed his mind and agreed that skin colour is the basic criterion. Both of these individuals were adamant that black people are the most inferior.

A single mother on welfare thought there were seven separate races: 'Pakis, Negroes, French Canadian, whites, Russians, Japanese, Chinese.' On reflection, she remarked: 'I'd say they're nationalities more than anything. I'd say that's a race more than anything: colours.' Her revised list included 'Negro, white, and Chinese people.' Unlike the previous couple, this woman did not believe that some races are more intelligent than others: 'It depends on your schooling. It has nothing to do with black and white, or whatever.' Another woman thought there were five races: 'Pakistans, blacks, Chinese, whites, Indians.' You could tell a person's race, she stated, by their skin colour, accent and clothes. One of her neighbours, after insisting that there was only one criterion – colour of skin – listed 'black, white and German.' She wasn't certain why she thought Germans were a separate race, but thought it might be because they assumed they were superior and kept themselves apart.

Turning to the middle of the class system, we find a man who began by listing 'white, Negro and yellow' and then added 'Jews.' Although he too thought skin colour was the basic way to identify the different races, he insisted that Jews were a separate race – in his mind the most despicable people on earth. Another individual, who was a university graduate, stated that there are three races, 'Asiatic, African and Caucasian,' and two basic criteria, 'skin colour and bone structure.' This man, who thought both Asians and Africans shared the bottom of the scale, remarked: 'I've heard Negroes have different aging processes. Their wrinkles would come on a different place on their face than a white person.' A college-educated man thought there were four races: 'Asians, Eurasians, whites, blacks.' As for the criteria, he stressed skin colour: 'That's your first way of identifying people.' But he also thought that secondary criteria had to be taken into account: 'Koreans and Chinese are different races. You can tell by the bone structure and language.' Another person listed six races: 'Asians, whites, blacks, Greeks, Phoenicians, Russians.' He stated: 'I figure each nation by itself is its own race.' In his opinion, blacks are undoubtedly the least intelligent. According to one young man, the main races are 'white, black, Chinese, Pakistan and Japanese. Chinese would be on the top.

And Japanese. Then East Indians.' Curiously, he did not have Rushton in mind here. Instead, he measured superiority in terms of sheer numbers: 'I just think there's a hell of a lot more of them, that's all.'

When I asked a highly tolerant woman if she thought there were different races, and if so, whether she could name them, she replied: 'I had this asked me before, and I know I was wrong.' The implication was that she assumed there was a correct scientific answer. After she and her husband struggled with the problem, they decided on the following: 'Germans, Japanese, Oriental, Caucasian, English.' They soon realized that they had confused race and nationality, and concluded that the one reliable measuring rod is skin colour.

People in the higher classes approached racial classification in much the same way as those below them. One wealthy woman who had graduated from university suggested there were four races: 'white, Caucasian, yellow, Negroid.' Her husband seemed a little embarrassed over her first two choices. Neither of these people expressed positive or negative attitudes about minorities. A successful merchant thought that skin colour was the main way of identifying races, and suggested there were four: 'black, white, yellow, red.' A secondary criterion, he stated, was financial. That is, one could identify races by their financial status. The richest race, he said, was obviously the white race, and the poorest 'the red race of North American Indians.' A highly educated professional man listed four races: 'Negroid, Caucasoid, Mongoloid, and Australian Aborigines.' But then he identified Germans, Swiss, and Japanese as separate races, and placed them at the top of the scale because he thought that was how these 'races' saw themselves. Conversely, he believed that blacks regarded themselves as inferior, and he put them at the bottom of the scale. This man actually was quite tolerant. Black people, in his opinion, lacked opportunity, not intelligence, which accounted for their low self-concepts.

Finally, according to a black woman there are only two races: black and white. After reflecting for a moment, she added: 'I think racism goes beyond colour. Racism, in my mind, means being completely against a culture – I mean, a nation.' At this point she had obviously become quite confused, but then she made a very sophisticated comment: racial categories, she thought, could be defined in terms of the *expression* of racism. Whenever racism between two people existed, by definition they represented different races. One of this woman's friends who had been listening to her thought there were many more races than she had indicated: 'Chinese, blacks, Italians, Greeks, and me.' He was partly British, French, and Aboriginal. As they argued between themselves, he asked how she would classify him. She joked that he didn't belong anywhere. Maybe, he suggested, every person is his own race.

In summary, the idea of separate biologically based races, which can be identified mainly by skin colour and ranked along a scale of superiority and inferiority, was almost universal among Paradise people. Such an approach to race and racism has been obsolete in academic circles since the Second World War. Most physical anthropologists and human biologists have discarded the attempt to establish a scientific taxonomy of races, and have happily handed the investigation of racism over to social scientists, who attempt to decode the social and political dimensions implicit in people's folk categories. Academics who continue to investigate biological types focus today on genes rather than physical appearances, and the genotypes that they create do not usually overlap with the famous phenotypes of the past: Negroid, Mongoloid, Australoid, and Caucasoid. The fact that lay people, such as those in Paradise, continue to think in terms of phenotypes, and to draw conclusions from them about intelligence and behaviour, could be characterized as the principle failure of anthropology in the contemporary world.

Deep and Shallow Racism

Contrary to the assumption that the relative lack of contact among the natives with minority groups would render them particularly intolerant, racism actually ran deeper among the newcomers. In this context, the distinction between racism and ethnocentrism may be relevant. 'Racism,' according to Banton (1970: 18), 'is the doctrine that a man's behaviour is determined by stable inherited characteristics deriving from separate racial stocks, having distinctive attributes and usually considered to stand to one another in relations of superiority and inferiority.' Ethnocentrism is the tendency to regard as inferior all ways of life that do not correspond to one's own. Racism, conceived in biological terms and amounting to an ideology, does not necessarily diminish when interaction between different population groups increases. Ethnocentrism, rooted in culture and amounting to a defence mechanism for parochialism, often withers in the face of experience with other ways of life. Some of the newcomers, with their attitudes forged in the multicultural city, tended to be racists. The natives tended to be ethnocentric. This helps to explain why it was rare to encounter newcomers who had softened their attitudes towards minorities over time, whereas a number of the natives, after becoming acquainted with some of the African and Asian Canadians, adopted a more positive attitude towards them.

Racism is a very crude term, and a more sensitive conceptual approach is to break it down into basic preconditions, general social structural determinants, and specific triggering factors. In this scheme, racism and ethnocentrism are not portrayed as separate entities. Instead ethnocentrism is subsumed within racism as one of its principal preconditions. The other preconditions are scapegoating, xenophobia, possibly sexual competition, certainly pan-human insecurity (the tragic mark of the species, the flip side of human sensitivity), and the inherent classificatory propensity of the human mind. This last factor needs to be clarified. My argument, following Needham (1979:57–60), is that to think is to classify. Classification, in other words, is an a priori mental operation. On this issue, I sharply disagree with Durkheim and Mauss (1963) who contended that the individual mind is incapable of classification, and that it was only when people became organized into groups, when they possessed social structure, that they began to order and categorize the world around them.

Durkheim and Mauss wrote (1963:8): 'Every classification implies a hierarchical order.' This could be interpreted to mean that racism is natural, but that too is implausible. Classification is merely a mental operation, devoid of empirical content. The propensity to classify may well have a distant influence on the tendency of people to think in terms of racial categories, but whether the content of a taxonomy acquires a racist, anti-racist or non-racist shape depends on a range of other factors, including the prevailing social and political currents in a society. The other preconditions of racism also play a part here, but they do not lead inevitably to racism. These preconditions are not confined to time and place. They are among the criteria that define Homo sapiens. Only if it could be argued that racism has existed everywhere and at all times – which it has not – would a contrary interpretation make any sense.

The general social structural conditions are more restricted in historical terms. Included here are colonialism, nationalism, social class (especially in relation to capitalism), and communications (especially media portrayal of minorities). Although racism undoubtedly predated colonialism and capitalism, it was significantly deepened with their emergence. The common element in the various social structural conditions is differential power, which is why it is reasonable to agree with Baker (1978:316): 'Race relations are essentially group power contests.'

The specific triggering factors, in turn, pertain to immediate social events; downward swings in the economy, changes in immigration patterns, celebrated incidents of minority persecution, and momentous national and international political strains.

This framework helps to illuminate a central problem with regard to race relations in small communities like Paradise: how can it be explained that in a setting where until recently almost everyone was British in origin and racial contests were virtually non-existent, that people nevertheless thought in racial terms, readily offered racial taxonomies, and expressed racial prejudice? The explanation, I suggest, is that such communities possess a 'racial capacity.' That is, by virtue of the preconditions of racism, plus the background social structural factors – and here I single out capitalistic class relations and the media as especially critical – racism as an ideology has already been fashioned, but lies dormant, ready to be triggered off by specific events such as the recent migration of visible minorities to the country-side. The big question, of course, is whether a progressive race-relations policy can prevent the racial capacity in small towns like Paradise – what might be labelled shallow racism – from being transformed into the deep racism that has been characteristic of urban centres.

At this juncture, it must be stressed that to some extent what appeared to be racism in rural Ontario was not racism at all. The lack of integration of minority people was partly caused by their status as strangers. Although social class and behaviour affected the length of time required to become accepted in the community, all newcomers, *because* they were strangers, were initially on trial. Some members of minorities were quite aware of this situation, and consequently were less inclined to read prejudice and discrimination into every brittle exchange with the natives.

The fragmented nature of contemporary rural society also had an impact. In the past, when the emphasis was placed on community cohesion in Paradise, the Jewish families that had lived there had no choice but to try to become integrated, and to the degree that they failed to do so (or were prevented from doing so) they were regarded as misfits. Today, not even the natives, for the most part, accept the fiction that Paradise consists of one big happy family. What many of the minority members, especially African Canadians, interpreted as racism may sometimes merely have been a manifestation of the weak calibre of social relations that affected everyone.

From the perspective of the natives, however, the African and Asian Canadians were not just ordinary newcomers. It might be suggested, indeed, that they constituted 'perfect strangers.' Lipset and Raab (1970), in their study of the extreme right wing in America, argued that the underlying target of fascists and racists was not blacks and Jews, but social change itself. Rose (1971) theorized that the basis of anti-Semitism can be found in the association of Jews with discordant urban life, and the passing of placid rural life. Similarly, the African and Asian Canadians who have settled around Paradise may represent to the natives the ultimate (perfect) sign that rural society, as a distinctive and superior way of life, has perished.

Finally, what does the comparative perspective tell us about Paradise? In terms of the proportion of visible minorities and people of European origin, Paradise does not even remotely resemble the community in southern United States studied by Davis and the Gardners (1944), where 50 per cent of the population in the town and 80 per cent in the surrounding countryside was black; and certainly the caste-like division between black and white portrayed in Dollard's classical study (1957) of another southern community in America has no counterpart in Paradise. Paradise, in fact, has little in common with Middletown, the name given by the Lynds (1929) to their community in the American Midwest. Not only was Middletown, with a population of 38,000 in 1924, much larger, but it also had at that time a thriving Ku Klux Klan presence, introduced 'by a few of the city's leading businessmen as a vigilance committee to hold an invisible whip over the corrupt Democratic political administration and generally "to clean up the town" ...' (Lynd and Lynd 1929:481). With its current heterogeneous ethnic composition, Paradise approximates more closely to Stymeist's study (1975) of the northern Ontario town of Crow Lake, although there the boundary lines among the various groups of white ethnics seemed to be more clearly drawn (despite Stymeist's emphasis that such lines were far from impregnable) and the principal visible-minority group was Aboriginal rather than people whose origins were African and Asian (albeit they were not entirely absent).

In terms of the racial motive for moving from the city to rural Ontario expressed by some of the newcomers, there is little in the literature that would suggest that Paradise is typical. However, Bradshaw and Blakely (1979:3) remarked in passing that rural America has begun to encounter increased levels of crime and racial tension. More to the point, Fliegel and Sofranko (1984) argued that it is plausible to describe the process of reverse migration in the American Midwest as white flight from urban to rural society, even though the people who were surveyed rarely mentioned racism as one of their motives for moving. In terms of history and demography, there appears to be no reason why Paradise should be a special case, which makes it plausible to suggest that its apparent uniqueness is merely a product of an inadequately investigated research problem.[3]

Chapter Twelve

Wider Issues

Paradise in 1990 is not the same community as it was in 1950. The good old days, as many of the natives remember them, were guarded by stability and cohesion. Stability, however, at least in a class-based society, normally is accompanied by inequality, and cohesion usually amounts to the ruling class's success in imposing its ideology on the rest of the population. We need only recall the different perspectives of people at the polar ends of the stratification system in the past to realize that these assertions amount almost to truisms. By the early 1970s Paradise's defences had been penetrated by the outside world, and the first casualties were stability and cohesion.

No community, of course, is completely isolated. In the 1950s young women and men left Paradise to seek their fortunes elsewhere, soldiers arrived back at the end of the Second World War, outside salesmen peddled their products to the local merchants, and radio and television, the latter in its early stages, brought the village into communication with the external world. By the 1980s it was no longer intellectually profitable to show that Paradise was tied to the wider society; that was all too obvious. By then a new question had surfaced: did anything remain in the community that was unique? Was it, indeed, still a community? In actuality, it would be more accurate to describe Paradise today as several communities – those of the natives, newcomers, and minorities being three of them – and rather than viewing the town in terms of tightly-knit layers of people arranged vertically according to social class, it now makes more sense to portray it as a patchwork of interest groups each of which extends, like so many spokes on a wheel, beyond the community to like-minded people who share their class and ethnic characteristics.

The intrusion of the provincial and federal bureaucracies has played its part in nibbling away at the autonomy of the small community, as have the migrants from the urban areas. The overall impact has been to bring rural society in line with urban society in terms of authority, class, and ethnicity. Traditional authority has been displaced by bureaucratic authority, status has given way to class, and racial and ethnic consciousness has expanded. With the arrival of the working-class commuters in rural Ontario, a rural proletariat, independent of the old paternalistic relationship of patron and client, or of subjective ties to land and place, has come into its own. At the present time a parallel proletariat among the minorities, one which under the influence of higher-class hegemony could serve as an instrument to divide and thus render more pliable working-class people to the dictates of capitalism, has not taken root in the countryside. The minorities who have moved there are marginalized both socially and politically, but they consist of a marginalized middle class. The only exception concerns the French Canadians in Paradise, but their numbers are insufficient to have much of an impact on the class system.

These last remarks bring us to the distinction drawn by Krauss between stratification and class. Stratification in Krauss's lexicon (and as I have employed it throughout this study) consists of a descriptive hierarchy of categories of people with similar characteristics. Strata are not organized and do not engage in collective action; moreover, there are as many strata in a population as the investigator wishes to distinguish. Social classes, in contrast, are organized in terms of their respective interests and are mutually antagonistic. As Krauss (1976:29–30) insists, classes only exist when there is conflict, or when people come together to contest institutionalized inequality. In my judgment, this is an inadequate conception of social class, because it restricts the concept to what Marx meant by 'a class for itself.' In Paradise there has been very little evidence of a class for itself, either in the 1950s or the 1980s. But it makes perfect sense to suggest that throughout the community's history there have been 'classes in themselves.' That is, people can be analytically located in terms of their relations to the means of production.

In the 1950s there were two main classes in themselves. One was a bourgeoisie consisting of the wealthy merchants and professional people who possessed economic power, buttressed by status power, and exhibited in political power (their control of both the formal administration of the community and the informal level of everyday influence). The second was the working class. Situated between these two classes was what could be labelled, following Wright (1978), a contradictory class of self-employed people with small businesses, such as carpenters, plumbers, and electricians, plus managers and supervisors who worked for the wealthy merchants, and some well-placed clerical staff. The major changes in the class system in the 1980s were the swelling of the bourgeoisie by professional people; the emergence of a more complex set of class fractions between the bourgeoisie and the working class, including people such as teachers and nurses in 'the marginal professions,' and those engaged in non-productive labour such as real estate agents; and, finally, the creation of an unpropertied underclass – the new poor of Paradise, often unemployed and existing on welfare.

At this juncture it is relevant to entertain the relationship between the transformed class system in Paradise and the transformed ethnic composition of the community. There is an unresolved debate between Marxist-oriented scholars such as Cox (1948) and Miles (1982) and liberal-oriented scholars such as Rex (1970) and Banton (1977) concerning the degree to which racial and ethnic prejudice can be reduced to a class analysis.[1] In many respects this debate parallels that concerning the extent to which *status* is independent of class. The Marxists generally contend that racism as an ideology is a direct outgrowth of the class system; racial antagonisms divide and weaken the proletariat, for the ultimate benefit of the ruling class. The liberals, for the most part, go along with this interpretation, but only up to a point; racism, they contend, is to some extent independent of class, and it is partly this autonomous zone that explains why shared class interests fail to prevail over ethnic divisions. A case in point, as Kuper (1975) indicates, is South Africa, where little sign of a united black and white proletariat has emerged, despite propitious circumstances.

The crux of this debate revolves around the causal status of (presumed) extra-class factors such as xenophobia, scapegoating, and ethnocentrism. Inasmuch as I included these factors among the preconditions of racism in the previous chapter, it might be thought that I fall clearly into the liberal camp. However, it must be remembered that my argument was not that these preconditions caused racism, but instead that they provide a psychological climate in which racism can grow.

In the final reckoning, it seems to me that racism is indeed to class as status is to class, but with one crucial difference. Just as status can distort social relations based on the market, the same is true for racism, but in both cases it is class that lies behind them and to which they ultimately respond. The difference concerns the polar opposite consequences of momentous social change for status and racism. Status, as we have seen, tends to evaporate under these conditions, providing a free rein to the market situation. Racism, in contrast, often deepens, or at least becomes more overt, when society is in turmoil. The explanation, I think, is twofold. It is precisely when people's lives become unanchored that xenophobia and scapegoating flourish. Equally important, a society in flux is a risky business for the dominant social class. Racial ideology, buttressed by the extra-class psychological propensities, and manifested sometimes in right-wing extremism, can serve as one of the ruling class's instruments to make sure it still is on top when the dust settles. It certainly would be controversial to jump from this argument to Nikolinakos's contention (1973) that racism as an ideology is an essential element in the contemporary capitalist state. But one thing is certain: ethnic heterogeneity, and the fusion of ethnicity and class within the stratification system, no longer mark urban society off from rural society, at least in the Paradise region.

The massive changes that have taken place in Paradise suggest just how silly it is to continue to talk about a rural-urban dichotomy, or even a continuum. Certainly there remain differences of degree in levels of education, crime, and divorce between urban and rural society, but these are quantitative differences. Qualitative ones are quite another matter. If the Paradise case tells us anything, it is that there are no social relationships unique to the small community per se. One does not study the small community because it constitutes a special sociological type around which a body of theory can be built. One does so because the small community (or village or settlement) is methodologically useful, a convenient setting in which to examine complex social relationships under manageable conditions. As Pahl (1966:309) stated long ago, the investigation of commuter communities like Paradise on the periphery of urban centres is especially appropriate for comprehending contemporary social change.

Finally, there is the sub-theme of the exotic and the bizarre. As Rabinow (1986: 241) has written: 'We need to anthropologize the West: show how exotic its constitution of reality has been, emphasize those domains most taken for granted as universal.' This quest has already begun, as anthropological research has switched from exotic societies, to employ Segalen's term (1983), to the investigator's own society, which for all practical purposes means Western society. The post-modernists would have us believe that the shift in emphasis towards one's own society has been engineered by their critical attacks on the authority of the anthropologist as writer and interpreter of other cultures, and on the embedded inequality in the researcher/subject relationship. Yet post-modernism in this respect amounts to little more than a rationalization after the fact for a change in fieldwork practice that had already been set in motion with the emergence of independent nations in the erstwhile colonial world.

The days when anthropology was identified with other cultures, which meant essentially the Third World, are gone, and that is a good thing, because all of human society should be the subject of its investigations. To swing completely in the other direction, however, and redefine the discipline as the study of Western society amounts only to an appearance of a solution to epistemological and political issues embedded in the field work enterprise.[2] What research at home does provide is an opportunity to exploit the insider/outsider relationship. In this situation the anthropologist is an insider in cultural terms, and the advantage of language competency can hardly be exaggerated. Armed with his or her comparative perspective, the anthropologist also is an outsider, which, among other things, enhances one's sensitivity towards the exotic and bizarre. Thus Varenne (1977:10), a French anthropologist who undertook a community study in the northern United States, advised: '... it is time ... to make more apparent the exoticism of our everyday life.'[3] Similarly, Nader (1982:301–2) wrote: 'For many students today, the experience of working in an international industrial complex would be more bizarre than anything a student anthropologist could find in a Mexican village, or in New Guinea for that matter. We anthropologists have studied the cultures of the world only to find in the end that ours is one of the most bizarre.'

Before turning to Paradise, we need a further clarifying note: the exotic is to ethnocentrism as the bizarre is to racism. Both the exotic and the ethnocentric fade in the face of experience. The exotic is a creation of the outsider; one person's exotic is another person's mundane, whether the setting is in North America or Borneo. Thus a young man who arrived in Canada from West Africa could hardly believe his eyes, as winter set in, when he first saw a dog dressed in a coat. That, he thought, was exoticism at its pinnacle. The bizarre, like racism, is more robust; it can persist even when it becomes familiar.

Little imagination and effort are required to marshall examples of the bizarre in Paradise, and the less apparent exotic as well: the inebri-

ated character who accidentally shot his faithful hound dog as it cring-
ed behind a sofa; an elderly barber who entertained his customers by
quoting poetry; a hard-drinking, hefty woman who habitually punched
out men at the local hockey games; the hog-calling and husband-
calling contests at the local fair in the 1950s; a single mother who
supplemented her family's diet by instructing her children to pick up
freshly killed animals on the road; an elderly woman who attended all
the funerals in order to have human contact; another woman who
went hungry in order that her dogs, several dozens of them, did not;
a wily mechanic who patched vehicles with cardboard rather than
metal, and sent his unsuspecting customers on their way with a friendly
pat on the back. On a different level, what could be more exotic and
bizarre than a society where people seclude themselves indoors and
relate to images on a screen rather than to their neighbours; where a
second car and an annual vacation in the Caribbean are sometimes
regarded as more important than the psychological needs of one's
children; where a single sports star is paid more than the entire staff
of a large school; where animal rights often take priority over human
rights; where almost every lofty value – be it marital fidelity, tolerance
of human diversity or compassion towards the unfortunate – and every
taboo – whether it concerns incest, spouse and child abuse, or alcoholism – is systematically contradicted by reality; and where people prove
to be geniuses at finding reasons to oppress each other, whether the
principle is class, ethnicity, religion, gender, age, or sexual orientation.

Although anthropologists, the romantics of the academic world, have
travelled to every corner of the globe in pursuit of the exotic, and the
bizarre too, they often end up falling over their own feet as they
scramble to demonstrate the mundane behind the exotic. It is partly
the desire to parade one's relativism that brings about this change in
emphasis, and partly the normal academic procedure of rejecting what
is apparent for a presumed deeper reality. Similarly, when anthropologists encounter the ordinary, the first impulse is to probe for the
extraordinary behind it. In arguing that rural Ontario is every bit as
exotic as Timbuctoo (which I have visited) I may have been guilty of
doing precisely that. Yet one thing is certain: in no other research
project that I have conducted – and these include living in a West
African Utopia where people believed they would never die, studying
the ritualized violence associated with the blood feud (or vendetta) in
Corsica, and investigating neo-fascists in Canada – have I found myself
in quite the same bizarre circumstances that occurred one day in

Paradise. A middle-aged woman whom I called on to interview took one look at me and immediately concluded that I had psychic powers, despite my protests to the contrary. As I soon learned, although she gave absolutely no indication that she was planning to do anything improper, she was extremely anxious to begin a new life without the burden of her bedridden husband.

She asked me if he would die within two months. I said no. Will he pass away by the end of the year? Again I answered in the negative, but in retrospect I'm not sure if I did that because of respect for a human being's life (her husband's) or because it enhanced my rapport with this unusual woman. Will he be gone within two years? As ethical principles flashed across my mind, and the sheer ridiculousness of the situation sank in, I again protested that I was not psychic (which she obviously refused to believe), and mumbled something to the effect that two years is a long time, and the wise person should be prepared for all eventualities. Although my remarks were intentionally vague, that did not appear to be the way she interpreted them. From the glint in her eye, she was already preparing for her husband's departure to a different kind of Paradise.

Appendix A

Methodology

The rough outline for this study took shape in my mind many years ago and far away. I was living, at the time, in a village in West Africa, almost identical in size to the one in rural Ontario where I had spent my youth, conducting my first anthropological field trip. Although the two communities were drastically different – the West African one was a religious Utopia, where private ownership and even the family had been banned (see Barrett 1977) – I often found myself comparing them mentally, the better to understand the singular properties of the West African village.

By the mid-1980s I had begun to do sporadic research in Paradise with stratification as my primary interest, but it was not until 1988 that I turned to the project on a full-time basis. During May and June of that year I lived in the village, examining the local archives and acting as a participant observer. This was the pilot study phase, and I emerged from it with the confidence that the project was feasible and significant, especially the focus on stratification. It was during this period that I also realized that the community of my youth had changed in ways I had not anticipated, namely by the presence of large numbers of newcomers, including visible minorities. As a result, the focus of the study was expanded to embrace the three themes of stratification, migration, and race and ethnic relations.[1]

Fieldwork on the project began in May 1988 and continued until August 1991. During the entire calendar year of 1990 I worked on the project full-time, living in the community except for most weekends. At other times, when research had to be squeezed in between teaching and administration duties, I commuted back and forth to the community once or twice a week.

For a variety of reasons, including the premature arguments in research proposals demanded by funding agencies plus the researcher's own psychological needs of security, one often begins a project with a rather simplistic model and an exaggerated knowledge about what one will find. That describes my own entry into Paradise, but after the pilot study had been completed, I consciously attempted to adopt a mental attitude which I call 'cultivated ignorance' (not to be confused with the real thing, which I possessed in abundance!). That is, I tried to push to one side my assumptions about the community in order to be flexible enough to recognize significant but unanticipated features.

Archival research, participant observation, and unstructured interviews dominated my efforts for about six months. The local archives were rich, with records of births, marriages, and deaths, plus council minutes and tax assessment documents going back to the turn of the century. Valuable data were also derived from the Ontario Archives, the Agricultural Museum in Milton, Ontario, local histories and newspapers, and federal censuses.

At the end of this period I turned to the major instrument employed in the project: the structured interview (see Appendix B). My initial efforts with it were far from successful. Although I should have known better – I suppose I was entranced by visions of scientific rigour – I followed the interview format literally the first few times, reading each question one after the other to the somewhat stunned interviewees. The problem with this procedure is that it creates a stilted atmosphere which discourages reflection and insight. My alternative was to memorize the questions, and to ask them as naturally as possible, not necessarily in the order they appeared on the interview form. The cost of this approach is that not every question is always raised or answered adequately. The benefit is more spontaneous, less guarded responses, and greater insight on the part of the investigator into the individual's personality, and how she or he fits into the wider society. Much the same problem exists in relation to attempts to force people to express themselves in a manner that is amenable to statistical analysis. For example, the natives were asked to respond on a five-point scale to a question about the friendliness of the newcomers. While the data derived from this exercise could have been summarized in a table, I nevertheless discarded the scale (but not the question) for the simple reason that material of immensely richer quality emerged merely by encouraging people to talk about their experiences with the newcomers. Validity, getting at the truth, and reliability, employing replicable research procedures, always seem to compete with each other, and my choice in this project has been to throw my weight behind the first, even if the final outcome is less elegant than it might otherwise have been.

It is the rule rather than the exception for field workers to find themselves torn among opposing groups and factions, each of them suspicious of the time their guests spend with their rivals. In Paradise there rarely were open battles among members of the three main groups that were investigated, but nevertheless I found it less contentious to focus on each of them in turn. The first phase of interviewing concentrated on the natives. When I switched to the newcomers, the research itself changed to a minor degree. Most of the natives were elderly men and women, and they preferred to be visited during the day. The newcomers, in contrast, were not only much younger, but also tended to be commuters. Interviews with them often had to be arranged during the evening or on the weekend. Almost without exception, the natives readily agreed to be interviewed. That was largely the case for the newcomers too, but occasionally one of them would ask to see my credentials.

The interviews with both the natives and the newcomers were arranged in a straightforward manner. Usually I simply telephoned them, explaining the nature of my research, and indicating who had given me their names. With the minorities, however, more background preparation was necessary. My usual procedure was to visit them informally once or twice before actually conducting the interview, and sometimes, when they showed interest, I left a copy of a book I had written on the subject of racism (Barrett 1987), which in most cases enhanced rapport when the interview actually was conducted (for obvious reasons, I remained silent about this book when interviewing those natives and newcomers who were especially prone to racism).

Actually, very little deception was necessary in this project. I openly explained that my interests lay in social change, stratification, and the presence of newcomers and minorities in the area. This does not mean that absolute honesty was possible at all times. For example, when interviewing a man whom others had described as a crook, or a woman who reputedly was sleeping with a local politician, I did not reveal what I had learned from other sources, or ask them if the rumours were true! The only occasion on which I employed tactics of dubious ethical standards concerned the subject of racism. Several African

Canadians had independently named the same individuals in an influential organization as extreme bigots. Towards the end of the field-work phase I decided I had to investigate these allegations. My tactic was to approach one of the secretaries of the organization with a general inquiry about how it operated, and allow her to select from the list of personnel, with my subtle guidance, the individuals whom I wished to meet (to protect their identities, I also interviewed other people in the organization). The interviews went well, enabling me to evaluate the claims of the African Canadians, but not without some humour. Despite my cautious approach, which meant avoiding any overt mention of racism, I ran into one of my former students, an employee in the organization, who asked me in the company of a person whom I was planning to interview if I had ever published my proposed book on white supremacists and neo-Nazis!

In none of the interviews did I use a tape recorder. While direct quotations certainly can add flavour and realism to an ethnography, our data are not confined to verbal reports, and our goal is not merely to provide the kinds of accurate information about people which would be acceptable in a court of law; instead, it is to analyse how individuals fit into the broader social structure, and ultimately to arrive at modest sociological generalizations and insights. Indeed, by the time the anthropologist has sifted and sorted the data, and drawn abstract relationships between seemingly unrelated variables, plus taking the normal efforts to protect the subject's identity, his or her written report usually only vaguely resembles particular actors. Transcribing tapes, moreover, is expensive in both money and time, and often the transcription is not done until several months have passed, by which time one can lose sight of the subtle meanings in the words. Besides, the tape recorder can render the interviewer inattentive: one knows it's all on record, and one's mind can lose the concentration required to probe and evaluate. I also think that the presence of the tape recorder can inhibit the respondent, but that may well be because of the fact that I am uncomfortable in its presence. At any rate, although I did not use a tape recorder, I not only was able to take notes openly during the interviews, but I also regularly recorded verbatim comments, especially the striking ones. All my finished field notes were written in duplicate on 5″ × 8″ index cards. The main reason for making a copy was to have a back-up if something happened to the original (anthropologists in previous generations used to joke about the possibility of their field notes being destroyed by white ants, the underlying implication being that that would serve as an unassailable excuse for avoiding the chore of turning them into a thesis or a book; nowadays, one's notes are more likely to be eaten by one's computer). If one has a copy, it also means that the field notes can be arranged according to the chronology in which they were collected, as well as by the basic analytic categories that guide the research.

One of the truisms of fieldwork is that it is never possible to predict how well an interview will turn out. Sometimes I would hardly be able to contain my impatience to meet a person whose story promised to be critical to the study, only to emerge deflated after having spent a couple of hours with a close-mouthed or unreflective individual. At other times I would arrange to interview a person almost as an afterthought, mostly because I had time on my hands, only to discover an unexpected goldmine. The interviews I enjoyed most were with people who seemed to be intrigued by questions about their community, usually because they themselves had often been curious about the same issues.

Each interview lasted between two and three hours, and it took the same length of time to write it up in formal manner afterwards. Each write-up included not only a record of the data, but also a final section in which I commented on the quality and peculiarities of the interview, analysed the content, and reflected on its wider theoretical significance (I also kept a regular diary on methodology, the basic source of this appendix). Usually I did two interviews each day, and occasionally three, but that was stretching it.

If an interview is done well, one adds very little by conducting a second one with the same person, at least on the same topics. It is much more useful to try to verify the remarks of the individual by collecting relevant data while interviewing others, or from observational opportunities. Occasionally, however, I did interview people twice when it was warranted. My purpose in the initial interview usually was to understand the individual and her or his place in the community. The purpose of the second interview was normally to probe in more depth specific issues about which the individual had expertise.

Most interviews were conducted with one person at a time. Whenever two people were present, normally a man and his wife, the quality of the interview sometimes suffered. In many cases, one of the spouses dominated the interview – among the older people it usually was the husband; among the young newcomers it more often than not was the wife – and I would depart wishing to arrange a second interview with the silent partner. On some occasions I would be halfway through an interview when the person's spouse joined us. The impact was generally dramatic. A man or woman who had previously been articulate, insightful, and frank would often dry up, in some cases overwhelmed by what turned out to be the more aggressive partner, or at least inhibited by his or her presence. Occasionally, it should be added, both spouses would be sharp, sensitive, and inquisitive, and when that happened I felt like a privileged guest as I listened to their mutual efforts to unfold the mysteries of Paradise.

By the end of the project I had conducted formal interviews (albeit under informal guise) with 122 natives, twenty-nine ex-natives (people who had moved away from the community), 107 newcomers and eighty-three members of minorities, or a total of 341 people. If added to this are the interviews done twice with some people, plus those conducted with various specialists, such as social workers and outside government officials, the final number would be closer to four hundred.

One of the flaws in this study is that the people who were interviewed were not selected on the basis of a random sample. My procedure, instead, was to construct a taxonomy of the community based on the major groups that interested me (the natives, newcomers, and minorities), and the major residential areas throughout the community (reflecting the stratification system), plus other criteria such as age and gender. Attempts were then made to select people from all of the cells in the taxonomy. Having gained entry to a specific cell – for example, upper-class newcomers living in the most elegant subdivision in the town – I then used the snowball sampling method; that is, every person who was interviewed was asked to name two or three others whom I might contact. With a couple of exceptions, I think I can claim that the interviews are reasonably representative of the various dimensions of the community. One exception concerns women, who are under-represented in my samples, reflecting, I assume, the normal manner in which the field worker's gender influences a project. The other exception concerns young natives, who were overshadowed in my sample by the elderly natives who helped me to reconstruct Paradise's past.

A further attempt to assure that the data would be representative involved the selection of informants. The characteristics of the four-teen people whom I regularly visited for information and explanation were as follows: eight men and six women; three upper class, seven middle class, and four lower class; ten British in origin, two Asian, one

African, and one eastern European; nine natives and five newcomers. In addition to their representativeness, most of these fourteen people also possessed another characteristic: they were particularly curious, reflective, and objective about the community in which they lived. One of the important lessons of post-modernism is that an ethnography always is dialogical, the collective product of the researcher and the researched. While all the people whom I interviewed and observed helped to shape this book, which means that it is as much theirs as mine, the contributions of the people who were my informants were especially outstanding.

As the fieldwork phase of the project, after a period of three years, drew closer to the end, I began to have doubts about my research procedures and about the quality of the data. In particular, I wondered whether I should attempt to complement my data by administering a questionnaire to a random sample of the population. At the same time I was torn in another direction. The structured interviews, on which I had relied so heavily, produced systematic data, some of it quantitative. Yet the interview technique is one step removed from the natural setting, and I began to worry that the data from the interviews were not adequately imbedded in observational materials of social life as it unfolded. It is perhaps not always appreciated – especially by quantitative-oriented social scientists – that a crucial type of data is that collected spontaneously during casual meetings with people on the street corner, or watching who talks to whom in the coffee shop. Such data, often amounting to a page or less, build up over the months and fill in the cracks between the formal interviews. At any rate, much of my efforts during the last months of research were devoted to participant observation and reliance on informants. Whether my decision was correct to turn in this direction, rather than to administer a questionnaire, is something the reader can judge.

In Paradise in the past, when the community was smaller and the population more homogeneous, the participant observer could have reached all corners without too much difficulty. But in Paradise today, not only larger but also fragmented, the task was less straightforward, which was one of the reasons that I had turned to the structured interview as a principle technique. Some of my best data came from hanging around a few of the stores and restaurants. This gave me an opportunity to chat with dozens of natives and newcomers, although rarely with minorities. When conducting participant observation, I never took notes openly, because the success of the technique depends on the degree to which the role of researcher is rendered invisible. This was perfectly recognized by one of my brightest informants who operated a store which I frequently visited. Research on these occasions was truly a team activity, as my friend, with a twinkle in his eye, engaged his customers in conversation on topics of my interest, subtly including me in the group.

From the outset of the project one problem in particular had concerned me: was Paradise typical of the communities that surrounded it, or was it in some way unique? Over the course of the three years I conducted interviews, examined records, and made observations in a half-dozen surrounding communities, concentrating especially on two of them; I also spent a considerable amount of time talking to farmers in the area. In many respects, this has been a study of a region, not just of a single town. My strong impression was that Paradise was a typical community in the area, and that the research findings could be legitimately generalized across the nearby towns and villages, and possibly to some degree across the frontier of communities on the fringe of metropolitan centres.

There always is the decision about anonymity. Should the real name of the community be used in publication? I had assured people whom I interviewed that their identities would be protected, and to help keep that promise I have used the fictitious name, Paradise. Of course, the real identities of the renowned community studies of the past – Middletown, Springdale, Yankee City, Crestwood Heights – are common knowledge to specialists in the field, and anyone determined enough can also discover the concealed name of Paradise. As an extra precaution to provide anonymity, I have included in this study some of the interviews with people in the other communities. What this means is that the reader can never be absolutely certain that any particular individual is a resident of Paradise, although this will be highly probable, or a resident of a nearby town or village. This precaution was particularly necessary in the case of African and Asian Canadians, given their relatively small numbers.

Another decision has to be made about how much writing to do while still in the field. One of the innovative features of the Ph D program organized by Professor F.G. Bailey at the University of Sussex in England, where I had been a student, was the submission of regular article-length field reports. My reaction to that exercise has always been ambiguous. On the one hand it was evident that such reports helped to focus one's labours, and to reveal the gaps in one's data; on the other hand I resented the time spent writing reports instead of collecting more data. About halfway through the Paradise project, I took time out to write a paper for a conference presentation. This forced me, with the benefit of several months of fieldwork under my belt, to clarify precisely what I was trying to achieve in the study, and what the end product might look like in theoretical terms. In other words, the exercise proved to be more than a little valuable. One note of caution, however, should be added. The researcher can develop a love affair with her or his own prose, and the field report or conference paper, particularly if well done, may be difficult to reject, even if by the end of a project some of the ideas have become obsolete.

Early in the course of fieldwork, I encountered the two types of people whom I had been expecting. The first were the deviant individuals, those who did not fit in and had few friends, sometimes because of an ascriptive factor such as an unusual religious affiliation, and sometimes because of personality quirks. Such people are usually the first ones to seek out the researcher. While often it is necessary to avoid too much public exposure in their company, otherwise the researcher too may be labelled an oddball, and while one must be careful not to base one's general interpretations on their perspectives, their viewpoints are nevertheless significant, because they throw into relief the more typical views of their neighbours. In some cases, too, their deviant vantage points enable them to dissect the community with particular skill. One such man, for example, who lived on the psychological edge of the town, possessed a greater perception about what made it tick than almost anyone else I met.

The second anticipated type consisted of those individuals who were especially protective of the community, and presented only an idealized version, rather than what people think and do in the back stage. When I was a younger fieldworker I used impatiently to dismiss these idealizations as misleading nonsense. But this was a mistake, because the ideal structure of belief and action is as much a part of reality as the actual structure of belief and action. Unlike the case of the deviant individual, one is not likely to encounter, or at least to recognize, the public relations spokesperson at an early point in the research, for the simple reason that at that stage almost everyone presents a fictionalized version of their lives. At a later point in the research, after entry has been made into the back stage, it is not difficult to recognize the type. On one occasion, for example, I had just completed an interview with an upper-class woman who had painted an idyllic picture of the

community, explaining the lofty values that held it together, and
describing the virtuous and happy people, free from conflict and envy,
abstainers all. As I prepared to depart, the woman remarked, somewhat smugly, that she was afraid that she hadn't given me much useful
information. On the contrary, she had provided me with the clearest
picture of what the community *ought* to be like that I had received up
to that point.

There was nothing extraordinary about my encounters with the
deviants and the guardians of the public image. All fieldworkers run
across them in due course. What was peculiar about my project was
that the community I had chosen to investigate used to be my home,
even though that was only during my childhood. In terms of research
focus, then (but certainly not in terms of methodology, since I have
employed such old-fashioned techniques as interviewing), this project
is thoroughly post-modern, because I am part of 'the other' who has
been investigated.[1] Some of my colleagues thought that my past association with Paradise would make the research more difficult. I might be
reluctant to probe deeply into sensitive areas, and numerous ethical
problems, involving old friends and acquaintances, would arise. These
anticipated obstacles would make little sense to a post-modernist,
because by conducting research at home – *really* at home, where a
portion of my biography is implanted – epistemological and ethical
dilemmas normally associated with research in other cultures should
be minimized, if not eliminated altogether. Yet some of the reserva-
tions expressed by my colleagues were well-founded. I did find it
impossible to conduct objective interviews with individuals with whom
I had grown up and counted as my friends. On the few occasions
where I experimented with such interviews, it quickly became apparent
that only if I was prepared to convert the relationship from one of
friend to stranger – which I was not willing to do – could such interviews proceed. However, virtually never were the number of people in
particular categories and roles so few that the selection of alternatives
to old friends was precluded. Moreover, in the majority of cases people
remembered my parents or grandparents, not me, with the result that
rapport was simply increased. Sometimes, however, even these people
would be confused as to whether they were talking to a researcher or
to the son of old acquaintances. Such role ambiguity tended to reduce
the quality of the interview because it inhibited me from probing
analytically. On the odd occasion, my past residence in the town took
a humorous turn. As I indicated earlier, newcomers repeatedly com-

plained that they could never say a bad word about anyone, because everyone in the town seemed to be related. More than once, long-term residents asked me if I was kin to such and such a person before proceeding to tear their characters apart. During one interview an influential newcomer had just finished explaining that you have to be careful what you say about any of the natives, because they all are intermarried. I could barely suppress a smile when in his very next breath he began to criticize one of my own relatives.

Heilman (1980) has written that the researcher who investigates his or her own group is likely to become somewhat estranged from it, rather than going native as sometimes happens when studying strangers. I think that partly describes my own orientation in Paradise. In retrospect, however, it is my strong opinion that my past association in the community was more an asset than a liability. I did not find it unusually difficult to probe behind the scenes, or to retain as much objectivity as can be expected in the fieldwork enterprise. What I did find was that I had a headstart *by virtue* of my past association. Not only did doors among the natives open more quickly than usual, but I was in possession of rudimentary knowledge of great value. For example, during my first visit to the town hall one of the secretaries, after telling me her name, added that she did not belong to the family in town with the same name. The reason for her comment was immediately clear: the other family's reputation was just about the worst in the community. Shortly after, the name of one of the unfortunate alcoholics in the town at present was mentioned in my presence. I recognized the name as belonging to one of the most powerful families of the past, and immediately arranged an interview. It turned out to be an eye-opener about just how much had changed for the old elite, but it is probable that I would have failed to recognize the significance of this person's tragic story had I not once lived in the community. My background, of course, did not help in my research on the newcomers and minorities. Indeed, I rarely made an issue of it with these people, especially among those who held 'the old guard' responsible for rendering life in rural Ontario less pleasant than they had anticipated.

Note

1 Could a thoroughly post-modernist study of Paradise have been produced? Of course. But that would have meant seeing the community

through the eyes of a handful of residents, probably presented in the form of life histories, plus an effort to pull off a textual analysis of the meanings of their stories. Issues of representativeness and scope would then be problematic. Who would be included in the select number of life histories: natives, newcomers or minorities; upper, middle- or lower-class people; men or women? Yet what one would lose in scope, one might gain in depth; moreover, the controlling voice of the researcher would be muted. In the end, the book I have produced is only one kind of book, quite conventional in its approach, and only one kind of conventional approach at that.

Appendix B

Interview Schedule for Natives

Date

Name

Case Number

1 Age

2 Sex

3 Education (exact grade completed)

4 Marital Status

5 Religion (plus frequency of worship)

6 Place of Birth (and whether city, town, village or rural)

7 Ethnic background

8 How long have you lived here? Did your parents live in or near the town? If near, specify

9 Membership (and exact positions held) in organizations and clubs

10 Have you travelled to other provinces and countries? Specify.

11 Occupations in past and present. If you are employed, do you work in town or commute? Are you self employed? What about your spouse?

12 What have been the most important changes in the town during the last three or four decades?

13 How would you rate the quality of life here in past and present?

14 Why do you think so many newcomers have moved to town?

15 Are most of your friends and acquaintances in town long-term residents like yourself or newcomers or both?

16 What has been the impact of the newcomers and the new subdivisions on the town? Have the changes been good or bad for the town?

17 Do you find the newcomers friendly?

18 When is a newcomer no longer a newcomer?

19 Some people have suggested that in the past, before the town began to change, there were areas where 'good families' lived, and areas where 'poor families' lived. Do you remember anything about that? Is it the same today? If not, what has changed?

20 How many levels or classes did there used to be? Can you describe them? Do we find the same thing today? If not, how has the class system changed? What was your (or your parent's) class position in the past? What is it today?

21 What kind of people had influence on how the town was run in the past? Did they have to be from good families? Did they have to be wealthy? Could they be from one of the poor families?

22 What kind of people have influence on how the town is run today? Have the criteria changed? Who has power today?

23 As you know, we now have a woman as mayor – the first woman in that position in the town's history. How do you feel about that?

24 This is a small community. Can you define 'community'? What does it mean to you? Do you think that this place still is a community?

25 There's a lot in the news about towns and cities that have declared themselves English only. What do you think about that?

26 Do you remember the Jewish families that used to live here? Have you any idea why they all left?

27 It seems that Indian, Pakistani and black families are starting to move up this way from the city. What do you think about that? Have you met any of these people?

28 What do you think about Mounties wearing turbans?

29 Do you think Sikh kids should be allowed to wear the ceremonial knife in school?

30 Do you remember the Ben Johnson affair? What do you think about it?

31 Have you heard about the Donald Marshall case – the Indian in Nova Scotia who spent ten years in jail for a murder he never committed? Why do you think so many Native People are in jail?

32 Do you remember reading or hearing about that professor (Rushton) at the University of Western Ontario who argued that Orientals are more intelligent than whites, and whites are more intelligent than blacks? Do you think he's a bit wacky or do you think there's something to his argument?

33 Are there different races? If so, how would you classify the world's population? What criteria would you use to separate them?

Notes

1 Appropriately modified versions of this instrument were composed for the newcomers and minorities.
2 Although this was the final version of the schedule used for the natives, I was still modifying it several months after I began to use it, which partly explains the large number of 'unknown' cases in some of the tables.

Notes

2. The Framework of the Study

1 Not all academics would agree with me here. Indeed, Miles (1982) has argued that since concepts such as race and race relations are based on misleading and unscientific folk beliefs, such concepts must be excised from the sociological vocabulary, because to retain them is indirectly to legitimate racism.

2 For another example of the rather arbitrary way of erecting the class structure, see Bourdieu (1984). In his scheme there are three main classes – the working class, the middle class, and the upper class – and the first two classes contain four subclasses or class fractions.

3 While many of the manifestations of these market forces will be examined in later chapters, I take as given the nature of the capitalist state, rather than attempting an analysis at that level, which would amount to a book in itself.

4 Here I follow Weber's lead in distinguishing between legitimate power (authority), which I interpret as an aspect of ideology, and power, which means the capacity of a person to realize his or her will even against the opposition of others.

5 Marx, as Raymond Williams (1973:302) has indicated, held ambiguous views about the impact of capitalism on rural society. On the one hand it was capitalism that had rendered rural society subordinate to urban society. On the other hand the overthrow of capitalism by socialism was not the only solution to the unequal relations between city and country. Marx also thought that even before the socialist revolution would occur, the city bourgeoisie's shadow would stretch across the countryside and

help to put an end to 'the idiocy of rural life.' It has been this second solution that has shaken the Paradise region to its roots.

6 In putting this model together, I have not forgotten my criticisms, inspired by post-modernism, against macro-theoretical orientations. Not even by the greatest stretch of imagination could this model be described as a macro-theoretical orientation. It grew directly out of my research on Paradise, and is meant to apply solely to this community. To the extent that it can be generalized beyond Paradise to other settlements on the fringes of metropolitan centres, that is a bonus.

3. Stratification

1 It may be thought that the variability (and ambiguity) was merely an inevitable result of the efforts of people to reconstruct the class system as it had existed a generation ago. I disagree. If the passing of time had any effect, which surely was the case, it would have been to smooth out the inconsistencies in the class system, to make it seem more neat and systematic than it actually had been. To argue such is merely to recognize the tendency for people's beliefs to represent their lived-in worlds as tidy and predictable.

2 Like Warner, Williams argues that the seven classes are subjectively real, because they represent how the people of Gosforth saw themselves. The same criticisms that have been levelled at Warner's work also apply to Williams's study.

3 Although Williams uses the term class, it would appear that he is in fact measuring prestige and esteem, and thus status is the more appropriate term.

4 This distinction seems to correspond to the differences between status and role in the older literature on stratification. Status connoted position; role referred to how one acted in the position.

5 Newby himself (1977:323–27) has suggested that when there is a conflict between attributional and interactional status, the former takes priority.

6 Virtually every reeve in the community up to that point had been a Conservative, which was the party of preference for most people in Paradise. A repeated joke in the community was that if the Progessive Conservative party's candidate was a pig, it would still win in a landslide. As for religious affiliation, one did not have to be an Anglican in order to gain a position on the council – indeed, the famous reeve who had just resigned belonged to the United Church – but as will be indicated below,

the most wealthy and powerful people in the community tended to be members of the Anglican Church.

7 On the basis of interviews with 122 natives who had lived in the community at that time, I estimated that the upper and lower classes respectively contained 2.5% and 17% of the population. See appendices A and B for a description of these interviews.

4. The Great Escape

1 Winks (1969:1), for example, remarks that 'a process of natural selection in all probability sent to Canada more energetic, enterprising, and imaginative Negroes than often remained in the American South.' In view of the above, he continues, the less aggressiveness of Canadian blacks compared to American blacks is all the more surprising. In my judgment, the explanation concerns the dubious assumption that migrants are more intelligent and enterprising than non-migrants, plus the more rigid social structure and political system in Canada.

2 For a succinct summary of the literature dealing with the issues of intelligence and migration, see Ember and Ember (1981:139–41).

3 This more modest measuring rod is itself not without ambiguity. The statistical presentation in table 5 provides a pseudo sense of precision. It assumes a knowledge of the class system and a capacity to quantify it beyond which I wish to claim. What I think I can claim is that the general trends indicated in the table are reasonably accurate, and the figures themselves are close approximations to reality.

5. Modern Pioneers

1 Ballard and Fuguitt (1985) caution that by the late 1970s the population turnaround in the United States had slowed, and since 1980 urban areas have once more been growing more rapidly than rural areas.

2 My estimate is that about one-third of the fifty-three newcomers placed in the middle class in table 7 actually belong to what I have labelled the aspiring-middle class. Certainly these people *appear* to belong to the middle class, judging by their houses and vehicles, and in their own minds they belong there, but in financial terms they are stretched to the very limit.

3 A generation earlier, as Clark (1966) showed, it was to the commuter suburbs that people from the city moved in search of cheaper houses and a better environment for their children.

4   The decision of newcomer mothers to remain at home with the children actually went against the local trend. As indicated in 'Dufferin Child Care Study' (ARA Consulting Group, Inc., 1990), in over half of the families in the county with children under age thirteen, both parents worked (or studied) outside the home.

5   As indicated in the previous chapter, I have some idea why people left Paradise in the past and why others remained. My data on newcomers are less complete. While I hopefully have explained what has motivated them to move to small-town Ontario, I have no data on people who stayed in the city, and cannot comment on their motivations.

6   In contrast, eccentrics among the natives abounded.

6. The Commuting Life

1   I am grateful to the Transportation Demand Research Office, Ministry of Transportation, for supplying me with these data.

2   There are no reliable figures on the proportion of natives and new-comers in Paradise in the labour force. But if it is assumed that half of them are natives and half of them are newcomers, then 40% (16 + 63 / 2) of the people in my two samples were commuters, which is exactly the proportion given in the 1986 census. Even if it is assumed that there are proportionately more newcomers (let us say 60%) than natives in the labour force, the combined commuting rate for newcomers and natives still works out to only 44%, which is not much different from the census estimate. The data derived from my interviews, thus, would seem to be plausible.

3   According to Statistics Canada, 1986, the industry of employment in Paradise was an follows: agriculture and related 3.3%, logging and forestry .7%, mining .4%, manufacturing 26%, construction 6.3%, transportation and storage 3%, communication and utilities 1.5%, wholesale trade 1.9%, retail trade 13.4%, finance and insurance 3.3%, real estate 1.9%, business service 3%, government service 3.7%, education service 6.2%, health and social service 11.9%, accommodation, food and beverage service 6.7%, other services 6.3%. Industry of employment data were not included for Paradise in the 1951 census, but some indication of the changes that have taken place is revealed in the employment profile of Dufferin County as a whole in that year: agriculture 52.8%, forestry and logging .3%, fishing and trap-ping .02%, mining and quarrying .08%, manufacturing 9.3%, electricity, gas and water 1.5%, construction 6.8%, transportation and communica-tion 4%, trade 11.1%, finance 1.7%, service 12.4%.

4   There were no records in the community on the rate of turnover among
     the newcomers, and the task of tracing those who had departed was daunt-
     ing, especially since few of them had left friends behind. As second-best
     sources of information about the turnover rate and the motivations for
     leaving the community, I relied on two other tactics. One was to knock on
     doors of houses which had 'For Sale' signs on their lawns (some of the
     data from this source in the form of case material have already been pre-
     sented). The other was to call on real estate agents (seven of them), asking
     whether their clients were newcomers or natives, and why these residents
     had sold their houses, or were in the process of doing so. Although the
     real estate agents thought that the departing newcomers were motivated
     primarily by factors related to commuting, the majority of their clients
     actually were natives, some moving into larger homes in Paradise, some
     into senior citizens' apartments, others leaving the town itself. How repre-
     sentative these findings are is beyond my knowledge; they may merely have
     reflected the profile of clients at the time of my inquiry.

7. Growing Pains

1   I lack data for the remaining individual.
2   As Schwarzweller (1979:17) has remarked, 'Newcomers almost always
     press for more services: police and fire protection, medical care facilities,
     garbage pickup, snow removal, improved roads, larger schools.'
3   In a report entitled 'Dufferin Child Care Study,' prepared by A.R.A.
     Consulting Group, Inc., 1990, the authors state that about half the peo-
     ple contacted in a telephone survey about child care refused to answer
     any questions; the reason, according to the authors, was the fear that the
     safety of their children would be jeopardized by providing the informa-
     tion requested by the interviewers.
4   This analysis owes a great deal to Brenda Dusome, a student in my
     course on qualitative methods, who investigated the crime rate in the
     town as part of her course assignment.
5   Remember, however, that an estimated one-third of the newcomers
     placed in the middle class actually constitute the aspiring-middle class.
6   Similarly, Vidich and Bensman (1960:94–95) pointed out that newcomers
     to Springdale from the city, most of them commuters, enjoyed a degree
     of freedom regarding class and status because the long-time residents
     had difficulty ranking them.
7   In 1982 the mayor's basic salary was $6,833, plus additional payments for
     attending meetings.

8   I have not forgotten that successful businessmen ran for mayor in 1982 and 1988. The fact is, however, that they no longer had the support of their class equals, who did not seem very concerned about who was elected.

8. British Subjects and Aliens

1   In the township of Mono in 1850, 80% of the 2,300 residents were Ulster stock (Harris 1975:3).
2   Because the assessment roll for 1916 was missing from the archives, I do not know if the new category was added that year, rather than in 1917.
3   Given the small number of members of minorities in Paradise, in order to have an adequate number of cases while simultaneously protecting identities, it was necessary to include people in the sample who lived in the surrounding countryside and villages.
4   Additional interviews were conducted with ten members of minority groups who had been born in Paradise, or at least on the periphery of the area, or who had lived there since the 1950s or earlier, meaning that they were natives. These included six African Canadians, two Jews, and two French Canadians. The results of these interviews will be presented where relevant in the following chapters. It should be added that the bias in the sample of eighty-one minority members towards males was almost identical to the bias in the sample of 122 natives: 57% and 58% respectively.

9. African and Asian Canadians

1   I had also been forewarned to expect a hostile reception. When I first knocked on their door, they were indeed aloof; but after I explained the nature of my business they were perfectly accommodating, and when I interviewed them again a week later they could not have been more hospitable.
2   In order to protect this individual's identity, I shall not provide much biographical information about him. It should be added that I interviewed more than a dozen teachers in Paradise, and since on the surface there was little to distinguish the person under analysis, his identity should be further obscured. Finally, while racial problems in the school did exist, they were not unusually severe in comparison to many other schools, especially those nearer Toronto with large numbers of minorities among the student body.

3 It would be an error in judgment to make too much of this issue. Euro-pean-origin Canadians, including many in the universities, also some-times leave Canada to retire in countries of their birth, and nobody raises an eyebrow.

4 These remarks are aimed solely at the two largest groups in the area – those from India and Pakistan. The handful of other Asian-origin people who had settled in and around Paradise, such as the Chinese and Ko-rean Canadians, were not part of this community.

10. Jews and French Canadians

1 This same source indicates that a further 110 residents of the town were a mixture of British and French origins, but surprisingly only ten people in the community were indicated as French under the category 'Mother Tongue.'

2 For an analysis of Keegstra, see Bercuson and Wertheimer (1985) and Barrett (1987).

3 As I learned in a previous study (Barrett 1987), it is not unusual to find a person who is apparently an exemplary citizen but at the same time is soft on anti-Semitism and racism.

4 These anti-French sentiments pervaded the entire community; there were no significant differences in terms of social class, ethnicity, new-comer-native status, or age and gender.

5 The 1951 census indicates that 2.9% of the population of Dufferin County was German in origin. According to the 1986 census, 2.2% of Paradise's population was German, the single largest ethnic group be-sides the British. Only .02% of the county's population in 1951 consisted of Aboriginal peoples, while in Paradise in 1986 the figure was .2%.

6 The implication is that ethnicity for Aboriginal people played a greater role in their lives than it did for people of German descent.

11. Patterns of Prejudice

1 Throughout this study I have cautioned the reader to be sceptical about the quantitative data which I have presented, and nowhere is that advice more pertinent than here, because the task of evaluating people's orien-tations to race relations is necessarily subjective. On the other hand, I do not think there is any greater reason to question the validity of these data, derived for the most part from in-depth interviews which allowed the subtle exploration of racist comments and opinions and placed them

in the context of cognate information about the interviewees, than data gathered by survey techniques. In both cases there is an artificial sense of precision. In the end, all that I claim about this table, based as it is on my subjective reading of the data, is that it provides a crude picture of the different degrees of tolerance and intolerance between the natives and the newcomers.

2   Unfortunately, I have insufficient information about the caste background of each of these individuals to know whether it too was instrumental in determining who became their friends and acquaintances.

3   Although it may be self-serving to suggest it, I think that further research on this problem should be dominated by qualitative methods, which allow the investigator to probe subtly and deeply. Alternatively, an extremely sensitive survey instrument must be devised, otherwise the investigator is reduced to the murky task of trying to decide, as did Fliegel and Sofranko, whether people really meant they were trying to escape from blacks when they merely stated they were concerned about the level of crime in cities.

12. Wider Issues

1   For an example of a writer who classifies the scholarship on racism into Marxist and liberal perspectives, see Prager (1972), who adds a third perspective – the radical perspective – in which racism is traced primarily to colonialism rather than capitalism.

2   As Rabinow (1977: 241) cautioned, we must 'avoid the error of reverse essentializing; Occidentalism is not a remedy for Orientalism.'

3   In Varenne's case, however, after stating that a main goal of his book was to make what appears familiar to be in reality strange and surprising, he ended up with the lame conclusion (1977: 209): 'Part of the surprise may lie in the fact that there were no surprises.' This author also contended that as an outsider he was better equipped to study the American community than an insider. Not only is that claim dubious, but it also echoes the anthropology of the colonial era.

Bibliography

Ankli, R., and K. Duncan. 1984. 'Farm Making Costs in Early Ontario.' In
D. Akenson, ed., *Canadian Papers in Rural History*, pp. 33–45. Gananoque,
Ontario: Langdale Press.

Arensberg, C. 1954. 'The Community-Study Method.' *American Journal of
Sociology* 60: 109–124.

Baker, D. 1978. 'Race and Power: Comparative Approaches to the Analysis
of Race Relations.' *Ethnic and Racial Studies* 1: 316–35.

Ballard, P., and G. Fuguitt. 1985. 'The Changing Small Town Settlement
Structure in the United States, 1900–1980.' *Rural Sociology* 50: 99–113.

Banton, M. 1970. 'The Concept of Racism.' In S. Zubaida, ed., *Race and
Racialism*. London: Tavistock Publications.

– 1977. *The Idea of Race*. London: Tavistock Publications.

Barrett, S. 1977. *The Rise and Fall of an African Utopia*. Waterloo: Wilfrid
Laurier University Press.

– 1987. *Is God a Racist? The Right Wing in Canada*. Toronto: University of
Toronto Press.

Bell, C., and H. Newby. 1972. *Community Studies*. New York: Praeger Publishers, Inc.

Bendix, R. 1962. *Max Weber: An Intellectual Portrait*. New York: Anchor Books.

Bendix, R., and S. Lipset. 1953. 'Karl Marx' Theory of Social Classes.' In R.
Bendix and S. Lipset, eds., *Class, Status and Power*, pp. 26–35. Free Press of
Glencoe.

Bercuson, D., and D. Wertheimer. 1985. *A Trust Betrayed: The Keegstra Affair*.
Toronto: Doubleday.

Bibby, R. 1987. *Fragmented Gods*. Toronto: Irwin Publishing.

Blakely, E., and T. Bradshaw. 1981. 'The Impact of Recent Migrants on

Economic Development in Small Towns.' In M. Fazio and P. Prenshaw, eds., *Order and Image in the American Small Town*, pp. 30–49. Jackson: University Press of Mississippi.

Bottomore, T. 1965. *Classes in Modern Society*. London: George Allen and Unwin Ltd.

Bourdieu, P. 1984. Trans. Richard Nice. *Distinction*. Cambridge, Mass.: Harvard University Press.

Bradshaw, T., and E. Blakely. 1979. *Rural Communities in Advanced Industrial Society*. New York: Praeger Publishers Inc.

Carstens, P. 1991. *The Queen's People: A Study of Hegemony, Coercion, and Accommodation among the Okanagan of Canada*. Toronto: University of Toronto Press.

Cashmore, E., and B. Troyna. 1983. *Introduction to Race Relations*. London: Routledge and Kegan Paul.

Clark, S.D. 1966. *The Suburban Society*. Toronto: University of Toronto Press.

Clifford, J., and G. Marcus. 1986. *Writing Culture: The Poetics and Politics of Ethnography*. Berkeley and Los Angeles: University of California Press.

Cohen, A. 1969. *Custom and Conflict in Urban Africa*. London: Routledge and Kegan Paul.

Cohen, A. 1989. *The Symbolic Construction of Community*. London: Routledge. First published in 1985 by Ellis Horwood Ltd. and Tavistock Publications Ltd.

Corbett, G. 1981. *Barnardo Children in Canada*. Peterborough, Ontario: Woodland Publishing.

Cox, O. 1948. *Caste, Class and Race*. Garden City, NY.: Doubleday.

Dahrendorf, R. 1959. *Class and Class Conflict in Industrial Society*. Stanford: Stanford University Press.

Dasgupta, S. 1988. *Rural Canada: Structure and Change*. Lewiston-Queenston: The Edwin Mellen Press.

Davis, A., B. Gardner, and M. Gardner. 1944. *Deep South*. Chicago: University of Chicago Press.

De Jong, G., and J. Fawcett. 1981. 'Motivations for Migration: An Assessment and a Value-Expectancy Research Model.' In G. De Jong and R. Gardner, eds., *Migration Decision Making*, pp. 13–58. New York: Pergamon Press.

Dewey, J. 1960–1. 'The Rural-Urban Continuum: Real but Relatively Unimportant.' *American Sociological Review* 66: 60–6.

Dodds, E. 1983. *The History of Education in Dufferin County, 1834–1983*. Grand Valley: The Star and Vidette Printing Ltd.

Dollard, J. 1957. *Caste and Class in a Southern Town*. New York: Doubleday.

Dufferin Child Care Study. 1990. A.R.A. Consulting Group, Inc.

Durkheim, E., and M. Mauss. 1963 (orig. 1903). *Primitive Classification*. London: Cohen and West.

Ember, C., and M. Ember. 1981. *Anthropology*. 3rd. ed. Englewood Cliffs, NJ: Prentice-Hall, Inc.

Fitzsimons, J., ed. 1991. *Recreational Needs Assessment*. University School of Rural Planning and Development, University of Guelph.

Fliegel, F., and A. Sofranko. 1984. 'Nonmetropolitan Population Increase, the Attractiveness of Rural Living, and Race.' *Rural Sociology* 49: 298–308.

Foote, R. 1979. *The Case of Port Hawkesbury*. Toronto: PMD Books.

Frankenberg, R. 1957. *Village on the Border*. London; Cohen and West.

Fuller, A. 1974. 'Critique.' In M. Troughton, J. Nelson, and S. Brown, eds., *The Countryside in Ontario*, pp. 17–20. Conference proceedings, University of Western Ontario.

Gans, H. 1962. *The Urban Villagers*. Glencoe, Ill.: The Free Press.

– 1967. *The Levittowners*. New York: Random House.

Geertz, C. 1973. *The Interpretation of Cultures*. New York: Basic Books.

Gerth, H., and C. Mills. 1958. *From Max Weber: Essays in Sociology*. New York: Oxford University Press.

Glaser, B., and A. Strauss. 1967. *The Discovery of Grounded Theory*. Chicago: Aldine Publishing Company.

Glazebrook, G. de T. 1968. *Life in Ontario: A Social History*. Toronto: University of Toronto Press.

Gold, G. 1975. *Saint-Pascal: Changing Leadership and Social Organization in a Quebec Town*. Toronto: Holt, Rinehart and Winston of Canada.

Gordon, E. 1988. 'Stress in the Farm Family: Implications for the Rural Human Service Worker.' In G. Basran and D. Hay, eds., *The Political Economy of Agriculture in Western Canada*, pp. 143–53. Toronto: Garamond Press.

Halbert, M. 1984. *Memoirs of an Old Cog*. Vol. 3. Sheldun Press.

Harris, R. Cole, et al. 1975. 'The Settlement of Mono Township.' *Canadian Geographer* 19: 1–17.

Hauser, P. 1965. 'Observations on the Urban-Folk and Urban-Rural Dichotomies as Forms of Western Ethnocentrism.' In P. Hauser and L. Schnore, eds., *The Study of Urbanization*, pp. 503–17. New York: John Wiley and Sons.

Heilman, S. 1980. 'Jewish Sociologist: Native-as-Stranger.' *American Sociologist* 15: 100–8.

Heller, C., ed. 1987. *Structured Social Inequality*. New York: Macmillan Publishing Company.

Hillery, G. 1955. 'Definitions of Community: Areas of Agreement.' *Rural Sociology* 20: 111–23.

Hughes, E. 1943. *French Canada in Transition.* Chicago: University of Chicago Press.

Huxtable, T. *Down Memories Lane.* No date or publisher indicated.

Kelling, E. 1981. *The Roots of Amaranth.* Erin, Ontario: Boston Mills Press.

Klineberg, O. 1935. *Negro Intelligence and Selective Migration.* New York: Columbia University Press.

Kornhauser, R. 1953. 'The Warner Approach to Social Stratification.' In R. Bendix and S. Lipset, eds., *Class, Status and Power,* pp. 224–55. Free Press of Glencoe.

Krauss, I. 1976. *Stratification, Class and Conflict.* New York: The Free Press.

Kuper, L. 1975. *Race, Class and Power.* Chicago: Aldine Publishing Company.

Leitch, A. 1975. *Into the High Country.* Published by the Corporation of the County of Dufferin, Ontario.

Leung, H. 1990. ' "Big Brother" and Small Town Planning.' *Municipal World* Nov.: 14–18.

Lewis, O. 1965. 'Further Observations on the Folk-Urban Continuum and Urbanization with Special Reference to Mexico City.' In P. Hauser and L. Schnore, eds., *The Study of Urbanization,* pp. 491–503. New York: John Wiley and Sons, Inc.

Lipset, S., and E. Raab. 1970. *The Politics of Unreason: Right-Wing Extremism in America, 1790–1970.* New York: Harper and Row.

Lupri, E. 1967. 'The Rural-Urban Variable Reconsidered: The Cross-Cultural Perspective.' *Sociologica Ruralis* 7: 1–20.

Lustig, N. 1990. 'A Study of Newcomers to Barcliffe: A Small Ontario Town Experiencing Growth and Change.' MA thesis, Department of Sociology and Anthropology, University of Guelph.

Lynd, R., and H. Lynd. 1929. *Middletown.* New York: Harcourt, Brace and World, Inc.

Mann, S., and J. Dickinson. 1987. 'One Furrow Forward, Two Furrows Back: A Marx-Weber Synthesis for Rural Sociology?' *Rural Sociology* 52: 264–85.

Marshall, J. *Fifty Years of Rural Life.* No date or publisher indicated.

– 'Half Century of Farming in Dufferin.' No date or publisher indicated.

Marx, K. 1975. Trans. Rodney Livingstone and Gregor Benton. *Early Writings.* New York: Vintage Books.

Marx, K., and F. Engels. 1970. Edited by C. Arthur. *The German Ideology.* New York: International Publishers.

Miles, R. 1982. *Racism and Migrant Labour.* London: Routledge and Kegan Paul.

Miller, M., and A. Luloff. 1981. 'Who is Rural? A Typological Approach to the Examination of Rurality.' *Rural Sociology* 46: 608–25.

Mills, C. 1967. 'The Social Life of a Modern Community.' In C. Mills, *Power, Politics and People: The Collected Essays of C. Wright Mills*, pp. 39–52. Edited by I. Horowitz. New York: Oxford University Press.

Miner, H. 1963 (orig. 1939). *St. Denis: A French-Canadian Parish*. Chicago: University of Chicago Press.

Motz, A., ed. 1990. *Reclaiming a Nation: The Challenge of Re-Evangelizing Canada by the Year 2000*. Richmond, BC: Church Leadership Library.

Nader, L. 1982. 'Up the Anthropologist – Perspectives Gained from Studying Up.' In J. Cole, ed., *Anthropology for the Eighties*, pp. 456–70. New York: The Free Press.

Needham, R. 1979. *Symbolic Classification*. Santa Monica: Goodyear Publishing.

Neuwirth, G. 1969. 'A Weberian Outline of a Theory of Community: Its Application to the "Dark Ghetto".' *British Journal of Sociology* 20: 148–63.

Newby, H. 1977. *The Deferential Worker*. London: Allen Lane.

Nikolinakos, M. 1973. 'Notes on the Economic Theory of Racism.' *Race* 14: 365–81.

Pahl, R. 1966. 'The Rural-Urban Continuum.' *Sociologica Ruralis* 6: 299–326.

– 1967. 'The Rural-Urban Continuum: A Reply to Eugen Lupri.' *Sociologica Ruralis* 7: 21–9.

– 1970. (orig. 1964). *Whose City?* London: Longman.

Ploch, L. 1978. 'The Reversal in Migration Patterns – Some Rural Development Consequences.' *Rural Sociology* 43: 293–303.

Poulantzas, N. 1975. *Classes in Contemporary Capitalism*. London: New Left Books.

Prager, J. 1972. 'White Racial Privilege and Social Change: An Examination of Theories of Racism.' *Berkeley Journal of Sociology* 17. 117–50.

Rabinow, P. 1977. *Reflections on Field Work in Morocco*. Berkeley and Los Angeles, California: University of California Press.

– 1986. 'Representations Are Social Facts: Modernity and Post-Modernity in Anthropology.' In J. Clifford and G. Marcus, eds., *Writing Culture*. Berkeley and Los Angeles: University of California Press.

Rayside, D. 1991. *A Small Town in Modern Times: Alexandria, Ontario*. Montreal and Kingston: McGill-Queen's University Press.

Redfield, R. 1947. 'The Folk Society.' *American Journal of Sociology* 52: 293–308.

Rex, J. 1970. *Race Relations in Sociological Theory*. New York: Schocken Books.

Rose, A. 1971. 'Antisemitism's Root in City Hatred.' In L. Dinnerstein, ed., *Antisemitism in the United States*, pp. 41–7. New York: Holt, Rinehart and Winston.

Saunders, L. 1960 (orig. 1941). *The Story of Orangeism*. Toronto: Britannia Printers.

Sawden, S. *History of Dufferin County.* No date or publisher indicated.

Schaff, A. 1970. *Marxism and the Human Individual.* New York: McGraw-Hill.

Schatzman, L., and A. Strauss. 1973. *Field Research.* Englewood Cliffs, NJ: Prentice-Hall, Inc.

Schnore, L. 1966. 'The Rural-Urban Variable: An Urbanite's Perspective.' *Rural Sociology* 31: 131–43.

Schwarzweller, H. 1979. 'Migration and the Changing Rural Scene.' *Rural Sociology* 44: 7–23.

Seeley, J., et al. 1956. *Crestwood Heights.* Toronto: University of Toronto Press.

Segalen, M. 1983. *Love and Power in the Peasant Society.* Trans. by Sarah Matthews. Chicago: University of Chicago Press.

Selsam, H., et al. 1970. *Dynamics of Social Change: A Reader in Marxist Social Science.* New York: International Publishers.

Sinclair, P., and K. Westhues. 1974. *Village in Crisis.* Toronto: Holt, Rinehart and Winston of Canada, Ltd.

Stacey, M. 1969. 'The Myth of Community Studies.' *British Journal of Sociology* 20: 134–47.

Strathern, M. 1982. 'The Village as an Idea: Constructs of Village-ness in Elmdon, Essex.' In A. Cohen, ed., *Belonging: Identity and Social Organization in British Rural Cultures,* pp. 247–77. Manchester: Manchester University Press; and ISER, Memorial University of Newfoundland.

Strauss, A. 1987. *Qualitative Analysis for Social Scientists.* Cambridge: Cambridge University Press.

Strauss, A., and J. Corbin. 1990. *Basics of Qualitative Research (Grounded Theory Procedures and Techniques).* Newbury Park: Sage Publications.

Stymeist, D. 1975. *Ethnics and Indians: Social Problems in a Northwestern Ontario Town.* Toronto: Peter Martin.

Varenne, H. 1977. *Americans Together: Structured Diversity in a Midwestern Town.* New York and London: Teachers College Press.

Vidich, A., and J. Bensman. 1958. *Small Town in Mass Society: Class, Power and Religion in a Rural Community.* Princeton: Princeton University Press.

Vidich, A., J. Bensman, and M. Stein. 1964. *Reflections on Community Studies.* New York: John Wiley and Sons, Inc.

Warner, W. 1949. *Social Class in America: A Manual of Procedure for the Measurement of Social Status.* Chicago: Science Research Associates.

Weber, M. 1953. 'Class Status and Party.' In R. Bendix and S. Lipset, eds., *Class, Status and Power,* pp. 63–75. Glencoe, Ill.: The Free Press.

– 1964. Edited by T. Parsons. *The Theory of Social and Economic Organizations.* New York: The Free Press.

Whittaker, E. In press. 'Decolonizing Knowledge: Towards a Feminist Cross-

Cultural Methodology and Ethic.' In Hugh Johnston and J.S. Grewal, eds., *East and West: Perspectives on Canada and India.* New Delhi: Sage.

Wilkinson, K. 1986. 'In Search of the Community in the Changing Country-side.' *Rural Sociology* 51: 1–17.

Williams, R. 1973. *The Country and the City.* New York: Oxford University Press.

Williams, W. 1969. *The Sociology of an English Village: Gosforth.* London: Routledge and Kegan Paul.

Winks, R. 1969. 'The Canadian Negro: A Historical Assessment. Part II: The Problem of Identity.' *Journal of Negro History* 54: 1–18.

Wirth, L. 1938. 'Urbanism as a Way of Life.' *American Journal of Sociology* 44: 1–24

Wright, E. 1978. *Class, Crisis and the State.* London: NLB.

Index